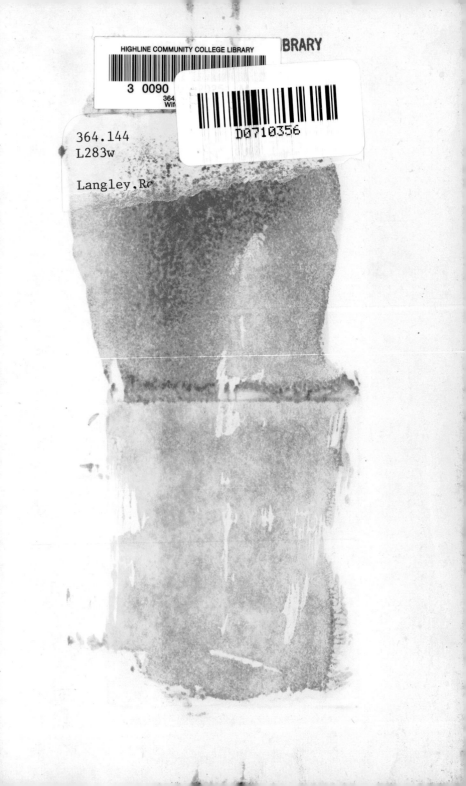

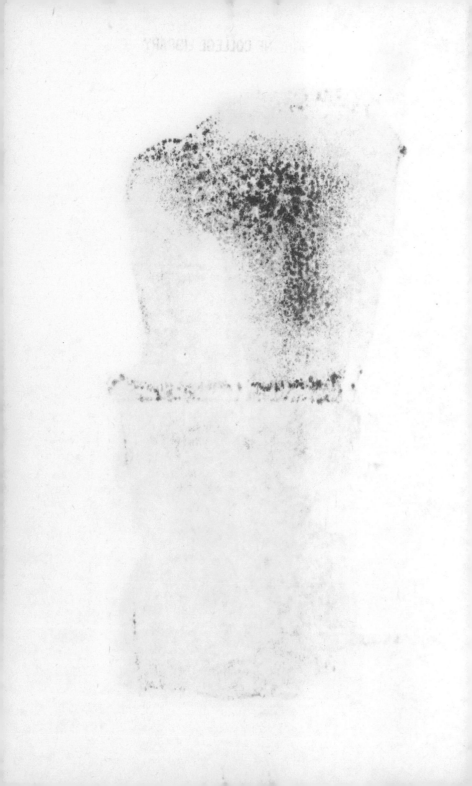

Wife Beating: The Silent Crisis

Wife Beating:
The Silent Crisis

ROGER LANGLEY and RICHARD C. LEVY

A Sunrise Book

E. P. DUTTON | NEW YORK

GRATEFUL ACKNOWLEDGMENT IS GIVEN THE FOLLOWING FOR PERMISSION TO QUOTE FROM COPYRIGHTED MATERIAL: *American Jurisprudence,* 2nd ed. Copyright © 1968 by Jurisprudence Publishers, Inc.; Susan Brownmiller, *Against Our Will: Men, Women and Rape* (New York: Simon & Schuster, 1975). Copyright © 1975 by Susan Brownmiller; Richard J. Gelles, *An Exploratory Study of Intra-Family Violence.* Copyright © 1973 by National Council on Family Relations. Reprinted by permission; Emily Jane Goodman, "Abused by Her Husband—and the Law," *The New York Times,* October 7, 1975. Copyright © 1975 by Emily Jane Goodman; Karen Horney, *Feminine Psychology* (New York: W. W. Norton & Co., 1967). Copyright © 1967 by Karen Horney; Susan Jackson, *In Search of Equal Protection for Battered Wives.* Copyright © 1975 by Susan Jackson; Leo Kanowitz, *Women and the Law* (Albuquerque, N.M.: University of New Mexico Press, 1969). Copyright © 1969 by Leo Kanowitz; Wayne LaFave and Austin Scott, *Handbook on Criminal Law.* Copyright © 1972 by West Publishing Co.; Ann Landers, *Gaithersburg* (Md.) *Gazette,* May 13, 1976. Copyright © by Field Enterprises, Inc.; John O'Brien, "Violence in Divorce-Prone Families," *Journal of Marriage and the Family* 33 (November 1971). Copyright © 1971 by National Council on Family Relations. Reprinted by permission; Rodney Stark and James McEvoy, "Middle Class Violence." Copyright © 1970 by Ziff-Davis Publishing Co. Reprinted by permission of *Psychology Today* magazine; Ann Steinmann and David J. Fox, *The Male Dilemma* (New York: Jason Aronson, Inc., 1974). Reprinted with permission; Robert Calvert, "Criminal and Civil Liability in Husband-Wife Assaults," in *Violence in the Family,* edited by Suzanne K. Steinmetz and Murray A. Straus (New York: Harper & Row, 1974).

Library of Congress Cataloging in Publication Data
Langley, Roger.
  Wife beating.
  "A Sunrise book."
  Bibliography: p.
  1. Wife beating. 2. Wife beating—Case studies.
I. Levy, Richard C., joint author. II. Title.
HV6626.L36 1977   364.1'55   76-54285
ISBN: 0-87690-231-X   L 783
Published simultaneously in Canada by Clarke, Irwin & Company Limited, Toronto and Vancouver

10 9 8 7 6 5 4 3

To my wife, Sheryl, who makes my life
complete and great; Love *mucho*.
                            Richard

To my wife, Norma, with much love.
                            Roger

Contents

Acknowledgments

A book of this kind depends heavily on the cooperation and assistance of many people. During the course of our nationwide research, we contacted an extensive array of husbands and wives (both the batterers and the battered), law-enforcement officials, academics, sociologists, hospital administrators, psychologists, attorneys, volunteers and psychiatrists. Their warm reception, hospitality, and understanding have made our research an assignment we will fondly remember.

While many of those who have helped us are mentioned at appropriate places, we do want to express special thanks to Dr. Suzanne Steinmetz, University of Delaware; Richard J. Gelles, University of Rhode Island; Murray A. Straus, University of New Hampshire; Dr. John P. Flynn, Western Michigan University; Sue E. Eisenberg and Patricia L. Micklow, University of Michigan; John O'Brien, Portland State University; Rosalie Novara, Kalamazoo Consultation Center, Kalamazoo, Michigan; Pamela J. Zagaria and Carolyn DeCoster, Community Planning Organization, Saint Paul, Minnesota; Patricia Bowser, County Council Office, Montgomery County, Maryland; and Attorney Sue Jackson, San Francisco, for the unselfish sharing of their time and research.

Thanks also to Andrew Loman, director, Dial Help, Bangor, Maine; Phyllis Nobel, Place, Boston, Massachusetts; Tom Peters, director, Community Mental Health Center, Spokane, Washington; Attorney Louise B. Raggio, chairman, Section of Family Law, American Bar Association; Attorney Arnold J. Gibbs, chairman, Practicing Lawyers Committee, American Bar Association; Ken Sproles, director, New Orleans Crisis Center, New Orleans, Louisiana; Dr. Matthew Dumont, director, Chelsea Mental Health Center, Chelsea, Massachusetts; Dr. Richard F. Lyles, Atlanta, Georgia; Dr. B. L. Daley, Columbia, South Carolina; Dr. Marguerite Fogel, Washington, D.C.; Maria Roy, executive director, AWAIC, New York, New York; Ellen Barnett, director, Passage Crisis Center, Silver Spring, Maryland; Mike Versace, director, Connections, Washington, D.C.; Charles Brogan and Frank Barnako, Jr., WRC-AM, Washington, D.C.; Lt. Harry Cox, Topeka Police Department, Topeka, Kansas; Dr. Mary Saddoris, director of Emergency Services, Hill Crest Medical Center, Tulsa, Oklahoma; Mary Kay Massay, librarian, Sociology Division, Martin Luther King Memorial Library, Washington, D.C.; Richard Greenfield and Larry Boyer, Law Section, Library of Congress, Washington, D.C.; and to dear Donna Cottone, our typist, for her patience and accuracy.

And now a few personal words to our families, who have given us the happiest moments of life. To my wife, Sheryl, thanks for bringing to this project the research, organization, enthusiasm, and love you bring to each endeavor we pursue. And to Sid and Bettie (the Beck) Levy, my parents, who fired my imagination for life, thanks for always being there.

R. C. L.

Thanks to all the members of the Langley household for accepting with good grace the disruption in their lives, to Norma Langley especially for all her extra efforts in so many areas, which made it possible for the book to progress on schedule, and to David, Jennifer, and Michael Langley for respecting their father's erratic work habits.

R. L.

Authors' Note

The most difficult task in researching this book was to keep reminding ourselves that everything about it is actual, documented, confirmed. Many of the incidents are so eerie, so outrageous, so tragic, that in treating the subject we kept wondering whether the public at large would ever believe the magnitude and severity of wife abuse in our country. However, regardless of personal isolation, a major social fact of our time, the evidence pointing to a wife-beating syndrome in America is overwhelming and cannot be denied.

We are not sociologists. Nor do we have any empirical experience beating our wives, associating with wife beaters or beaten wives (to the best of our knowledge), or in witnessing such aggressions within our family structures. We have approached this assignment as investigative journalists with a reporter's license to interview anyone and travel anywhere.

We have designed this book in a fashion to stimulate interest, provide thought, and offer a central information bank about what we feel to be a predominantly neglected subject. Every effort has been made to present sound, carefully documented data and, at the same time, to write it in a style readable by the greatest number. To simplify matters, we have used the term "battered wife" to apply to both married and unmarried women involved in violent relationships.

We accept the full responsibility for the point of view, the opinions, and the conclusions drawn from the evidence. They are entirely our own. Our purpose in writing this book is to focus attention on the subject of wife beating. If the book raises more questions than it answers, then it will have served its purpose well.

Wife Beating: The Silent Crisis

CHAPTER ONE

The Problem

> A spaniel, a woman and a walnut tree,
> the more they're beaten the better they be.
>
> *Old English Proverb*

Mary Agnes lives on a street of wooden, two-family houses in Gary, Indiana. Martha has a $100,000 home next to a former presidential candidate in a fashionable section of Washington, D.C. Charlotte is black; her home is a Chicago ghetto. Deliah is 65 and lives in a retirement trailer village in Florida. Sharon is a nurse working to put her husband through a Los Angeles medical school. Nora is a college professor at a Midwestern university. Nancy is a former 4-H queen trying to make ends meet in rural Pennsylvania. Tomi can't speak English, and as a Japanese war bride she had never developed roots in the red clay of Georgia. Lisa's penthouse overlooks New York City's Central Park.

These women form a diverse group, yet there is a tragic commonality among them.

Mary Agnes's husband works in a steel mill; Martha's is a lawyer and a successful lobbyist; Charlotte's husband is a laborer; Deliah's mate was a salesman before retiring; Sharon's is a student; Nora's husband is a college professor; Nancy's is a farmer; Tomi's works in a hardware store; Lisa's is a psychiatrist.

These men are equally diverse, yet they, too, share a commonality.

The women are battered wives, and the men are the husbands who beat them. Diverse individuals, yet they all share a bizarre bond of violence.

Wife beating, still thought by many to be the brutish sport of society's dregs, is present everywhere in American life.

"Wife beating in the United States is almost as much a national pastime as baseball," reports the handbook *Women in Transition,* compiled by researchers who spent three years counseling women seeking separations and divorces.

Estimates of the number of battered wives vary widely. The simple truth is that no one knows how many American women are being routinely beaten by their husbands, ex-husbands, boy friends, common-law spouses, and dates.

A number of researchers have made futile attempts to collect this information. Two University of Michigan law researchers, Sue Eisenberg and Patricia Micklow, in their study *The Assaulted Wife: Catch 22 Revisited,* report: "No national or state statistics are available on the incidence of wife assault crimes."

John O'Brien, in his work *Violence in Divorce-Prone Families,* notes:

> In the index for all editions of *The Journal of Marriage and the Family,* from its inception in 1939 through 1969, not a single article can be found which contains the word "violence" in the title. . . . Apparently violence . . . was either assumed to be too touchy an issue for research or else thought to be unimportant as a feature in "normal" families.

Drs. Suzanne K. Steinmetz and Murray A. Straus, in their anthology *Violence in the Family,* observe: "Amazing as it may seem, we could not locate even one research giving figures for a representative sample of the percentage of couples who get into violent fights. Just about every other aspect of family life has been the object of many studies by social scientists."

Battered women are the missing persons of official statistics.

Wife beating has been difficult to document not because it does not exist but because of the public's attitude toward it.

Wife beating is so ingrained in our society that it is often invisible. It is so pervasive that it literally does not occur to people to report it or collect statistics on it. Many police officers would no more file reports on battered wives than they would on the number of telephone poles they pass on a given day.

✳ Dr. Steinmetz has done the only spouse-abuse study with a scientifically selected random sample. The families studied were representative of the population as a whole. Using both interviews and questionnaires and checking the results against each other, she probed the violent behavior of fifty-seven families living in New Castle County, Delaware.

Dr. Steinmetz discovered that an incredible 60 percent of the families reported that the husband and wife engaged in some form of violent physical behavior. Ten percent admitted that they regularly engaged in extreme physical abuse of their spouses.

Extrapolating Steinmetz's findings produces some startling projections. The U.S. Census Bureau reports that as of 1976 there were 47.5 million married couples in the U.S. If one accepts Steinmetz's figure of 10 percent as applying to the whole population, then there are at least 4.7 million badly battered wives in the U.S. today. Most experts feel this is a conservative figure.

Some of the most important research on wife beating is being conducted by Dr. Richard J. Gelles, a sociologist at the University of Rhode Island. Dr. Gelles produced a landmark study on physical violence between married persons that contained several revelations.

He studied eighty families. Forty were identified by the police and social agencies as likely candidates for violence, and the remaining forty were neighbors with no history of violence. The results showed that forty-four families—55 percent—engaged in one or more violent acts of spouse assault. Twenty-one percent beat their spouses regularly. The frequency of these beatings ranged from daily to six times a year.

But Gelles's most unexpected finding was in the control group—the forty families with no history of violence—in which more than one-third reported spouse assaults. Extrapolating from Gelles's low figure—one-third of the control group that engaged in spouse assaults—suggests that there are at least 15 million battered wives in
✳ the U.S. today.

Estimates that 50 percent of all American wives are battered women are not uncommon.

Stewart Oneglia, a judge in Prince Georges County, Maryland, and an attorney who specializes in domestic relations, says: "I estimate that 50 percent of all marriages involve some degree of physical abuse of the woman. I use the words battering, beating and abuse synonymously to mean the regular systematic practice of violence and torture. I don't classify a scuffling match, where a man holds a woman's arms or pushes her away as a beating."

Another expert, Gladys Kessler, an attorney for the Women's Legal Defense Fund in Washington, D.C., says: "Fifty percent of all husbands beat their wives."

And a report prepared by the National League of Cities and the United States Conference of Mayors notes: "The incidence of wife assault is so pervasive in this society that half of all wives will experience some form of spouse-inflicted violence during their marriage, regardless of race or socio-economic status."

Wife beating is almost impossible to document since it is often listed under "assault and battery" or "disputes."

San Francisco is typical. Susan Jackson, a feminist attorney, investigated police records there and discovered: "There are no separate police statistics available on the number of family-violence calls received by the police, the number of calls responded to, the average time lapse in responding to family calls, the number of cases for which no report is filed, the number of repeat calls, the number of arrests arising from a family-violence call, the number of aggravated assaults and homicides resulting from repeat-call situations, the percentage of cases involving female victims, and the percentage involving victims who are male.

"It should be emphasized that as long as an unknown number of family-violence cases are unreported by police, . . . there will be no clear picture of the extent of the problem."

Police records, where they exist, give some indication of the problem.

Police records in Salt Lake City, Utah, show approximately 1,125 cases of wife beating a year.

In New York State, the courts handle over 17,000 family-offense cases per year involving violence or threats of violence.

The Dade County, Florida, Citizens Dispute Settlement Center handles more than 1,000 cases of battered women a year.

Records in Fairfax County, Virginia, show more than 4,000 family-disturbance calls per year. Jared Stout, chief of Planning and Research for the Fairfax County police department, estimates that over half of these calls involve husbands beating wives. "But this may understate the problem," he admits. "Probably forty percent of the daily fights aren't recognized as such on police records."

Assaults between husbands and wives make up 11 percent of all aggravated assaults in St. Louis and 52 percent in Detroit.

These police statistics, no matter how alarming, seriously under-report the extent of wife beating in America today.

Dr. Morton Bard, an expert on police crisis-intervention training at City College of New York, says: "Accurate estimates of the scope of this police function are difficult to determine with any precision: Usual police statistics reflect recognized crime categories and do not report incidents which do not involve a reportable crime.

"However, personal communication with experienced police officers attest to the frequency of the occurrence of family-disturbance calls."

The authoritative law-enforcement magazine *Police Chief* reports: "Repeated studies have revealed that urban police spend the majority of their time on service related functions and the most frequent of these details is the handling of domestic disturbances."

Raymond Parnas did a study in Chicago entitled *The Police Response to the Domestic Disturbance* in which he concluded that more police calls involve family conflicts than do calls for all other criminal incidents, including murders, rapes, nonfamily assaults, robberies, and muggings, combined.

The FBI's *Uniform Crime Report* lists 10 million reported crimes a year but does not collect statistics on wife abuse. If Parnas is correct in his estimate, then there are more than 10 million "family trouble calls" answered each year by the nation's police. It should be remembered that "family trouble" is often the official euphemism for wife beating.

Another aspect of the problem is the failure of battered women to make any report at all to the police.

Some of the reasons for this gross underreporting of wife assaults are discussed in the report *Violence in the Family:*

> Many police officers attempt to dissuade wives from filing assault charges and many wives do not see an attack by a husband as a case of legal assault. Therefore, one cannot tell from these data on police calls and assault charges just what proportion of all husband and wives have had physical fights since it takes an unusual combination of events to have the police called in.

The President's Crime Commission estimated that the volume of unreported crime may be as great as ten times the number of reported crimes, depending on whether the crime involved is the type that shames the victim, or whether it is the kind the police are thought likely to solve.

Clearly, wife-assault cases have the former characteristics.

"There is a great deal of stigma involved in publicly reporting this crime, but there is in addition the very real danger of retaliation by the husband if the assault is reported. Also there is little the police can do to actually prevent the assault from happening or recurring," writes Mindy Resnik in the National Organization for Women (NOW) counselor training manual distributed in Washtenaw County, Michigan.

Sociologist Dr. Murray Straus, one of the leading experts on spouse abuse, says: "The family is pre-eminent in every type of violence from slaps to torture and murder. There are informal norms that make a marriage license also a hitting license."

Police know that wife beating occurs in the tree-shaded suburbs as well as in the ghettos. For example, in Washington, D.C., the Citizens Complaint Center reports that between 5,500 and 7,200 husband-wife assaults are reported each year. The argument has been made that the District of Columbia is populated largely by blacks, many of whom are poor and living in crowded, wretched conditions that lead to subhuman behavior.

But just a few miles away, in Montgomery County, Maryland, one of the wealthiest suburbs in the nation, official figures show police responded to 4,225 cases of "family trouble," including 285 verified assaults by husbands on wives.

Dr. Maxwell Boverman, a psychiatrist who practices in Washington and lives in Potomac, the posh Maryland horse-country suburb, flatly states: "Wife beating is a very common problem, and it's not confined to poor blacks. I see a lot of it in Potomac."

A recent study showed that there are roughly the same number of wife-abuse complaints in the city of Norwalk, Connecticut, a city with a population of 85,000, and a precinct in Harlem of about the same size.

Those who work with battered women report victims among the wives of physicians, lawyers, college professors, and even clergymen.

In Dr. Gelles's spouse-abuse study, the families with the most violence were those with the highest incomes.

At the University of New Hampshire, sociologist Dr. Straus questioned 385 students about violence in their homes. The answers, given anonymously, revealed that 16 percent of these students had witnessed physical violence between their mother and father during the previous year. According to the U.S. Bureau of Census, the majority of college students come from families that are better educated and have higher levels of income than the general population.

No matter where you search, the figures and the expert opinions reflect that spouse abuse is far more common than generally supposed, yet the battered wife remains a little discussed, largely disregarded social problem. As Dr. Bard correctly observed: "The wife-beating issue is just beginning to come out of the closet."

"Society's attitude today towards wife abuse is about where it was a decade ago on child abuse," says Pat Micklow, co-author of a study on battered wives.

There is still a tendency in America to think of wife beating as a good thing. Still common are beliefs such as: "Some women need to be beaten." . . . "A good kick in the ass will straighten her out." . . . "She needs a punch in the mouth every once in a while to keep her in line."

A nationwide poll for the National Commission on the Causes and Prevention of Violence, conducted by Louis Harris, found: "One-fifth of all Americans approve of slapping one's spouse on appropriate occasions. Surprisingly, approval of this practice increases with income and education. . . ."

Even some wives believe that their husbands should beat them every once in a while for their own good. Some of the women interviewed by Dr. Gelles said they thought it was all right for their husbands to hit them when they "deserved it," or when they needed to be "snapped out" of a hysterical or depressed state.

"Violence between family members is by far the most common type of violence a typical person is likely to experience," conclude three of the top experts in spouse abuse in a recent unpublished paper.

Audiences still laugh at Jackie Gleason in a "Honeymooners" sketch when Ralph threatens to let Alice "have it." Political writer Richard Reeves smirks with the assurance that he's made a well-turned phrase when he tells *Time* magazine: "Politicians, like wives, should be beaten regularly."

But there's nothing funny about wife beating in the real world. A wife-beating joke won't get a laugh from:

Elizabeth M., who was hacked with a ceremonial sword wielded by her husband, a West Point graduate, or from:

Rosemary G., who walks with a limp because her right leg was crushed when her husband pushed a refrigerator over on her as she lay unconscious on the kitchen floor, or from:

Niki R., who was blinded in the right eye by the rage in her husband's fists, or from:

Virginia K., whose baby was stillborn after her husband knocked her down and repeatedly kicked her in the stomach, or from:

Sue Anne B., whose right cheek has a deep depression in it because her husband extinguished his cigarette there.

Some clues to the extent of wife beating can be found by examining statistics that only tangentially touch on the silent crisis of the battered wife.

For example, in Los Angeles, Haven House, a nonprofit organization established to offer temporary shelter to the families of alcoholics, found that 80 percent of its women were also battered wives.

A hospital emergency room in Kalamazoo, Michigan, treats about five women per week who are the victims of spouse assaults. In the same county, a physician at a health clinic estimates it treats about 200 battered wives per year.

Divorce statistics show a high incidence of spouse abuse. In a study, *Violence in Divorce-Prone Families,* John O'Brien interviewed 150 couples of which 17 percent spontaneously revealed overt, violent behavior.

A study conducted at the School of Social Work, Western Michigan University, reports: "An attorney with a public legal service handling about 200 divorces per year estimated that half of these divorces involved spouse assault."

George Levinger conducted a study of 600 couples in Cleveland entitled *Physical Abuse Among Applicants for Divorce.* He found that 36 percent of the women gave physical abuse as the reason for ending the marriage. Among the violent couples, 48 percent revealed that the violence had been chronically recurring throughout the marriage.

The U.S. Department of Health, Education and Welfare estimates that there are 1.6 million divorces a year in the U.S. Extrapolating the figures from the various estimates and studies indicates that between 200,000 and 800,000 battered wives seek divorces every year.

Few, if any, of these women headed for the divorce court after one isolated assault by their husbands.

Eisenberg and Micklow conducted interviews with twenty known victims of wife abuse and fifty public officials who had dealt with such cases in one capacity or another.

Nineteen of the women they spoke with received their first beating during their first year of marriage, and as the years passed, the beatings became more frequent and more severe.

Of forty-four families that reported at least one incident of spouse assault in Dr. Gelles's study, twenty-one reported that it occurred regularly from twice a year to daily. Of the forty neighbors' families, fifteen reported at least one incident of spouse assault, and in five families it occurred regularly.

In Detroit, Commander James Bannon discovered from police records that in 144 cases of wife abuse studied, 54 percent had been victims in previous assaults.

Police in Kansas City found that half of their "domestic trouble" calls occurred in households that they had visited at least five times in the previous two years.

Elaine Weiner of Montgomery County, Maryland Women's Commission, who deals with half a dozen battered wives per week, said:

"You ask someone how long has this been going on, and you hear things such as fifteen years, twenty years, twenty-two years, and you know they finally reached the point where it's the straw that broke the camel's back.

"Now if that's the case, how many women are there who have been going through it for six months, a year, two years, who have not yet reached the crisis point where they're willing to take action?"

A recent development in our society—the crisis intervention center—is also helping to reveal the vast extent of wife beating in America today.

These centers, springing up across the land in big cities and small towns, use trained personnel to defuse explosive family discords, to prevent suicides and offer professional help when needed.

These crisis centers are uncovering an alarming number of battered women.

Dr. Jay Moran of the Los Angeles Crisis Unit says, "Wife beating is one of our greatest problems. It's an area where something really needs to be done and one where very little is getting done."

In Nashville, Tennessee, Patricia Higginbotham, crisis center director, estimates that between 30 and 40 percent of all calls into her center involve spouse abuse.

In Bangor, Maine, Andy Loman, director of the Emergency Services, Counseling Center, estimates that in 1975 between 25 and 30 percent of the marital-conflict calls to the center involved wife beating or direct threats of beatings.

The Tulsa, Oklahoma, crisis center averages about 210 cases of wife beating per month, yet James Cox, director of the Tulsa Psychiatric Center, claims, "Wife beating here is underreported."

Half of the 500 women seeking to find help each year at the Woman's Advocate, a Minneapolis-St. Paul nonprofit co-operative, are battered wives.

In South Bend, Indiana, Molly Reid, a specialist for the city's Hot Line crisis intervention center, says: "The number of battered women calling us has increased greatly, but it's just the tip of the iceberg because most battered wives are afraid to call. We discover a lot of cases after women come in to discuss drug problems or some other family problem. After a while they break down and tell us about the beatings their husbands give them."

Ken Sproles, director of the New Orleans' Crisis Center, says: "When we do get a call from a battered wife, it is never the first time she has been beaten. By the time she gets around to calling us, she's desperate and searching for a way out. Most of them have already sought psychiatric help or have been to a marriage counselor and given up when these methods failed to solve their problem."

Wife beating often escalates to wife killing.

"If you're going to be killed in America, it's more likely to happen by someone in your own family," says Dr. Gelles.

Dr. Straus observes: "I don't think we are going to understand violence in American society until we understand violence in the family. Violence in the family is where it primarily occurs."

Family violence also has a deadly effect on the police. According to the FBI, more law-enforcement officers are killed breaking up personal disturbances than in any other area of police work. Chasing armed robbers ranks second.

One-quarter of the assaults on Chicago police occurred during domestic disputes.

The problem of making an accurate examination of wife beating is somewhat akin to a game children play in upstate New York's snow-belt region. When the snows are high and the drifts are deep, kids amuse each other by trying to correctly guess what an object is by the shape of the mound of snow covering it. From the outlines and shapes, children make assumptions that lead them to conclusions about the nature of the object. Sometimes they are exactly right, and other times they are only partially correct. For example, it is often easy to identify a buried automobile but extremely difficult to be specific about the year and the model.

This is similar to the problem of determining the extent of wife beating and spouse abuse in the U.S. today. From the information available it is possible to determine some broad facts but very difficult to be precise. For instance, without uniform police-reporting procedures and a central collection agency, it is impossible to get an accurate record of the amount of wife beating in our society. And even if uniform police statistics were available, the figure would not accurately reflect the scope of the problem because there are a great many more unreported cases than reported ones.

Drs. Gelles, Straus, and Steinmetz have obtained a grant from the National Institute of Mental Health and are in the process of doing a nationwide study with a random sample of 22,000 persons. This study could supply some of the comprehensive data that is now missing. However, it will be several years before this information is compiled, analyzed, and made available.

Sociologists and others active in spouse abuse research are convinced that in the U.S. today, the extent of wife beating is seriously underestimated. Abuse is an inexact term, but when it is defined to include physical violence ranging from an occasional slap to a severe beating, the experts believe that more than half of all U.S. couples engage in it. Drs. Steinmetz and Gelles believe that about 60 percent of all U.S. couples engage in some form of spouse abuse. Seven studies using small samples indicate that between 55 and 65 percent of the married population engages in spouse abuse. If one accepts these findings as representative, then there are between 26 and 30 million abused spouses in the U.S. today. Obviously severity and frequency are important factors. Nevertheless any activity occupying up to 30 million Americans is worthy of serious study.

CHAPTER TWO

Anne's Story—
A Case History

A wife isn't a jug . . .
she won't crack if you hit her ten times.

Russian Proverb

Anne Jessup's head snapped backward from the force of the blow. At first, she stared in utter disbelief. She was shocked. Then, in rapid succession, she began to cry, scream, and swing wildly at her husband Nelson.

For six months their marriage had been idyllic. All their friends commented on how well suited they were to each other. They shared common interests in politics, sports, and films. They were both college graduates, both good-looking, both vital, ambitious people who were going to make their mark in the world.

They both worked. She planned to get a toehold on a career before taking some time out to have a family. They were agreed on that.

After a storybook marriage in the church in which Anne was baptized—complete with Nelson's fraternity brothers and her sorority sisters in attendance—they moved to New York, ready to take on the world together.

The world was a lot tougher than they expected. Anne wanted to get into publishing. She settled for a typing job with an insurance company. Nelson was working with a big accounting firm and studying for part one of the CPA exam. He was one of a dozen young men hired by the firm to fill four permanent jobs. It was a shakedown drill for four months, after which the lucky four would be dubbed "suitable material" for the firm; the rest would be cut loose to begin again somewhere else.

It was more pressure than Nelson had ever faced. Up until now, all of life's milestones had been automatic and effortless—including college, which turned out to be a lot easier than he had anticipated.

Now Nelson faced the first real test of his life. The other young men were all very bright. In fact, some of them were brighter than he. Several had attended better colleges. Most of them seemed to have sharper survival instincts and were quicker to exploit a weakness or a mistake. It was cutthroat poker played with a false veneer of civility. They all hated each other. Each one was ready to seize advantage—fair or foul—to get ahead of the pack.

Less than two weeks into the competition, Nelson realized that he was definitely an underdog. He could see five or six guys who were going to beat him out unless he got a break—or made one for himself. It was a lot of pressure for someone in his early twenties to bear.

Nelson was almost as surprised as Anne the first time he hit her. Her day had been a disaster. She arrived late for work and was dressed down by the head of the secretarial pool. She typed a letter and put one of the carbons in backward, and when the supervisor saw her mistake, she made an elaborate display of explaining how to do the job properly, embarrassing Anne in front of the other girls. From there things just got worse, as Anne made one stupid mistake after another all day.

She hurried to their apartment after work. Once there, she threw a couple of frozen TV dinners into the oven for their supper. She was looking for some clean silverware when Nelson arrived.

He said something about always having TV dinners, and she called him a name. That's when he hit her.

When Anne recovered her senses, she unleashed her fury. Nelson took a couple of slaps on the arm he'd put up to protect his face, then really got mad. All the pent-up fury he felt for that "goddamn accounting firm and all those Ivy league creeps" who were deliberately undercutting him, ganging up on him, making him look bad, came rushing to the surface.

The next blow sent Anne reeling against the refrigerator. Nelson shuffled in after her like a prizefighter ready for the kill. His right fist smashed into the left side of her neck, just below the jawbone. His left fist sunk to the wrist in her soft, fleshy stomach. His right hand plummeted her breast. The next left just grazed her as she fell to the floor.

Nelson stood over her, flushed with rage, breathing like a bull. Anne doubled over and, unable to speak, stared up at him. She began to sob uncontrollably.

Nelson couldn't believe what he had done. If only he could wake up and have it be over. But it was no dream. He was living under tremendous pressure, and he just cracked. Mr. Nice Guy, well educated and cold sober, just beat up his wife. He was overwhelmed with guilt.

Anne lifted herself to her feet, ran from the kitchen, and threw herself on a couch that converted into their bed.

For a long time neither said a word. Anne, prostrate on the couch, cried without letup. Nelson took a can of beer from the refrigerator and sat at the kitchen table looking out into space. He wanted the earth to swallow him up.

A half an hour passed, the the TV dinners began to smoke. Nelson went to the oven and pulled them out.

"Anne," he called, "do you want one of these?"

She didn't answer. He asked again, but there was still no answer.

He couldn't eat, either. He threw them both into the sink and walked into the other room and knelt down beside his wife. She turned her head away from him.

"I'm sorry, honey," he said softly. "I'm sorry . . . God, I can't tell you how sorry I am." He said it over and over.

It was a long time before Anne spoke. Her body ached. A large bruise was forming on her neck. Her head roared, and her hands shook. She felt dirty, ashamed, and worthless.

Through the night Nelson told her he was sorry. He said he didn't know what came over him, that he would never, never do it again. Eventually, they fell asleep, Anne on the couch and Nelson in their one soft chair.

In the morning, they cleaned up, and each got ready for work.

Anne arranged a scarf around her neck to cover the bruise. Neither said much, and they were both glad when they eventually parted for work.

When they met again that evening, neither mentioned what had happened the night before. The conversation was forced and polite, but they were both trying to put their life back in order. The honeymoon was definitely over.

For a while, they both pretended that first night of violence never happened. They rationalized it as a temporary aberration that occurred because they were both upset. Nelson was under considerable pressure. They were both nice, respectable people. It couldn't happen again.

But it did. Neither one can remember any specifics about the second time Nelson beat his wife. Or the third, fourth, or fifth. The exact sequence that led up to the violence is forgotten, who hit first, how many blows were struck. It's all a blur now.

But both Anne and Nelson agree on one thing. The beatings grew more violent as they increased in frequency.

From the outside looking in, their life seemed typical of the upward-bound, split-level-in-the-suburbs set. Nelson wasn't selected by the first firm, but he got another job, passed the first two parts of the CPA exam, flunked the third once, then passed it.

Anne never made it in publishing, but she became a mother twice—a boy, then a girl. She busied herself at home and in volunteer work. Nelson made reasonable progress on the job. They acquired wall-to-wall carpets, stereos, stationwagons—all the accouterments of middle-class respectability.

But they made few close friends. Most of the people they knew they met through Anne's activities or through their kids.

"As time went on, I gradually withdrew from the human race," Anne said. "I felt so ashamed, so guilt-ridden that I never wanted to see anyone. Most of the time Nelson was clever enough to hit me where the bruises wouldn't show, but sometimes he would forget, and I'd have to stay out of sight with a black eye or a cut lip. It got too hard making up lies to tell my friends. It was easier to stop seeing them.

"Sometimes he would go for months without beating me, and

then something would set him down. Sometimes one of the kids could get him to stop.

"One time he came home drunk and wanted something to eat. I had fixed a big dinner earlier—roast beef, potatoes, the whole number—and he didn't show up, and he never called.

"I knew I was playing with fire, but I'd spent all day in the kitchen, first making a nice meal, then cleaning up. When he stumbled in around midnight demanding something to eat, I told him to go to hell.

"He punched me in the face and knocked me cold. When I woke up, I lifted my head and banged into something. I couldn't figure out where I was. My head seemed to be inside a black metal box, and my body and feet were hanging outside.

"Then suddenly I realized that my head was in the oven. Nelson had dragged me over and shoved my head in the oven. He was trying to turn on the gas, but he was too drunk to figure out how the stove worked.

"He saw me trying to wiggle out, and he jammed my head back in hard against the back wall of the oven. He was a lot bigger than me, and when he was mad, he seemed to have superhuman strength.

"Somehow I got out of there, but he cornered me in the kitchen and began punching me. I heard my jaw shatter, and I spit out a tooth.

"I picked up a bowl and swung at him, but he took it away and jammed it down on my head. My knees buckled, and I was dazed and confused.

"He stood there grinning at me, panting: 'Want some more, baby?'

"He looked completely insane, and I knew I had to get out of there. I moved toward the door, and he lunged after me. Ironically, he slipped on my blood—which was all over the floor—fell down, and wacked his head on the edge of the kitchen table.

"I ran as fast as I could out the side door and jumped into the stationwagon. Luckily, I always left the key in it—despite repeated protests from my husband.

"I backed out of the driveway and stopped to shift into a forward gear. By then he was out of the house and racing across the lawn screaming every filthy name he could think of at me. He reached for the car door, but by then I was moving forward. I roared down the street with Nelson chasing after me for about a block.

"I had no idea where I was going. My body ached, my face was bloody, and the tears flowed without end.

"I drove all night, not really thinking about where I was going. The next thing I knew I was pulling into the driveway of my sister's house, about forty miles away from my own."

Anne was not prepared for her reception. Desperate and hurt, she had counted on sympathy and help from her older sister and her husband. Instead, she was treated with cool disdain.

"At first, they were very concerned because they could see that I was badly hurt. Bob, my sister June's husband, drove me to a hospital emergency room. I was admitted to the hospital, and my jaw was set, and I was given something to make me sleep. The next day, June checked me out and drove me to her home.

"We didn't say much during the ride. It was difficult for me to speak because my jaws were wired shut, and we were both embarrassed. When we got to June's home, she explained what was to happen.

"Bob had driven my car back to my house, where he would pick up Nelson, and they would drive back together, and then Nelson would take me home.

"I told her that I didn't want to go back there with him. Then, in a deluge of tears, I told her of Nelson's repeated beatings and that he had tried to kill me. She comforted me, then explained Bob had talked to Nelson and gotten the 'real' story.

"I was shocked. My own sister didn't believe me. The gist of the 'real' story was that I had been acting strange lately, refused to cook for my husband, went into a hysterical rage, began throwing and breaking things. According to Nelson, he had tried to reason with me, but I was too hysterical. He slapped me—he guessed harder than he should have if my jaw was broken—to try and snap me out of it.

"He said I took a heavy metal frying pan and hit him on the side of his head from behind and ran out of the house screaming.

"Then came the crowning blow. My sister revealed that my husband, the decent sort that he was, was willing to forgive me and take me back. Bob had allowed as this was very kind of him since Nelson had a mild concussion from the blow to his head—which was true, but it was caused when he slipped and struck his head on the kitchen table.

"Nelson said, 'Sometimes a woman needs a good slap or two to get her back in line,' and Bob had readily agreed. But when June told me she thought the men were right, the last vestiges of hope oozed out of me.

"There was no hope. I cried and cried and cried. What could I do? Who could I turn to? I showed up at my sister's house a bloody, battered mess, and everyone assumes that it must have been me who did something wrong. Every woman deserves a good beating every once in a while. God, I wanted to die."

The next months were filled with quiet tension. Anne and Nelson never spoke of the incident. Anne's jaw mended, and she had her tooth recapped. Nelson came and went normally, and Anne went through the motions of running a normal home. There was very little conversation. The kids—now both teen-agers—spent most of their time away from the house. They never brought their friends home. Anne had long since stopped going through the motions of urging them to "bring your friends over here sometimes."

Anne had dropped out of her volunteer activities. She no longer attended church. She seldom saw anyone. Her contact with the outside world was reduced to an occasional passing of remarks with the woman next door if they both happened to be in their yards at the same time. Nelson spent more and more time away from home. Anne didn't know who his friends were, but she supposed they were people he had met at work. He also had a girl friend—or several; she didn't really care.

She was happiest now during the afternoons. Her housework completed, the kids at school, Nelson safely at work and a minimum of an hour away by train, she would curl up by herself, read Book of the Month Club novels, and be at peace.

Around four she would become apprehensive. She would have to come out of her peaceful cocoon and deal with the real world. The

kids would be home, dinner to fix, and Nelson . . . Nelson might
be home and she might have to face another night of violence and
agony.

Nelson began a war of nerves. He made sarcastic references to
Anne's trip to her sister. He mocked their words. He hinted that he
was building up to another thrashing. When they were alone, he
would talk out loud to himself and ask hypothetical questions such
as: "Will her sister believe her next time?" and then answer them:
"No, Nelson is such a sweet guy, and Anne is sooo crazy, no one
would believe he'd beat her."

Sometimes Nelson would act the model husband. He would
come and go on a routine basis. He was pleasant and polite. Several times, when he was in these moods, Anne had tried to approach him about seeing a marriage counselor or a psychiatrist.
Usually, Nelson ignored the request or simply said, "No, I don't
need a psychiatrist. If you want one, why don't you go."

Finally, she decided that this might be the best thing to do. Several times she started to call the mental health clinic or a psychiatrist listed in the phone book, but each time she hung up before the
call was completed.

"I began thinking about what I should do, but somehow needing
to see a psychiatrist seemed almost disgraceful or too extreme, and
I couldn't bring myself to do it.

"Then it occurred to me that a clergyman might be the best person to approach. I thought about it for a while, and then I called the
minister of the church that we had attended years ago. He seemed
warm and personable over the phone, and we made an appointment
to meet one afternoon.

"I arrived at the manse at the appointed hour, and the house-
keeper let me in. She directed me to a warm, pleasant room, lined
with books. Reverend Thomas was standing, waiting for me, a
smile on his face and both arms outstretched in front of him.

"His two hands enveloped one of mine, and he guided me over
to a settee, and we sat down together facing each other.

"We spent a few moments in pleasantries, and then he asked me
how he could help me. His voice was so full of compassion and understanding that I just knew I had done the right thing.

"I poured out my whole wretched story. He listened attentively and said nothing except for an occasional 'I see' or a 'yes.' When the tears came, he offered me his handkerchief. I laid it all out for him, and I felt weak and vulnerable.

"He asked me if I still engaged in sexual relations with my husband. I told him no, that for some time we hadn't. The reason being that his repeated beatings made it impossible for me to be warm and loving toward him. That I feared so I could never relax enough to have sex with him now.

"Then he asked me about other things. Was I a good cook? Did I keep the house neat and clean? In my opinion, was I fulfilling my role as a wife and mother?

"Gradually, the tone of our conversation shifted. We had drifted away from the problem of my survival—of what I could do to try and maintain my sanity and my health while living with a man who liked to beat me—to what was I doing to cause all this trouble.

"When I realized what was happening, my heart plummeted. He didn't believe me, either. He implied that a woman who refuses to sleep with her husband should not only expect a beating or two but no doubt deserved it. He was a clergyman but nevertheless a man first. He had the same attitudes of the society at large, that I was here to serve my husband, and if I got slapped around some, I ought to search my soul and find out what I was doing wrong.

"It never occurred to this man of God that I might be in the right. That I might be married to a sadistic beast who needed a shrink . . . no it had to be me . . . the woman was always wrong.

"And although the reverend could never condone violence, he did understand how it might flare up between two people living under constant tension. What was I doing to relieve the tension, to mitigate the violence?

"I was guilty until proven innocent. Didn't it matter that this man had tried to kill me? Surely I exaggerated. Nice suburban people don't do that sort of thing. That happens only in the ghettos.

"I stormed out of this conference livid with rage. I was betrayed by God's minister. I had put out my hand for God's help and received a male reprimand.

"Reverend Thomas called out after me, but I didn't turn back. I knew I'd wasted my time.

"That was the final straw. I knew that if I was ever going to get relief, I'd have to do it myself. I made up my mind then and there that there would be no more cover-ups, no more pleas to relatives or clergymen for help.

"The next time Nelson hit me he was going to jail. I would have him arrested. To hell with the neighbors, and to hell with what anybody thinks. I have my rights as a human being, and I don't have to meekly submit to beatings from my husband or anyone else."

Anne didn't have to wait long for the next flare-up. Nelson didn't show up for dinner. She fed the kids and cleaned up and sat down for an evening of television. Around 10 o'clock the kids went to bed, and she followed them after the 11 o'clock news.

She was in bed but not asleep when she heard Nelson come in. He was making a lot of noise—deliberately trying to provoke her, she thought. She said nothing and pretended to be asleep.

Suddenly, the bedroom door burst open. Nelson stood in the doorway and shouted: "Where the hell is all the bourbon?"

"Whatever we have is in the liquor cabinet." she answered, and rolled over on her side with her back to her husband.

"Well, there's none there."

"Then we must be out," she said.

"You've been drinking it all up during the day!"

"No, I didn't drink it. I don't care for bourbon."

"No, I don't care for bourbon," he mocked her. "Listen to you . . . 'I don't care for bourbon'. . . . Who'n hell do you think you are? You think you're too goddamn good to drink bourbon? You got to have champagne or Scotch or some other fancy son-of-a-bitch drink. . . ."

Anne didn't answer. She knew the scene was rapidly accelerating toward violence, but she could do nothing to reverse it.

"Well?"

"Well what?"

"You think you're too goddamn good to drink bourbon?"

"First you accuse me of deliberately drinking it all up, then you say I think I'm too good to drink it. . . . Nelson let's not have one of our stupid arguments."

"You call me stupid?"

"No . . . I just don't want to talk about it anymore."

"The hell you didn't. . . . Stupid, am I?"

Nelson dove on the bed, sending it crashing to the floor. He rained punches down on Anne's head. She instinctively pulled up the covers, but they offered scant protection from the fury of his blows.

She struggled out of bed, but her husband grabbed her arm and hauled her back. He twisted her arm behind her, and it felt like it was being pulled out of the socket. She screamed, and he hit her in the solar plexus. The wind knocked out of her, she rolled up in a little ball and moaned. Nelson gave her a final shot in the kidneys and stomped downstairs.

Both children held their breath and pretended to be asleep. They were used to the violent battles of their parents and had developed a defense mechanism that allowed them to pretend they didn't know what was going on.

Anne lay weeping in the wreckage of her bed. This was it. She'd had it. She rolled over across the bed and picked up the phone from the night stand and dialed 911. When the voice answered, she said she wanted to report a man beating his wife and gave her address and hung up.

She watched out the window until the police car drew up. Two officers climbed out and rang the front bell. She rushed down the stairs to tell them what happened.

"They came in and were very polite," she said. "But you should have seen Nelson. He was the picture of civility. Butter would have melted in his mouth. He was friendly and nice and told the cops that he understood they had to answer these calls even though they had no basis in fact.

"I was furious. I couldn't control myself. I sputtered out something about him beating me and showed them some welts.

"All of the time Nelson was doing his Mr. Nice Guy routine, calling me 'dear' and 'honey' and saying things like, 'These officers have more important things to do.'

"We were a study in contrast. I was screaming and yelling, and he was calm and serene. The cops were patronizing.

"I demanded that they arrest him. One cop asked me: 'Are there any witnesses to this alleged assault?' I said, 'No. It happened in my bedroom. He burst in and beat me up while I was trying to sleep.'

"The other cop told me, 'Well, lady, if there are no witnesses, you'll have to get a warrant.' 'How do I do that,' I asked. 'You'll have to get a judge to issue one.' I asked how I could do that in the middle of the night, and he said it would be very difficult, that I would have to get a judge at home and have him come down to his chambers and issue a warrant. He said I could come down to the station the next day and swear out a warrant.

" 'You mean there's nothing I can do to prevent this gorilla from beating me up all night?' I asked. I'll never forget the cop's answer: 'Look, lady, he pays the bills, doesn't he?' he said, motioning toward my husband. 'What he does in his own house is his business.'

" 'You mean you're going to leave me here? You won't protect me?'

" 'Lady,' the cop said, 'why don't you two kiss and make up and forget the whole thing. Everything will seem a lot different in the morning. We see this sort of thing all the time. A woman gets her husband arrested, then the next day she drops the charges. My advice is try and work out your problems yourself.'

"Nelson smiled and thanked the officers and apologized for taking up their time. The cops smiled back and said they 'understood' and 'to think nothing of it.'

"I sat on the stairs, my mouth open in utter disbelief. Once again no one believed me. I was just a woman. I didn't count. A man's home is his castle, and if he wants to whip the servants, well, then all well and good. I felt humiliated, dirty, and ashamed. I was beyond crying. I just gazed off in space, not knowing what to do.

"Nelson walked to the police cars with the officers. There was handshaking and smiling and good old boy camaraderie. They drove off, and he waved good-by. He turned and walked up the path and back into our house.

"He wasn't smiling anymore. He closed the door and leaned up against it. I was still sitting on the stairs. His eyes narrowed, and he hissed at me: 'This time you're really going to get it.' "

The next morning Anne struggled to read the yellow-page telephone listings under "Lawyers." She could scarcely see because both eyes were swollen nearly shut. Both breasts were deep purple. Her head ached, her teeth ached, her whole body ached. She was tatooed with bruises from her eyes to her buttocks. Her index finger moved slowly down the page. She automatically rejected most of the names until she came to Bartlett, Martha. She wanted a woman lawyer. Anne was desperate. She knew that Nelson might beat her to death any night, and there was nothing she could do about it. She had tried relatives, the clergy, and the police and received the same reaction from all. "It's okay for a man to beat his wife, and if he does, it proves there is something wrong with you."

Anne put aside her shame and humiliation. She was motivated by fear. She wanted a divorce. She had to get away from Nelson, and perhaps another woman might believe her if she could see her condition today.

Anne dialed the number and got a secretary who asked a lot of questions. Anne said she had to talk to Ms. Bartlett, that she didn't want to explain her situation to a secretary. The secretary was implacable. The best she would do is take Anne's name and number and have Ms. Bartlett return the call when she was free.

"This was more than I could stand," Anne related. "It was the absolute bottom, the pits. I couldn't even cry. I felt totally worthless, less than human. There was absolutely no place for me to turn. For the first time in my life I seriously considered suicide. I sat staring blankly into space, trying to decide how I should kill myself.

"I distinctly remember having this thought: You're such a klutz that you won't be able to even kill yourself. Nelson couldn't have said it better.

"I kept thinking over and over, God, I hate me. Why am I so worthless?

"I remember thinking quite dispassionately that a gun fired in my mouth would be the most foolproof way. We didn't have a gun, or I'd probably be dead now. I knew I didn't have the nerve to cut my wrists or jump off a bridge or building. I decided that for me the best way was probably an overdose of sleeping pills. I checked the medicine cabinet. There were twenty tablets, but I didn't know if they would be enough.

"I sat on the toilet seat with my head in my hands wanting to die but too much of a coward to actually do it. I can't begin to describe my depression."

Anne was startled when the phone rang. She walked over to the bedroom extension and picked up the receiver. She didn't speak. The voice on the other end said hello several times. It was a woman's voice—firm and businesslike.

Weakly, Anne said, "Hello." The voice on the other end belonged to Martha Bartlett. Indeed, she would take her case. No, don't worry about the money now. Yes, she would not only get Anne a divorce, but she would see to it that Nelson never beat her again.

The sound of a human voice offering support and hope was therapeutic to Anne. For the first time someone believed her. Oh, God, maybe there is a way out of this mess, she thought.

Anne's lawyer told her that she was sending a cab around to pick her up. The next hours were filled with activity. First Anne and Ms. Bartlett met briefly at her office. Next came the photographer, who took dozens of color photographs. Ordinarily, Anne would have felt strange standing naked before a male photographer, but the last remnant of schoolgirlish modesty had been beaten out of her.

Next she was taken to a hospital emergency room. Ms. Bartlett explained that it was important to have medical records to document the charges of wife beating.

Then Ms. Bartlett telephoned a judge. She talked easily in a friendly offhanded way. She explained the sequence: the first beating, the call to the police, the second beating, the photographs, medical reports, and now the request for a bench warrant. She casually mentioned that she hadn't called the press—yet.

Judge Abrahams was most cooperative. He would issue the warrant immediately along with an order for Nelson to vacate the house until after a formal hearing on the assault charge was held.

Nelson was arrested and immediately posted bail. He called Ms. Bartlett "to tell her about Anne because she might not understand the situation." Nelson was a model of understanding and sweetness. However, Ms. Bartlett wasn't buying it. "I saw what you did to your wife," she snapped. "I suggest you get yourself an attorney. See you in court."

The case never got to court. Anne agreed to drop the charges in return for a quick, uncontested divorce. She got the house, custody of the kids, and $200 a month child support. Nelson paid all the legal fees and court costs.

The judge also issued a court order restraining Nelson from seeing his wife. Child visitations were to be arranged by telephone at a time and place agreeable to both parties.

Suddenly it was over. Her marriage, her life style, her place in our society. She would have to find a new way. She would have to go to work. She was near 40, with no significant work experience except as a secretary. Her college degree meant little, her hopes of a career in publishing even less. Perhaps she would sell the house and move someplace cheaper to live, but this meant taking the kids away from their friends. There was so much to do, so much to think of.

Then the front door flew open. It was Nelson. "What are you doing here?" Anne yelled. "I can put you in jail if you come here."

Nelson just grinned and slammed the door.

"You've won for now," he snarled, "but don't you ever think that I'm ever going to leave you alone. You're too dumb, too stupid to make it without me. You'll have everything so screwed up in a week you'll be begging me to come back.

"And I'll be back. Don't you ever forget it. I'll be back, and I'll settle things with you once and for all. You've got a good one coming after this cute little trick.

"Mark my words, lady. You'll live to regret what you've done. You'll pay and pay, and you know I mean what I say."

Then he pulled out the court order and waved it in front of her face.

"You know what I think of this?" he said.

He crumbled the paper into a tight ball. He shoved Anne up against the wall and grabbed her throat at the rear of her jaw and squeezed until her mouth popped open. Then he took the crumbled court order and stuffed it into her mouth.

"Eat it, you son of a bitch," he said.

Nelson turned and walked out of the house.

Anne has had all the locks changed, and she has added chain bolts and new window locks. But she knows these will be of little use the night Nelson decides to break in and beat her again. She also knows that may very well be her last night on earth.

She told the cops about the threat, but they told her there was nothing they could do about it. "People say a lot of things, lady," they told her. "Let us know if he tries to get in."

Sometimes in the dead of night, Anne wakes up with start. Was it just another bad dream? Did a dog knock over a garbage can? Did the wind rattle a shutter?

She tries to calm her pounding heart with a cigarette. All is quiet again. Try to get some sleep. Everything is okay—this time.

CHAPTER THREE

The Social and Legal
History of Wife Beating

> Ye wives, be in subjection to your husbands . . .
>
> *New Testament I Peter 3*

Nature in the raw operates on the simple rule that for something to live, something else has to die.

The gazelle eats the plant, and the leopard eats the gazelle. The big fish eats the little fish and is in turn eaten by a bigger fish. Survival is based on brute force and violence.

Under these harsh conditions, the human race made its debut somewhere in Asia, anthropologists tell us. Humans survived—like the other creatures—through violence.

At some point, the first building block of civilization—the family—was formed. Stronger males naturally dominated the weaker females. Man literally took his wife and ruled her by physical force. The classic cartoon of the caveman dragging a woman off by the hair depicts a scene that is anthropologically accurate.

Women had little choice but to try and make the best of the situation. Author Susan Brownmiller theorizes that women chose to remain with one man in hopes that he would protect her from being beaten and raped by the brutes. "The price of woman's protection by some men against an abuse by others was steep," she writes in her book *Against Our Will: Men, Women and Rape.*

> Disappointed and disillusioned by the inherent female incapacity to protect, she became estranged in a very real sense from other females, a problem that haunts the social organization of women to this very day. And those who did assume the historic burden of her

29

protection—later formalized as husband, father, brother, clan—extracted more than a pound of flesh. They reduced her status to that of chattel. . . .

As the first permanent acquisition of man, his first piece of real property, woman was, in fact, the original building block, the cornerstone of the 'house of the father.' Man's forcible extension of his boundaries to his mate and later to their offspring was the beginning of his concept of ownership.

Sheer physical strength was critical to these early arrangements. Violence, or the threat of violence, kept women in their place. Other physical differences were also important. Early man was a hunter, and as a hunter, a woman's usefulness was curtailed during times of pregnancy or menstruation. When she wasn't always able to travel with the hunt, she remained back at the camp. Eventually, it evolved that she would stay behind and take care of the children, tend the fires, tan the skins, and perform the other early household chores while man hunted and provided not only for himself but for his wife and family.

"Role differences developed between the sexes which originally stemmed from the physiological differences relating to strength, menstruation and pregnancy," write sociologists Anne Steinmann and David J. Fox in their book *The Male Dilemma*. "Then as social systems developed, these physiological differences and the functional role that proceeded from them, combined with the actual postures of the two sexes during intercourse, led to value judgments concerning the dissimilarity of the two sexes, with man seen as superior and woman inferior."

These judgments became formalized in customs, religions, and the laws. The Old Testament states that no lesser a being than God put woman in her place. In the Book of Genesis it is written: "Unto the woman He said, 'I will greatly multiply thy pain and travail; in pain thou shalt bring forth children; and thy desire shall be to thy husband, and he shall rule over thee."

Women were given this message following the first sin in the Garden of Eden. The first sin has been interpreted as tempting Adam to try sexual intercourse.

Some psychologists have argued that characterizing the woman as the heavy for the first sin—the sex act—has contributed mightily in making her the object of antagonism and aggression throughout the centuries.

The Old Testament repeatedly testifies to woman's inferiority. Among Orthodox Jews, women still play a very minor role in the religion. Until recently, Jewish men said a prayer of thanksgiving to God for not making them women.

The Biblical story of creation squarely places woman in a secondary role since she was created both *after* man and *from* man. The significance of this event is continued and reinforced in the New Testament. For example, St. Paul wrote in Timothy, Chapters 11–15:

> A married woman must learn in quiet and in perfect submission. I do not permit married women to practice teaching or domineering over a husband; she must be kept quiet. For Adam was formed first, and then Eve; it was the woman who was utterly deceived and fell into transgression.

St. Peter, the rock upon which the Christian church was built, also admonished women. He told them: "Ye wives, be in subjection to your husbands. . . ."

In fact, all of the great religious works—the Old Testament, the New Testament, the Talmud, the Koran, the Book of Mormon—put men above women and give men the authority to dominate. Women are still excluded from the priesthood of most religions, and their inferior status has been underscored by rules requiring them to be segregated at services or to hide themselves under veils or other specified coverings.

The concept of male superiority was carried over to secular laws when they developed. From the days of Moses to ancient Babylon to Rome to feudal Europe to twentieth-century America the idea that men are superior to women was officially incorporated into the laws.

Examples of this attitude found in societies throughout history include the right of men, but not women, to own property, to vote, to divorce, to inherit wealth and titles.

The existence of civil and religious laws giving men superior rights over women nurtured the belief—born in the dim past in the smoke-filled caves of primitives—that men also had the right to beat their wives.

Over the course of time civilization has moved toward abolishing the practice, but it has been accomplished by degrees and slowly. "There is no specific time which one can point to as the year or decade when the husband lost his authority to beat his wife," writes Robert Calvert in his contribution to the book *Violence in the Family.*

British common law—which is also the origin of U.S. law—gave husbands the right to "chastise" women, children, and apprentices.

The noted English jurist and legal scholar, Sir William Blackstone, observed:

> The husband, by the old common law, might give his wife moderate correction. For as he is to answer for her misbehavior, the law thought it reasonable to entrust with this power of restraining her, by domestic chastisement in the same moderation that a man is allowed to correct his apprentices or children. . . .

The Middle Ages were violent times when feudal armies constantly battled each other; the church condoned whippings and torture; and wife beating was rampant.

But even in those brutal days, a man's right to beat his wife was being abridged. Recorded in the book *Women in the Middle Ages* is the passage: "In marriage the wife was always subordinate to the husband; he had the right to punish her, though only in the event of misdeeds on her part, not arbitrarily."

During these times a single woman had some right to own property, but when she married, it became her husband's, and he had the right to keep it or sell it as he saw fit without consulting her. The right of unmarried women to own property gave rise to a curious custom known as "stealing an heiress." Poor but ambitious knights could obtain wealth and respectability by attacking and raping a rich virgin.

As the centuries passed, the woman's plight improved, but the pace was slow and the progress slight. The truth of this is illustrated by the story of an Englishwoman named Margaret Neffeld of York, recorded in the book *Marriage Litigation in Medieval England*. In 1395, she tried to divorce her husband because of his brutal treatment and was given the chance to prove her case in court. She produced witnesses who testified that her husband had attacked her with a knife, forcing her to flee to the street "wailing and in tears." Another time he attacked her with a dagger, slashed her, and broke her arm.

In court, Margaret's husband protested that whatever he had done was honest, reasonable, and solely for the purpose of "reducing her from errors."

The court agreed and ruled in favor of the husband. No divorce was granted, and Margaret was compelled to continue to live with her brutal husband.

Over the next 200 years, official attitudes softened slightly. During the fifteenth century, it was still legal for men to beat their wives, but "severe violence" and "extreme brutality" began to be considered bad form.

Another 100 years passed and brought some improvements for women.

"In James I's reign (1603–25), in the case of Sir Thomas Seymore, who was in the habit of beating Lady Seymore, the judges expressed an opinion that a wife might have a remedy against her husband for 'unreasonable correction,' " according to a report published in *The Effects of Marriage on Property and the Wife's Legal Capacity*.

> But even this limited right of chastisement began to fall into discredit in the days of Charles II (1660–85). Sir Matthew Hale held that the moderate "castigatio" which the old authorities had declared to be permissible, was not to be understood to be a "beating but only an admonition. . . ."
>
> Yet there continued to be jurists, even in the following century, who still maintained a husband's right to beat his wife, so long as he did not do it "outrageously."

In Wales, the common law provided that a husband could beat a disrespectful wife a maximum of three strokes with a rod of the length of his forearm and thickness of his middle finger."

Blackstone later recorded the English "Rule of Thumb," which referred to a husband's right to "chastise his wife with a whip or rattan no bigger than his thumb, in order to enforce the salutory restraints of domestic discipline."

Even in death there was no equality between the sexes. English common law stated: "Whilst only punishing the husband who killed his wife with the ordinary penalties of murderer, regarded for the woman who killed her husband as guilty of Petit Treason and condemned her to the flames," according to *The Effects of Marriage on Property and the Wife's Legal Capacity*.

But the times were not without some mercy. "For several generations . . . it had become the invariable custom to delay the actual burning until after death had been produced by strangulation."

While Western civilization held tenaciously to its ancient prerogatives, the conditions endured by females in the Orient were far worse.

Women had no rights in Far Eastern cultures and were at one time so despised that newborn baby girls were routinely killed because they were considered worthless. But the most outrageous practice was the systematic crippling of all Chinese women through the act of foot binding.

This practice, though long since discontinued, still stirs strong passions among modern feminists. Andrea Dworkin, in her book *Woman Hating,* cried out: "The bound foot existed for 1,000 years. In what measure could one calculate the enormity of the crime, the dimension of the transgression, the amount of cruelty and pain inherent in that 1,000 years?"

Throughout Europe, the concept of women as property continued to flourish. When someone other than her husband assaulted a woman, her husband was allowed to sue for damages much as he would if a prized cow or horse had been injured.

The legal work *Of Feme Coverts,* first published in England in 1732, noted: "If a married Woman be assaulted and beaten; if the Husband is thereby deprived of her Conversation and Service, he alone may commence an Action. . . ."

Most women apparently accepted their lot, but a few, determined not to endure physical cruelty, tried to escape. Most often their escapes failed. The fate of one such wife was chronicled in the book *The Hardships of the English Laws in Relation to Wives,* published in 1735.

> An unfortunate Wife who had been so cruelly treated by her Husband, that Life itself was become a Burthen to her, at last made her Application to her Brother, who was a Clergy-Man, and inclined by all the Motives of Christianity to assist her. He received her into his House, with her Spirit quite opprest and sunk by her Husband's Severity, which had so far affected her Constitution, that she was in a very bad State of Health. He went to her Husband, and in the softest Terms represented his unmanly Treatment of his Wife, and the sad Effects it had had upon her; and endeavor'd by all possible Arguments, to awaken in his Mind some Sentiments of common Humanity towards her; adding, that (with his Leeve) she should be welcome to stay at his House, till she had recovered her Health, of which he would be at the sole Expence. But Alas! how unavailing is Reason, and soft Persuasion, when opposed to *Insolent Power and Arbitrary Will*. The Husband insisted upon his *Right to Controul;* it was an Invasion of his *Prerogative Royal* for his Wife to pretend to espostulate, and in short, he ordered her Brother to send her Home again, or keep her at his *Peril*. This was the unhappy Creature's last Effort; and this ill success flung her into a lingering *Fever,* of which she languished a Fortnight, when her Husband came in Person, and demanded his Wife. Her Brother was forced to deliver her up, being as unable to contend with her Husband, as the Senator of *Rome* with the Emperor, when he declared he was never ashamed to give up an Argument to a Man, who was master of fifty Legions. Thus the miserable Wife, was carried Home again where her Husband, exasperated by her Complaint, treated her with greater Harshness which gave her, her *Coup de Grace* in less than a Month; when she left her Sufferings to be avenged by Heaven, though they were disregarded by Men, from whom she could find no Redress, . . ."

One of the most bizarre Catch 22 conditions imposed on women by men was the legal concept that when two people married, they became one in the eyes of the law. This prevented a woman from suing her husband—regardless of what he did to her property or her person—because under the law a man and wife were one, and it is impossible to sue yourself.

"By marriage the husband and wife are one person in law, that is, the very being or legal existence of the woman is suspended during marriage or at least is incorporated and consolidated into that of the husband," wrote Blackstone in 1768.

And by extending this concept, it was easy to conclude that a husband couldn't be charged with beating his wife because he and his wife were one. How can you arrest someone for beating himself? And a nonperson whose "very being" was "legally suspended" certainly could have no business before the courts. How can someone who isn't there be beaten?

More than one hundred years later, lawyers were still trying to clarify these points. The interpretation that evolved split the difference. A man couldn't be sued by his wife, but at the same time he couldn't beat her up with impunity on the ground that she didn't legally exist.

"The law does not carry the doctrine of conjugal unity to the extent of ignoring *all* physical injuries that a husband may inflict upon his wife" was the opinion contained in *The Effects of Marriage on Property and the Wife's Legal Capacity,* written in 1879.

> For such act he may be criminally liable; and the law even aids her in prosecuting him for them, by suspending the rule which usually renders her incompetent to appear as a witness against him in criminal proceedings. But acts which would amount to an assault if committed against a stranger, may be legally innocent when committed by a husband against a wife.

For decade after decade women continued to be conditioned by the religious, social, and legal concepts that held them to be naturally inferior to men. The combined forces of God, society, and the law were a formidable enemy to resist. Most women acquiesced and came to think of themselves, at worst, as mere property, or at best, as pets that needed to be disciplined and trained. John M. Briggs in his *Concept of Matrimonial Cruelty* wrote:

> Indeed it would seem that in the 19th century women were brought up in the belief that a larger license should be allowed to

their husbands than to themselves and that it was the destiny of a wife to bear with as much fortitude as she could muster all but the most extreme acts of oppression by her lord and master.

Women who turned to the church for justice found little. In 1831 an ecclesiastical court ruled in *Neeld* v. *Neeld* that it was assumed that conduct, which was undoubtedly wrong, still had to be endured for better or worse by a long-suffering wife.

Of course, not all women suffered their fate with equal acceptance. A spunky lady named Mrs. Norton wrote a book in 1854 about her life with a battering husband that provides an excellent insight into the times.

> After our honeymoon, we lived for a short time in chambers Mr. Norton had occupied as a bachelor in Garden Court, Temple, and on the first occasion of dispute, after some high and violent words, he flung the ink-stand and most of the law books, which might have served a better purpose, at the head of his bride. We had no servants only an old woman who had taken care of these chambers for some years and who offered me the acceptable consolation that her master was not "sober" and would regret "by-and-by." . . .
>
> We had been married about two months when one evening after we had all withdrawn to our apartment, we were discussing some opinion he had expressed, I said (very uncivilly) that "I thought I had never heard so silly or ridiculous a conclusion." This remark was punished by a sudden and violent kick; the blow reached my side and it caused great pain for many days and being afraid to remain with him, I sat up the whole night in another apartment. . . .
>
> On another occasion, when I was writing to my mother, Mr. Norton (who was sipping spirits and water, while he smokes his cigar) said he was sure "from the expression of my countenance" that I was "complaining." I answered that "I seldom could do anything else." Irritated by the reply, Mr. Norton said I should not write at all, and tore the letter up. I took another sheet of paper and recommenced. After watching and smoking for a few minutes, he rose, took one of the allumettes, I had placed for his cigar, lit it, poured some of the spirits that stood by him over my writing book, and, in a moment, set the whole in a blaze.

Mrs. Norton's story had a sad but typical ending for those times. Mr. Norton eventually charged that his wife was having an affair with a high government official. The matter went to court, but it was so obviously a trumped-up case, the jury ruled against Mr. Norton without even waiting to hear the defense arguments. But it was a pyrrhic victory for Mrs. Norton. She soon discovered that she could not obtain a divorce from her husband because of a technicality, and the custody of her children went to her husband. She continued to mount legal battles, but they were to no avail. She was forced to stand by and watch powerlessly as her children were taken out of the country by her husband's sister. She never saw them again but heard sickening reports that they were being beaten and mistreated. There was nothing she could do to help them.

Conditions in America were not much different. The U.S. legal system had evolved from the British system. In America, as in Britain, the common-law tradition held that husbands had the right to "chastise" their wives.

The first U.S. court case to acknowledge this ancient prerogative was in 1824, *Bradley* v. *State*. The Mississippi Supreme Court held that a husband should be permitted to "moderately chastise his wife without subjecting himself to vexatious prosecutions for assault and battery, resulting in the discredit and shame of all parties concerned."

The gist of this ruling seems to be: A man should be able to beat his wife without a lot of problems from the courts.

In 1864, a North Carolina Court followed the same logic when it ruled, in *The State* v. *Black,* that wife beating was a matter best left out of the courts. The court decided it should not interfere unless "some permanent injury be inflicted or there be an excess of violence. Otherwise the law will not invade the domestic forum or go behind the curtain . . ." preferring to "leave the parties to themselves as the best mode of inducing them to make the matter up and live together as man and wife should."

The prevailing attitude was that beating was for the wife's benefit. It was assumed that all women were flighty and biologically unable to decide the right thing to do, so it was up to the husband to straighten her out from time to time. It was his duty and for her good.

In America, however, pioneer women who helped settle the West won a large measure of admiration from their men as they repeatedly proved that they not only "could take it" but were capable of great endurance, forbearance, and ingenuity. They repeatedly demonstrated these qualities in overcoming the problems of their harsh lives.

Shortly after the Civil War, the Married Women's Acts began to be passed by state legislatures. These new laws allowed separate property ownership and began to erode the absolute dominance of men over women, at least in the strict legal sense. In addition to property rights for both single and married women, the woman gained the right to enter into contracts, to keep her own earnings, to sue under her own name, to write her own will, and to establish her own separate place of residence, with or without her husband's permission.

Court decisions began to limit rather than reinforce the "husband's right to chastisement." Then, in 1871, in the landmark decision of *Fulgham* v. *State,* an Alabama court ruled that men no longer had any right to beat their wives. The decision said, "The privilege, ancient though it be, to beat her with a stick, to pull her hair, choke her, spit in her face or kick her about the floor or to inflict upon her other like indignities, is not now acknowledged by our law."

Similar cases followed. In New Hampshire, in *Poor* v. *Poor,* the court ruled: "The moral sense of the community revolts at the idea that the husband may inflict personal chastisement upon his wife, even for the most outrageous conduct."

In 1882, Maryland enacted a law to punish wife beaters by giving them forty lashes with a whip or a year in jail. In Baltimore, after the first man was punished under this law, the district attorney observed "the crime ceased as if by magic." This statute remained on the books until it was repealed in 1953.

The law has not always been consistent. The courts established that a man had no right to beat his wife, but it was also held that a woman couldn't bring a suit against her husband for beating her.

In fact, the U.S. Supreme Court ruled in 1910 that a wife had no cause for action on an assault and battery charge against her husband because it "would open the doors of the courts to accusations of all sorts of one spouse against the other and bring into public notice complaints for assault, slander and libel.''

The peace and sanctity of the home were considered too important to be dragged through the courts. This created the paradox that the courts would allow violence in order to keep the peace.

Leo Kanowitz notes in his book *Women and the Law: The Unfinished Revolution:*

> The new reason for denying them the right to sue one another for personal injuries was allegedly to prevent damage to domestic tranquility. . . . A husband could beat his wife mercilessly . . . but the law in its rectitude denied her the right to sue her husband because such a suit, it claimed, could destroy the peace of the home.

Eventually, courts began to recognize this inconsistency. In California, in 1962, the court observed in *Self* v. *Self,* ''The contention that immunity is necessary to maintain conjugal harmony is unsound because after a husband has beaten his wife, there is little peace and harmony left to be disturbed.''

The legal right of a husband has clearly been abolished. Under the heading ''Authority of husband over wife,'' the standard legal reference *American Jurisprudence* unequivocally states:

> Under the modern law, the husband has no authority, apart from that as head of the family, over the person of his wife. The aim of the Married Women's Acts is, in general, the equality of the spouses and the emancipation of the wife from her common law subordination, or what has been called her common-law slavery. (*Austin* v. *Austin,* Miss. 1961) It has long been established that the husband has no legal right to chastise his wife physically or restrain her person by confinement for the purpose of compelling her obedience to his wishes, . . .

But wife beating still presents a dilemma. Robert Calvert notes in *Family Violence:*

> Even today the only recourse for a wife is the criminal law or divorce. The former is difficult to invoke and the latter is an extreme

step. Nevertheless, despite the ambiguity of the law on this matter, it seems as though the right of husbands to use physical punishment is no longer present.

Over the centuries a great change has occurred. What was once an absolute right of men no longer has any legal sanction in the U.S. It has been an evolution. No law has ever been passed revoking the ancient privilege, but change has come nevertheless. "Husbands have lost the right by change in customary usage more than by legal change," wrote Calvert. Perhaps this is to the good since the mere passing of laws does not guarantee change.

For example, three states—California, Hawaii, and Texas—have enacted laws making it a felony for a husband to assault his wife, but a deluge of felony convictions under these laws has yet to materialize.

Having a law on the books is one thing; enforcing it is another. A 1961 case in California, *People* v. *Jones,* is a case in point.

A woman who had suffered a number of beatings from her husband was attacked by him again. She took a gun to defend herself, shot and killed him.

Under California law it is justifiable homicide to kill someone while resisting a felony. Nevertheless, Mrs. Jones was convicted.

The court ruled: "In creating the statutory felony of wife-beating the purpose of the legislation was not to issue a license for a wife to kill her husband but to provide a means of dealing with a particular family situation."

Sue Eisenberg and Pat Micklow reviewed this case and many others in their remarkable study *The Assaulted Wife: Catch 22 Revisited* and concluded: "Although present laws may be adequate, their applications were found to be misleading and inconsistent to victims seeking aid, and thus, assaulted wives are assured of little or no protection from violent husbands."

Others have made similar observations.

Dr. Judd Marmor, former president of the American Psychiatric Association, said: "There was a time in the history of Western culture when a man had the right to beat his wife as part of the privilege of being a husband. It wasn't considered a problem. Today, when we are moving toward an egalitarian role between man and women, this is no longer acceptable behavior. There's always a cultural lag, and many husbands still think they should be lord and master.''

Susan Jackson, a lawyer with the California Rural Legal Assistance Program, agrees: ''The tradition of spousal immunity is now formally relaxed in the area of family violence, but in behavioral terms the situation seems practically not to have changed much at all since the days of Blackstone. . . .''

It has been more than 200 years since the learned jurist Blackstone declared wife beating ''antiquated,'' but neither the custom nor the attitude that fostered it has disappeared.

Cary D. Pollak, a city lawyer who deals with spouse abuse daily at the Washington, D.C., Citizen's Complaint Center, confirms it. ''Some men still believe they have a God-given right to beat their wives,'' he said. ''There's wide-mouth shock when they're told they don't have that right. They can't believe it.''

CHAPTER FOUR

What Kind of Man Beats His Wife?

"Now we are even," quoth Steven,
When he gave his wife six blows to one.

Jonathan Swift

What kind of man beats his wife? Is he sick, mentally disturbed, or emotionally troubled? What are the conditions that foster acts of violence against a spouse? Is society the cause, or is it an individual problem? Are wife beaters mentally deficient, insane, abnormal?

Conventional wisdom depicts the wife beater as a lower class, beer-drinking, undershirt-wearing, Stanley Kowalski brute. Nowadays, he's also probably black, on welfare, and living in a teeming ghetto.

This stereotyped wife beater does exist, but he is far from representative. Research shows that wife beaters come in all sizes, shapes, and colors and from both sides of the tracks.

"Battered wives definitely are not mainly from the poor and lower class," says Judge Stewart Oneglia. "My worst case was the wife of a physician in Montgomery County, Maryland, the richest county in the nation, whose husband jumped on her spine causing paralysis because she left the door open and let the cool, air-conditioned air escape."

After studying our own empirical data and numerous independent investigations, we are convinced that persons taking part in such conflicts are of all ages, communities, income levels, races, religions, employment situations, and marital status. In other words, we could find no definitive characteristics of the wife beater. The crime of spouse assault and battery knows no social, geographical, economic, age, or racial barriers.

The occupations of the husbands we studied included high government officials, members of the armed forces, businessmen, mechanics, policemen, truck drivers, blue-collar workers, the unemployed, physicians, and lawyers.

In Arlington, Virginia, Police Officer Thomas Hoffman reports: "My beat encompasses some low-income neighborhoods and some pretty good ones where the people are wealthy. When it comes to wife beating, we go into the wealthy homes almost as often as we do the poorer ones."

In New York, Maria Roy, director of Abused Women's Aid in Crisis (AWAIC), says: "We see abuse of women on all levels of income, age, occupation, and social standing. I've had four women come in recently whose husbands are Ph.D.s—two of them are professors at top universities. Another abused woman is married to a very prominent attorney. We've counseled battered wives whose husbands are doctors, psychiatrists, even clergymen."

Ellen Barnett, director of Passage Crisis Center in Silver Spring, Maryland, relates: "We had a battered wife whose husband was a high official in the State Department. She was in her late thirties, and her husband had been beating her for about six or eight months. She showed up here with two black eyes and a sprained ankle. She had a little boy eleven and a daughter eight. Finally, she took them and left her husband and went to California."

In Washington, D.C., Michael Versace, a crisis line director, claims there is a prominent divorce lawyer in the nation's capital who has designed a special weapon that allows him to beat his wife and leave no incriminating marks.

The wife of a space-program scientist admits: "I've been hit in the pit of my stomach until I vomited blood for two or three days. Last year I had a cast on my arm from an automobile accident. He broke that cast twice."

In Michigan, writer Sue Shelley compared police statistics on battered wives in Detroit and in suburbs such as Livonia, Birmingham, and Grosse Pointe. She writes: "The percentages and general problems involving wife abuse are similar throughout the metropolitan area."

However, most studies involving only official records, such as police reports, show the poor have the highest number of wife-assault cases.

Richard Gelles, in his study of eighty New Hampshire families, concluded that there is an inverse relationship between both income and family violence and between education of the husband and family violence. The lower the income, the higher the amount of violence. The same rule applies to education: The less schooling, the greater the violence. Dr. Gelles also noted that violence is more likely to occur when the husband's education and occupational status are lower than his wife's. He found a high level of violence when the wife had attended college and the husband had not or if the wife had graduated and the husband had not.

Dr. Gelles also discovered the highest incidence of violence in families in which the husband had an unskilled or semiskilled job with low occupational status. Ironically, Dr. Gelles found that unemployed men beat their wives less than men employed in low- or middle-status jobs.

In another study of family violence, researcher John O'Brien divided a sample of wife beaters into three socioeconomic categories based on the husband's income and education. He found that 24 percent were upper-middle class; 29 percent were lower-middle class, and 47 percent were lower class.

"We conclude that although intrafamily violence is probably more common in lower-class families, it is erroneous to see it as primarily a lower-class phenomenon," O'Brien says. "The greater the incidence of violence which occurs in ghetto areas reflects not a subcultural disposition towards violence but rather greater incidence of men in the father-husband role who fail to have the achievement capacities normally associated with the role."

The evidence supporting the proposition that wife beating is more common among the lower socioeconomic class is mixed according to the unpublished report, *Violence in the Family*.

Official statistics on assault—a substantial proportion of which are between spouses—show higher rates in the poorest areas of a city. However, officially recorded rates are by no means the same as incidence rates, as was clearly shown in studies of juvenile offenses.

The apparent class difference could be entirely a function of differences in public visibility and differences in willingness to call in the police to deal with family disputes. . . .

A similar argument is made by Michigan Judge Sue Borman, who says: "Wife assault crosses socioeconomic lines, but I would think that a woman who is middle class or upper class is going to be less apt to prosecute because of embarrassment. I mean, I think that person would be more embarrassed to go into court to testify against her husband. She might be more apt to end the marriage, but I think she would be less apt to bring a criminal charge. She has more ability to get away from the man, too."

In fact, some social scientists feel wife beating is more common in the middle class. Rodney Stark and James McEvoy III, writing in *Psychology Today,* claim:

> The poor and less educated are not more likely than the middle class to resort to physical forms of aggression. We have assumed that middle-class persons vent their hostilities through more sedate channels—they are supposed to be more verbally violent. Actually physical violence is reported as equally common among all income groups and education levels. This finding is also true for frequency of physical violence. The middle class is not only as likely as others ever to have engaged in physical aggression, but have done so often. If anything, the middle class is more prone toward physical assault than the poor.
>
> This finding directly contradicts police statistics that suggest that the poor commit more acts of assault, get embroiled in more violent family arguments and otherwise act out their aggression more frequently than the members of higher social strata. We suggest that altercations among the poor are simply more likely to become police matters.
>
> Middle class persons have recourse to friends and professional counselors to help settle their disputes, they report more effective intervention by third parties not the police. Further, lower-class people are denied privacy for their quarrels; neighborhood bars, sidewalks and crowded, thin-walled apartments afford little isolation. The privacy of the middle-class life-style preserves an illusion of greater domestic tranquility, but it is apparently, only an illusion.

Sociologist Suzanne Steinmetz adds: "You might find there is a larger percentage of increase of both child abuse and wife beating occurring in middle-class families than in lower class families. Middle-class people are suffering more frustrations today because there is a discrepancy between their expectations and the cost of living."

The study by Sue Eisenberg and Pat Micklow reveals:

> The personal data regarding the victims and assailants does not indicate that wife assault is confined to any specific age group, occupational level, educational achievement levels, physical sizes, duration of marriage or family size.
>
> The ages of the victims varied from 19 to 35, averaging 26 years. The husband-assailants tended to be older, averaging 32 years. The youngest assailant was 22 and the oldest 45.
>
> Eighty percent of the victims were housewives or employed as waitresses, nurses aides, and saleswomen. The sample also included a high school teacher, office manager, a real estate agent, a corporate officer in public relations and an administrator in higher education.
>
> The average number of years of education among the victims was 12.4 with four having college degrees and two presently attending college. Husband-assailants, on the other hand, encompassed a wider range of occupations and had accumulated a higher average of educational attainment. Although 25 percent of them were unemployed, 50 percent were earning middle incomes as skilled laborers and blue collar workers. The remaining twenty-five percent were white collar professionals, including two plant managers, an attorney, an engineer and the president of a corporation earning $40,000 a year. The average educational attainment of the assailants was 13.2 years. The male assailant's size and weights varied from 5'8", 155 pounds to 6'4", 238 pounds. The victims ranged from 5'1", 106 pounds to 5'9", 266 pounds.

Dr. Gelles found that the most frequent age for the husband in relation to violence is 41 to 50, followed by 19 to 30. For wives, the most frequent age period is also 41 to 50 followed by 31 to 40.

Far from being just the activity of the poor, wife beating is engaged in by the rich, the powerful, and the glamorous.

In 1974, the wife of Japan's former Prime Minister Sato—winner of the Nobel Peace Prize—publicly accused him of beating her.

Actor Humphrey Bogart was a famous Hollywood wife beater whose knock-down, drag-out fights with his third wife, Mayo Methot, are still talked about. And recently, pop singer Fabian was taken to court over a charge that he battered two women—his wife and his mother-in-law.

In the sports world, former football star Jim Brown has been involved in several well-publicized battles with wives and girl friends.

Erin Pizzey, founder of the Chiswick Women's Aid refuge for battered wives in England, claims wife beaters come in four categories: (1) alcoholics, (2) psychotics, (3) psychopaths, (4) plain bullies.

Dr. Marguerite Fogel, Washington psychologist, observes: "I agree with Erin Pizzey that all the types she listed are inclined to beat their wives, but I believe also that other types of men, if they are sufficiently frustrated, will resort to wife beating. Reasonably normal, well-adjusted people will, if they are badgered enough, eventually hit.

"The immature personality is more likely to explode into violence. One who has never learned to stand frustrations and cope with it in other ways will resort to violence. Extremely docile types, when pushed enough, will also resort to violence."

Dr. B. L. Daley, a counseling psychologist in South Carolina, says, "To Pizzey's four categories I would add a fifth called the ultramasculine type." Several studies of both wife abusers and child abusers indicate that the psychological characteristics of the assaulters and their victims may form a pattern.

In the study *The Wife-Beaters' Wife,* twelve couples from a middle-class suburban area were subjects of detailed study, including psychiatric evaluations. All of the husbands had been charged with assault and battery by their wives.

The study found:

1. The wives in all the cases were characterized as aggressive, efficient, masculine, sexually frigid, and masochistic.

2. The husbands were shy, passive, sexually ineffectual, reason-

ably hard-working "mother's boys" with a tendency to drink excessively.

3. A working equilibrium in such a marriage was achieved through frequent alternation of passive and aggressive roles in their relationship.

In another study involving twenty-three men arrested for seriously assaulting their wives, sixteen were found to be suffering from psychiatric disorders such as depression, delusional jealousy, anxiety states, and personality disorders.

The study *Men Who Assault Their Wives* by M. Faulk categorized the husbands into five types: (1) dependent-passive, (2) dependent and suspicious, (3) violent and bullying, (4) dominating, or (5) stable and affectionate. This latter group included couples that appeared to have a long-standing stable relationship. Violence occurred at a time of mental disturbance, mostly during a depressive episode. Representatives of all these groups were found among his twenty-three men, but the commonest was the dependent-passive type, with nine cases.

Faulk compared wife beaters and child abusers and found some clear-cut differences. Child abusers were found to be immature or aggressive, while wife beaters were apparently stable people responding to prolonged strain or psychotics responding to severe mental illness. Wife beaters also had a lower incidence of previous criminal offenses.

Dr. Steinmetz is leery of classifying wife beaters as psychotic and psychopaths except for a relatively few cases.

"Most of the studies have shown that they are not psychologically ill," she says. "In most respects, they would be just like anybody else. This might be called the psychopathology myth.

"This is the idea that all husbands who hit their wives are mentally ill. No doubt some are. But the studies indicate that such actions more often reflect the carrying out of a role model which the abusing parent or the violent husband learned from his parents and which is brought into play when social stresses become intolerable."

Dr. Steinmetz offers her own four categories. She claims when it comes to resolving family conflicts, people fall into four groups:

(1) screaming sluggers, (2) silent attackers, (3) threateners, and (4) pacifists.

The first group, the screaming sluggers, use a great deal of physical and verbal aggression in solving their problems.

The second, the silent attackers, don't say much but are prone to use violence often to settle conflicts.

The third, threateners, make use of a high level of verbal abuse but seldom get physical.

The fourth, the pacifists, are not very aggressive either verbally or physically.

All of these types are found among normal, everyday people. Dr. Steinmetz feels that giving wife beaters psychiatric classifications overlooks the point that spouse abuse is too widespread and occurs too frequently to be the work of a demented few. The answer to the question "What kind of man beats his wife?" is: *Every* kind, and they can be located in so-called "normal families."

"Evidence abounds to indicate that normal families are not conflict-free and that they use considerable amounts of both verbal and physical aggression in resolving these conflicts," says Dr. Steinmetz.

A number of studies have established firm links between battered children and battering spouses. Battered children grow up to become battering parents and battering spouses.

"Family violence is usually a learned pattern of behavior," says Dr. Daley. "Often the behavior is modeled on the father or other adult male figures. The mother also contributes by accepting this behavior."

Dr. Gelles found that people who saw their own parents use physical violence were more likely to use it themselves as adults. He also noted that those who were hit infrequently as children were less likely to participate in spousal violence than those who had been hit frequently.

A study directed by Dr. John Flynn at Western Michigan University in Kalamazoo found two-fifths of the wife beaters had been abused as children. At least one-third of them were also abusing their own children.

Eisenberg and Micklow also discovered a link of violence between spouse abusers and their parents. "The final significant factor derived from the study was that violent physical behavior occurred between the parents of 40 percent of the victims and 50 percent of the assailants. Twenty percent stated that violence occurred in both families."

Shirley M. Nurse found that in seven of the twenty cases of child abuse in her study, the abusing parent also physically abused his or her partner. Maurice Boisvert reports that in one-fourth of the cases he studied, the abusing parent had been physically abused by the spouse and then in turn had abused a child.

Fifteen of the professionals interviewed in the Kalamazoo study said that they knew of at least one case of spouse assault in which the child also was abused.

"The chances of a battered child becoming a battering adult are very, very strong," says Dr. Steinmetz. "I found that there were patterns that extended over three generations. So that if you had a grandmother and grandfather who perhaps screamed and yelled at each other and maybe occasionally slapped each other, they tended to use those methods on their children, and their children tended to use those methods on their brothers and sisters. And then when these children married, they tended to use the same methods on their husbands and wives and similarly on their children, and of course their children repeated it. So for three generations I found very consistent patterns on the way they resolved conflict . . . the monkey see, monkey do idea."

There have been some notable examples of this cycle of violence. Albert De Salvo, the notorious Boston Strangler, at his trial described how his father brutally beat him and knocked out his mother's teeth and broke every finger on one of her hands.

Researchers also believe that violence in so-called normal families can contribute to the creation of a wife beater. The Harris Poll for the National Commission on the Causes and Prevention of Violence recorded an almost unanimous approval of using force to discipline children.

Sociologists Murray Straus, Gelles, and Steinmetz report that 84 to 97 percent of American families use physical punishment at some point in a child's life.

They cited a number of studies that conclude that physical punishment leaves personality traits of aggression and guilt and attitudes approving the use of violence to affect social reform. Punishment becomes associated with love and violence. They report:

> The child learns that those who love him or her the most are also
> those who hit and have the right to hit. The second unintended con-
> sequence is the lesson that when something is really important, it
> justifies the use of physical force.
>
> The parents who use physical punishment to control the aggres-
> siveness of their children are probably increasing rather than de-
> creasing the aggressive tendencies of their child.

In short, there are grounds for believing that violence begets violence, however peaceful and altruistic the motivation.

David Bakan, in his book *Slaughter of the Innocents,* writes,
"Persons who engage in violence tend to have been the victims of
violence. . . . Every time a child is punished by the use of violence, he is taught that the use of violence is the proper mode of behavior."

Researchers have identified certain characteristics of personality
that seem to be present in many wife beaters.

"We have to rely upon victims for what little information we
have about wife beating," says Del Martin, former national board
member of NOW. "Physically punishing a wife, a hangover from
earlier days, is generally frowned upon today. Consequently, the
man who still practices this ancient custom is not likely to admit it
publicly. Those guilty of assaulting their wives are seldom arrested
and generally refuse therapy.

"Battering husbands are described as angry, resentful, suspicious, competitive, moody, and tense. They have about them an
aura of helplessness, fear, inadequacy, insecurity, alcoholism, jealousy, and frustration."

Many battering husbands are described as Jekyll and Hyde types.
Part of the time they are model husbands, gentle, loving, and considerate, and part of the time they are snarling, brutish, mean bullies.

"Attending one of the AWAIC meetings explodes some of the

myths about wife beaters," says Maria Roy. "Violence is usually a strictly behind-closed-doors situation, and many of the wives say that their husbands are the type of men that everyone likes and are the life of the party.

"Most men don't believe that they have a problem. They feel that this is their basic right—to treat their wives however they wish. In many ways, they're right—their behavior is condoned by our society."

Many wife beaters regard themselves as inadequate in some aspect of the prescribed male role in our society. Dr. Gelles notes that wife beaters often have trouble adequately filling the husband-provider role. Often, when the wife becomes the head of the household, the husband resents it and takes out his resentment on his wife.

A case from the police blotter of a large metropolitan city illustrates this point. "I was plaiting my husband's hair when I told him I was tired of supporting him," the woman told police. "At that he hit me on the left ear with a giant vaseline jar. I fell back against the wall; the jar broke. Since then my husband comes to my job, makes a commotion, and threatens me."

William J. Goode, writing in the *Journal of Marriage and the Family*, observes that men who command limited social, psychological, and verbal resources are likely to use more force on their wives than men who are well-educated, hold prestigious jobs, and earn a respectable income.

Dr. Marguerite Fogel says: "A wife beater would have great difficulty putting into words what he's really feeling, and in an effort to communicate the enormity of his passions, he would put it into action rather than words."

Ray Fowler, director of the American Association of Marriage and Family Counselors, says, "Wife abusers are generally obsessional men who have learned to trigger themselves emotionally."

But identifying the wife beater or the potential wife beater is a difficult task. The evidence suggests that they are everywhere and that the qualities that separate them from the rest of the population are not always discernible.

Perhaps the most acute observation on the subject was made by

Loman in Bangor, Maine. Every day he deals with wife beaters not as an abstraction but as real people in the real world.

"Inadequate and unsure males are more likely to abuse women than psychologically stable men," says Loman. "But any man is likely to be a wife beater."

True, some wife beaters are psychotic, but the evidence shows that most do not suffer from severe emotional disorders. Some battered wives tend to ascribe mental or emotional problems to their husbands to excuse them for their violent acts. But more often than not the American wife beater is not a "mental case." Most often he appears to be normal in almost every respect.

All of us—men and women—carry the seeds of violence. The difference between the raving savage and the genteel, civilized person may be less than most of us are prepared to recognize.

"How easy it is to deny that within all of us lies a potential for violence and that any of us could be unreachable," writes Dr. Sidney Wasserman, discussing child abusers. But his observation would seem to apply equally to spouse abusers.

> What is more repugnant to our rational "mature" minds than the thought of committing impulsive, violent acts. . . .
>
> We tell ourselves that the primitive, untempered instincts responsible for such acts could not erupt in us. But stripped of our defenses against such instincts and placed in a social and psychological climate conducive to violent behavior, any of us could do the "unthinkable." This thought should humble us: perhaps we are not battering parents only because conditions do not lead us to commit "unnatural acts."

Might not the same be said for spouse abusers? Perhaps we are not battering spouses because we have not yet faced the "right" set of conditions that would cause us to react with violence against our mate.

"Like it or not, we are bound each to the other and our destinies are interwoven," continues Dr. Wasserman.

> As we try to understand the battering person, we must look into ourselves to find out what there is in each of us, in our community,

our nation and the world that the battering parent takes as a sign that what he is doing is permissible.

To answer this question we must face up to the paradoxes in our moral code that condemn violence in one form, permit it in another. . . .

Wife beating is not only tolerated in the U.S.; it is nurtured in our violent American soil. National polls show an overwhelming acceptance of force and violence as acceptable conduct under certain conditions. As a people we deplore violence but show near unanimous approval of physical punishment for our children. We talk of equality between the sexes, yet significant numbers of us feel that men not only have the right but *should* use physical force on women "when they need it." Paradoxically, both men and *women* hold this view.

There have been a number of attempts to classify wife beaters into types, and all of these efforts are useful to some degree. But the mere act of classifying tends to set the spouse abuser aside, to remove him from "the rest of us" to be examined by "the rest of us." Spouse abuse needs to be examined as part of the whole fabric of violence in our society. The simple fact is that in America today almost every man is a potential wife beater.

Sometimes my anger is so great I want to hit someone or something but usually I hit myself. What stops me from taking this aggression out on someone? Why doesn't my brother have the same stopping mechanism? What makes him hit?

CHAPTER FIVE

Maria's Story—
A Case History

Man is the hunter, woman is his game.

Tennyson

Maria Arjona finished her drink and looked nervously up at the clock on the wall behind the bar. She had passed the afternoon sipping beer and listening to Spanish songs on the jukebox. It was difficult to make out the time because the large Budweiser sign obscured the clock's face. She squinted. It was four-thirty. Time to go home. Time to fix some supper for her husband.

Maria gathered up her packages and purse and hurried out the door. I will have to get something fast, she thought as she headed for her tiny apartment on Compton Street, one of Los Angeles's down-at-the-heels Spanish-black neighborhoods.

Maria Arjona called James Murphy her husband even though they were not legally married. They had been living together for five years. They never talked of marriage—it was "no big thing," they agreed.

At first, they lived together because of the physical attraction, then for convenience, and now out of habit. They had no thoughts about love. Their relationship simply existed.

From the start, Jimmy beat Maria. This did not surprise her. She expected it; it was the way things were in the world. Growing up in her father's house in Balboa, in the Panama Canal Zone, she often saw her mother beaten. It never occurred to Maria that men on the American mainland would be any different from the Zonians.

Maria put the key in her apartment door, but before she could turn it, the door fell away, yanked open from the inside. Her common-law husband stood in the doorway. His eyes, framed by his dark-brown skin, were moist and glistening. He was high on God knows what.

Jimmy slapped her and knocked her up against the doorjamb. Then he grabbed her by the arm, pulled her inside, and shoved her across the room; she fell on their tattered couch. Jimmy was a short man but powerful.

"Where you been?" he shouted.

"Shopping. I have been shopping."

"You lying. You've been out drinking beer and peddling your ass."

"I don't do that, Jimmy. I went shopping and had one beer on the way home."

"You lying cunt! I saw your ass in Junior's. You drinking up my money and making passes at every motherfucker in there."

"I was in Junior's, but I had only one beer . . . maybe two . . ."

She put up her arm and took his fist on her shoulder. She tucked her head under her arm and turned away from him. Jimmy laid another punch on her back as she moved to escape.

She hurried into the kitchen, and he did not follow her. "I'll get some supper. Watch TV. I'll have something for you right away."

"You've been jiving me," he muttered. "No chick gonna jive me."

She didn't answer. She busied herself in the kitchen.

The door slammed. She could hear Jimmy thumping down the front stairs. She raised her elbow to test the pain in her shoulder. It wasn't too bad.

She continued to work on the meal. He might come back, and he would be really mad this time if his supper wasn't ready.

When she heard his footsteps on the stairs, the rice and beans were cooked and ready to serve. She spooned a hot heap on a plate so that Jimmy could sit down and eat the second he walked in the door.

He came in carrying a gallon of wine. He walked directly to the table and sat behind his food. He unscrewed the top to the bottle and filled a water tumbler up to the brim with the red liquid.

He said nothing, took a big drink, and began shoveling in his food. Maria fixed herself a plate and sat down on the other end of the table and quietly began to eat.

Jimmy drained his first glass of wine and then another. When he finished eating, he got up from the table, hooked a finger into the jug, and picked up his glass with his other hand and walked into the living room. He turned on the TV and flopped in an overstuffed chair with broken springs that tilted his body to the left. Jimmy sat drinking the red wine and staring at TV. He was muttering under his breath.

It will be bad tonight, thought Maria as she cleaned up the supper dishes. He is like a boiling pot with a tight lid on it. Sooner or later he is going to explode. Holy Mother, pray for me.

She ran the prayer mechanically through her mind over and over, hoping it would ward off the evil. She went into the living room and sat on the end of the couch, as far away from Jimmy as she could get.

"You don't like this program, do you?" he said.

"It's okay" she answered. "We can watch your show. There is nothing I want to see better than this one."

They sat in silence. Suddenly Jimmy shouted: "How come you don't say nothing?"

"I'm watching the TV. This show has my interest, and I don't have nothing much to say, anyway."

"Shit," he snarled. "You thinking about how you're gonna cheat me."

"I was watching the TV program, that's all."

A long silence followed, punctuated only by the drone of the TV set and an occasional muttered remark from Jimmy.

He finished the wine, and his body fell slack in the chair. He began to snore.

Maria waited until she was sure he was asleep, then crept across the room and turned off the set.

Jimmy bolted up in his chair.

"What you doing?"

"You was asleep. I was just turning off the TV."

He had startled her, and she was nervous and shaking.

"You leave my fucking TV set alone."

"You was sleeping. . . ."

"You thought I was sleeping! You were getting ready to sneak out and go fuck somebody."

"No, Jimmy. I don't do that. I told you I'm your woman. I don't want no other guys."

Jimmy leaped from his chair and seized Maria by the throat. He choked her and shook her head violently. "You lying son of a bitch."

"No Jimmy . . . please . . . I can't breathe . . ."

He released her, and she fell to the floor.

"You're the one who's fooling around," she shouted. "You're out fucking everybody you can, and you accuse me all the time. Your girl friend probably threw you out today, and you're taking it out on me."

Jimmy was in the kitchen, poking through the refrigerator.

"Where's the beer I bought?"

"You drank it."

"Lying bitch! I buy beer, and you drink it up. I can't keep a goddamn thing in this house with you here."

"Jimmy, you ain't bought no beer since last week, and you drank it all watching the game. I didn't drink none of it."

She was shouting.

"Who you yelling at?" roared Jimmy.

"You! You son of a bit . . ."

The final expletive died half uttered in her throat. Jimmy's hands were on her neck again.

Maria gasped. Her eyes bulged with fright. He was going to kill her. She knew it. He was really trying to kill her.

Jimmy was choking her and beating her head against the wall. She was pulling at his hands, but he was too strong. She brought up her knee in a sharp, forceful kick, smashing Jimmy in the groin.

He screamed and grabbed his testicles, then dropped to the floor.

Maria sucked air into her lungs and screamed. "You crazy. You crazy. You're trying to kill me."

She tried to run around him and make her way to the door, but Jimmy caught her foot and brought her down with a thud.

"Help!" she screamed. "He's trying to kill me! Help! Help!"

They were both sprawled out on the floor. Maria was kicking with all her might, but Jimmy held on to her ankle. He pulled her across the floor with a sharp yank, raised himself up on his elbows, then lunged on top of her.

His eyes were filled with hatred and rage as he sat on his common-law wife and began to pound her face savagely with his fists.

Maria kept screaming for help.

Suddenly there was a knock on the door. "What's going on in there?" It was a man's voice.

"It's okay, brother," shouted Jimmy. "Nothing. Everything is cool."

Maria screamed, "He's killing me, call the cops."

"Stay cool, brother," Jimmy shouted. "Don't need no fuzz. She's high."

"Call the cops! Call the cops," Maria continued to scream.

They both heard the man at the door walk away.

By the time the first police car arrived, a crowd had begun to collect on the street outside the apartment.

When the ambulance got there, the street was choked with people. The revolving red and white lights, mounted on the roofs of the emergency vehicles, played across the expressionless faces as they watched the white-jacketed attendants rush through the narrow doorway and up the stairs.

When the ambulance attendants returned, they had Maria strapped to their stretcher. The crowd surged forward for a better look, and the police shouted: "Step back! Step back, please, and let them through."

A crack opened in the throng, and the emergency procession swiftly filed through. As Maria was being placed in the back of the ambulance, someone said softly: "Her throat's been cut."

The news buzzed through the crowd. Spectators craned forward for a look and stood watching until the ambulance sped off, its sirens shrieking. The crowd was still. No one spoke or moved until the shriek was gone, absorbed into the city's mundane clatter. A policeman's voice punctured the mood. "Did anyone hear or see what happened? Does anyone know if anyone else lives in the apartment?''

On cue, the crowd began to disintegrate. People started to move quickly. A tall man wearing a baseball cap turned to Jimmy and said, "You better get your ass out of here, brother.''

"Right on," said Jimmy. Keeping his blood-spattered hands buried deep in his pockets, he turned and walked off into the darkness.

Maria nearly lost her left ear. It took twenty-three stitches and the speedy and skillful work of the surgeons at the hospital to save it. She had lost a great deal of blood and was nearly dead on arrival. Two weeks later her head was still bandaged, but she was well enough to be released from the hospital.

Jimmy was not there. He did not come to visit her during her entire stay. She had heard from her good friend Aminta that Jimmy had been seen around the neighborhood but that he was avoiding the apartment because he feared the cops were watching it.

When it was time to go home, Aminta came to the hospital to pick up Maria. She waited impassively while Maria explained to the hospital people that she had no money, no job, no family here. She was an American citizen, but her family all lived in the Panama Canal Zone. She had a common-law husband who didn't work much. No, there was no money to pay for the hospital bills.

Maria hugged Aminta when they met, and they walked out together to Aminta's '65 Dodge.

"That man's crazy," said Aminta.

"I know this," agreed Maria.

"You going back to him?"

"No, I've had enough. He tried to kill me. I almost died, and he never once came to see me to see if I was all right. He does not care for me. I think you are right—he's crazy.''

"Did the cops talk to you?"

"Yes.''

"What you tell them?"

"I told them Jimmy tried to kill me. That I don't want to see him no more and that I want him arrested.''

"What they say?"

"They tell me that when I get out of the hospital to go down to the precinct house and swear out a paper for his arrest."

"You going to do it?"

"Yes."

Jimmy was arrested and brought before a criminal court judge. The judge questioned Jimmy and severely scolded him for taking a knife to his woman.

During the proceedings, Jimmy said little. He stood with his head down and called the judge sir every time he spoke to him.

"Mr. Murphy, do you realize the seriousness of what you've done?"

"Yes, sir."

"Do you want to go to prison?"

"No, sir."

"Are you still living with Maria Arjona?"

"No, sir."

"She doesn't want to live with you anymore, does she?"

"No, sir."

"She filed an affidavit so stating. Do you understand what a court order means?"

"Yes, sir."

"You understand that you are not to go near Maria Arjona anymore. If you do, you can be put in jail. Do you understand that?"

"Yes, sir. I don't want to see her no more."

"Well, good. Now James, will you promise me that you'll stay away from her? That there won't be any more trouble between you two?"

"Yes, sir."

"Yes, what?

"I promise I won't go near her no more."

"All right, James. I'm going to take you at your word. I think you're a smart enough young man to realize violation of my order can only lead to more trouble for you. I'm giving you a chance to put this mess behind you and to assume a role as a useful citizen."

"Yes, sir."

"Are you willing to do that?"

"Yes, sir."

"All right, Jimmy. Find yourself a new girl friend and stay away from your old one. This woman is nothing but trouble for you. Go on home now and stay out of trouble."

"Yes, sir. Thank you, sir."

Maria went back to the old apartment and picked up her clothes and a few other belongings and about $50.00 she had saved. Most of the things there were tattered and broken, and she was glad to leave them all behind.

Maria spent the next few days with Aminta and then went looking for a place of her own. She was carrying a folded newspaper and searching for numbers on a building when she was knocked to the pavement.

Dazed and confused, she felt another blinding flash of pain against her face. Then another. She groped through the pain and confusion and received another deadening blow, this one to the back of her neck. She struggled to her knees, and for the first time she caught a glimpse of Jimmy. He punched her head again and sent her sprawling.

She heard her fingers crack when Jimmy's Cuban-heeled shoes stomped on them. Then there was another electric shock in her face, a sunburst of light, then oblivion.

The attack had been so sudden and savage that she never had a chance to even cry out.

When Maria came to, she forced herself to walk to the same police precinct where she had previously filed charges against Jimmy. The desk sergeant was impassive. He took down the information and sent Maria home in a squad car.

Jimmy was again arrested, and once again he was brought into court. He appeared before a different judge, but the scene that followed was almost identical. The judge lectured, extracted a promise from Jimmy that he would leave Maria alone, and then released him.

More than two months passed without incident. Jimmy stayed away, and Maria's injuries healed. She got herself a job and found a new apartment. Soon she was settled into a new routine, and the memory of Jimmy's unwarranted violence began to fade.

Then one hot June night, Maria answered a knock on her door.

She opened it slightly to see who was there. Jimmy easily pushed it open the rest of the way and forced his way inside.

"Go away, Jimmy. I don't want nothing to do with you no more."

"You're still my woman," he said. His speech was slurred, his eyes were red, his breath reeked.

He snatched her wrist and pulled her toward him. Maria pulled and twisted and punched him on the chest with her free hand.

Jimmy tried to kiss her, but she shook her head violently.

"Go away, Jimmy. You hurt me. I don't want to be with you no more. Get out!"

Jimmy continued to force himself on her, and she continued to struggle.

"Don't give me that shit," he shouted.

"Get out of here, you son of a bitch," Maria screamed. "You leave me go!" She lashed out and dug her fingernails into Jimmy's cheek.

He retaliated with a right cross to her head.

She fell to her knees.

He smashed her with his left, and she fell to the floor. Jimmy jumped on top of her and began fumbling with her dress. She grabbed at him, and he punched her again and again.

He raped her on the floor of her own apartment. She cried uncontrollably.

Maria doesn't know who found her or how she got to the hospital. In fact, she can remember almost nothing for her first two days as a patient. She was totally unconscious for twelve hours and in shock for days.

Her eyes were swollen shut, and at first she thought she was blind. Her bottom teeth were driven through her lower lip, and her mouth was swollen and grotesquely twisted. She sustained a brain concussion.

As soon as she was able, Maria filed charges from her hospital bed. Once again, Jimmy was arrested and brought to court. The judge paroled him without bail, with the stipulation that he stay away from Maria. Jimmy promised that he would and was a free man in a matter of hours. Maria was hospitalized for twenty-six days.

After her release, Maria went to the police to complain. She was terrified of Jimmy and with good reason. She pleaded with them to help her. The cops listened politely and told her to call them if he bothered her again.

It wasn't until November that he returned. The moment she heard the knock she knew it was he. She held her breath and prayed to the Virgin that he would go away. He called her name. She didn't answer.

Over and over she silently prayed: "Holy Mary, make him think I'm not here."

"I know you're in there!" he shouted. "Don't try playing possum with me. I know you're in there."

In desperation she tried a bluff.

"I'm calling the cops right now, Jimmy," she yelled through the locked door. "Don't come in here."

She heard his body crash up against the door.

"I'm dialing the cops right now," she cried. "You better get out of here."

He smashed against the door again.

"Hello, police. This is Maria Arjona, Pico Boulevard. Jimmy Murphy is breaking into my house. Send the cops over right away."

He smashed against the door again.

"Yes. He is the one who beat me up before. That's right. Come and arrest him."

The door flew up as the flimsy moulding around the lock cracked and splintered.

Jimmy stood staring at her, then said: "You crazy woman? You ain't got no phone. You think you can fool me with that shit?"

"Stay away from me," she warned.

Jimmy glared at her and in a falsetto voice mocked her: "Come on over and arrest Jimmy Murphy, Officer . . . shit!"

Trembling, Maria slowly reached over to find a broken broom handle she had saved "just in case."

She found it and held it up, over her head, getting ready to swing it.

Jimmy laughed in open contempt. He moved directly across the room toward her, walking with an arrogant, casual shuffle. She swung the broom handle, but he caught her forearm before the blow landed, then easily disarmed her.

"What you got this thing for?" he jeered. "Gonna hit somebody up side of their head?"

Maria screamed before the first blow hit her. She laced her fingers together over her head and felt the wood sting them. Then she felt a wack to her forehead, one on her elbow and one on her head. Jimmy was flaying the club back and forth, hitting her head first on one side and then the other.

Maria made her body into a ball, grabbing the back of her head with her hands and hiding her face in her arms behind her elbows.

Jimmy clubbed her protective cover, and when her arms failed to drop away from her face, he began poking and jabbing her with the jagged end of the broom handle.

Maria's scream was a gasp of pain and horror.

The jagged stick was imbedded in her left eye.

She grabbed the stick and held it, too terrified to pull it out. Mercifully, she fainted. Murphy bolted out the door and ran as fast as he could down the street.

The surgeons could not save her eye.

Half of her head was covered with bandages as she once again filed charges against James Murphy from a hospital bed. Once again the police arrested him and brought him into court, and once again a judge released him on his own recognizance, without bail. The only thing required of Murphy was that he promise not to bother Maria again. He promised.

When her eye was sufficiently healed, Maria went to the hospital clinic and was fitted with a cheap glass eye. She anxiously inspected herself in the mirror, then burst into tears. It was grotesque.

"I didn't want anyone to look at me," she said. "I was ashamed of myself. I was always proud of how I looked. I was not real beautiful, but I considered myself good-looking. Now I looked fisheyed. I wanted to be pretty again, but there was nothing I could do.

"I went to the cops and complained that no one was doing nothing to save me from this man. I was now missing one eye, and he came and beat me whenever he pleased, and there was nothing I

could do about it. I wanted the cops to protect me. I even went to
the district attorney and complained, but nobody wanted to do
nothing for me.

"They told me they was doing all they could. They said that
when I complained that they arrested him as quickly as they could,
but they couldn't arrest him just because he might beat me up
again.

"They told me that they could lock him up after he beat me up.
It was up to the judge to put Jimmy in jail, they said. They just arrest them; the judges sentence people. The only one who could put
Jimmy away permanently was a judge, and right now he wasn't
even charged with nothing, so they could do nothing until I got beat
up again.

"He already took my eye. Do I have to wait for him to kill me
before the cops do something? They told me, 'We just enforce the
law, lady, we don't have anything to say what happens to somebody after we arrest them.'

"I told them I was scared. They said they understood and that
the best thing for me to do would be to move. They said if they was
me that they'd move as far away as they could. I told them I don't
know nobody nowhere else except L.A. and in Panama. They told
me: 'Well, it's up to you to do what you want. I'm just telling you
what I would do.'

"I left there. I felt like I was the one who was the criminal. I
didn't do nothing, but the cops tell me I should get out of town. I
didn't know what to do or where to turn."

Maria took the cop's advice. She didn't leave town, but she
found a new apartment. She got a job in a factory and began to
save a little money.

By February, she had saved enough to buy a new set of kitchen
furniture, and her life was getting in better order. She had no men
friends because she was too self-conscious about her "fisheye."
She spent most of her time at work or home alone watching TV.
Occasionally, she saw Aminta or one of the other girls from the
Compton Street neighborhood, but she was afraid to go over there,
afraid Jimmy would see her and beat her again.

She had lost a lot of weight after her last beating, and only now,
four months later, was she beginning to put some back on. She was

beginning to feel better—more human. She still hated to look at herself in the mirror. She felt ugly, freakish.

When the new furniture arrived, it gave her a tremendous lift. She carefully arranged it and stopped to admire it several times that day. She ate a good supper and thought about inviting someone over to show off her new possessions. She went to bed feeling better than she had in months.

Her peace was short-lived. She awoke with a start. He was pounding on the door and throwing his body against it with all his strength.

She was grateful she'd had a phone installed. She ran to it and dialed 911, the emergency number.

Jimmy was throwing himself against her door, and she could hear the wood begin to splinter. She screamed hysterically into the phone. "Come quickly. He's here to kill me. Send the cops! Send the cops!"

The police dispatcher got her to give him her name and address and promised help was on the way. He no sooner got the words out when the door gave way and Jimmy was in the room, cursing and swearing at the top of his lungs.

He snatched the phone away from her and ripped it off the wall. He smashed her across her right temple with the ear piece with such force that the broken instrument flew out of his hands.

She screamed, and he punched her in the stomach. He pounded her several times in her breasts and stomach until she dropped in a heap on the floor. Then he turned his fury on her prized new kitchen set. He tipped the table over; then he began kicking the legs until they broke off. Systematically, he worked his way around the table. Next he picked up the chairs and began pounding them against the sink until the legs broke off. He took all the chairs, one by one, and broke them all.

Maria lay sobbing on the floor, unable to move, powerless to do anything.

Jimmy took a kitchen knife from the drawer and cut a large X across the seat cushions of her living-room furniture.

He stood in the middle of the apartment and surveyed the scene. Apparently satisfied with his work, he gave Maria a final kick and walked out the door.

Only a few minutes passed before the police arrived. They helped her up and drove her once again to the hospital emergency room. This time she was lucky; she had several large bruises but no broken bones or cuts.

The police found Jimmy and arrested him. He was taken to court once again, but this time both the police and the district attorney appeared and testified to the repeated beatings.

They told the judge Maria Arjona lived in terror. That she was routinely beaten by a man whom she had severed all relations with months before. She had sustained extremely severe injuries, including the loss of an eye. She had made every effort to stay away from her tormentor. She had repeatedly asked the police for help because her rights as an American citizen were severely curtailed and her body threatened with grievous harm. The city recommended that James Murphy be incarcerated for a maximum sentence because he had repeatedly demonstrated that he was a threat to the woman he once lived with and that he had given no indication that he would abide by his many promises to the court that he would cease and desist from attacking her without cause or reason.

The judge listened, then turned to Jimmy.

"Have you learned your lesson, James?"

"Yes, sir."

"Have you finally realized that you can't go around beating up this woman?"

"Yes, sir."

"Can I count on you to stay away from her in the future?"

"Yes, sir."

"Well, I'm going to give you one more chance. I'm going to place you on parole without bail but with the stipulation—and I mean this—that you promise never to go near Maria Arjona again."

"I promise, Judge," Jimmy said. He held his head down so the judge could not see the smirk that crept across his face.

Maria sat in the back of the courtroom and cried.

The district attorney put his hand on her shoulder on his way out and said, "I'm sorry, Miss Arjona. I really am. I did everything I could."

Maria Arjona has since committed suicide.

CHAPTER SIX

Why Does He Beat Her?

"When did you stop beating your wife?"
"Who said I stopped?"

Vaudeville Joke

Why do men beat their wives?

Richard Gelles argues that it is impossible to single out one cause of wife beating. Other experts in the field agree that spouse abuse is caused by a combination of things involving social position, stress, self-concept, socialization, personal and community values.

For the purpose of examination, we have arranged the reasons for spousal violence into nine categories. They are:

1. Mental illness.
2. Alcohol and drugs.
3. Public acceptance of violence.
4. Lack of communication.
5. Sex.
6. Poor self-image.
7. Frustration.
8. Change.
9. Violence as a resource to solve problems.

Mental Illness

No one doubts that a certain percentage of wife beaters are suffering from serious mental disorders. The extreme cases, such as one in which a man pounded out his wife's teeth with a hammer, are probably the work of severely disturbed individuals. Erin Pizzey, a pioneer in providing havens for battered wives in England, does not hesitate to label many wife beaters as psychopaths. "That is exactly what they are," she says, "aggressive, dangerous, and deeply immature."

In apparent agreement are many of the abused wives. A study conducted by Western Michigan University at Kalamazoo reports:

> This study seems to indicate that there are certain psychological traits that are found as characteristics of assaulters. The most often mentioned were mental incompetence, alcohol abuse and extreme jealousy. . . .
> A majority of the women interviewed felt that their husbands were in some way mentally incompetent. That is, they were said to be either mentally retarded, psychologically or emotionally immature or extremely paranoid individuals. . . .
> The prevailing psychological theme . . . appears to be that they excuse or explain away their husbands' assaults by asserting that their mate does not know what he is doing. Mental illness and alcoholism have been given as the most prevalent reasons.

A commonly held belief is that many wife beaters are paranoid—exhibiting deep irrational fears—and schizophrenic—unable to tell reality from fantasy. A certain percentage are sadists who obtain pleasure from inflicting pain. Some psychiatrists believe that a wife is a surrogate for the assaulter's self-hatred. Wife beaters are often filled with immense feelings of guilt and become morose, despondent, and deeply depressed. Sometimes this leads to suicide or murder-suicide.

However, most researchers do not believe that mental illness afflicts the majority of wife beaters. Dr. Murray Straus says: "The proportion is no greater than the proportion of mentally ill people in the population at large." Dr. Straus does not believe that violent couples are acting out repressed fantasies. "I think that's a fantasy the psychiatrists have," he says.

Alcohol and Drugs

There is no shortage of evidence that alcohol and drugs—particularly alcohol—have a lot to do with wife beating. From 40 to 95 percent of spouse-abuse cases are estimated to be directly linked to alcohol.

Dr. Gelles found that drinking played a part in 47 percent of the cases of spouse abuse he studied.

In their study, Sue Eisenberg and Patricia Micklow report:

> In 60 percent of the cases, alcohol consumption by the assailant was always present at the time of the attack.
>
> In an additional 10 percent alcohol was present occasionally. Drugs, especially amphetamines, were used prior to the beatings in 20 percent of the cases, but always in conjunction with alcohol. The characterization of the drunken husband as a wife-beater has some merit.

Robert Flynn, Washington, D.C., assistant corporation counsel, says: "The overriding thing that comes out in the vast majority of cases is that most of the husbands have some sort of an alcoholic problem."

Andrew Loman reports: "At least 80 percent of the wife beating situations in Eastern Maine are alcohol related. Drugs play a far lesser role."

In Prince Georges County, Maryland, Marge Caswell of the county Women's Commission says "I would say in 75 to 80 percent of the cases, alcohol is involved."

Michael Verace, director of a Washington, D.C., crisis center, estimates: "Seventy to 80 percent are heavily alcohol related."

Maria Roy says: "These assaults, 95 percent of them, are the result of a husband's drinking. Only a minority of the husbands beat their wives when they're not drunk."

There is no doubt that alcohol and family violence are strongly connected, but not all of the experts are sure that alcohol is a *cause* of wife beating.

Dr. Gelles points out that "in most families husbands and wives drink without ever becoming violent. In others, violence occurs without any alcohol being drunk. And in some families where violence occurs when the offender is drinking, it also occurs when he or she does not drink."

One possible explanation is that cause and effect are the reverse of what is commonly supposed. Instead of men beating their wives because they've been drinking, they drink because they want to beat their wives.

Dr. Gelles said: "The drinker can use the period when he is drunk as a 'time out' when he is not responsible for his actions. Also alcohol can serve as an excuse . . . nothing is wrong in the family, it's 'demon rum' that's the blame."

According to the report *Violence in the Family: An Assessment of Knowledge and Research Needs:*

> There is reasonably good evidence that alcohol is associated with violence in the family. But what is not clear is whether people act violently because they are drunk or whether they get drunk in order to have implicit social permission to act violently. Empirical research on this issue will be extremely difficult because the actors themselves are committed to a definition of the situation in which violent acts are attributed to temporary loss of control due to alcohol.

Public Acceptance of Violence

"A large segment of society accepts and glorifies physical and verbal force under the *right* circumstances," argues sociologist Suzanne Steinmetz.

> This use of physical force is glorified in the media—television, movies, magazines and newspapers. It is abundant in art forms and literature. Nursery rhymes, and children's stories, for example Hansel and Gretel; There Was An Old Woman; Humpty Dumpty; all extol the glory as well as the fear of violence. . . .
>
> There is a general acceptance and the glorification of force. (For example, John Wayne, Mission Impossible, Mannix) in the name of law, order and the "American way."

Dr. Steinmetz's position is borne out by the findings of the Louis Harris poll previously cited. This poll shows that one-fifth of all adult American men have either punched or beaten another person or have been beaten. One-fifth of the population, including women, approved of a man slapping his wife.

There is other evidence that society sanctions violence, particularly violence between husbands and wives.

A series of fights were staged by three psychologists at Michigan State University. They found that men rushed to the aid of other men being assaulted by either men or women. Many also helped women being beaten by other women. But not one male bystander interfered when they saw a man apparently beating up a woman.

This study recalls the famous murder of Kitty Genovese a number of years ago. She was methodically stalked on a New York City street, beaten and killed while thirty-eight people saw and heard what was going on. Not one witness came to her aid. Many people later said they didn't help her because they thought the killer was her husband.

The media play a role in encouraging spouse abuse, many believe. "Violence is portrayed as normal on the TV screen," says Maria Roy, "and certain types of men think it's okay to use it at home."

Loman believes: "Society encourages the wife beater through such avenues as the electronic media, cultural values passed from generation to generation, and the machismo ego identity of males."

In general, our society condones the use of force. Law-enforcement agencies and the military have been granted the use of force in their jobs, and parents have the right to use force on their children.

Most people do not become concerned about force until it becomes violence—that is, when force is used beyond ill-defined prescribed limits.

Lack of Communication

Researchers find that in spouse-battering homes there is a serious lack of communication between the marriage partners. Dr. Marguerite Fogel tells her clients to avoid violence by talking to each other. She says frank discussion should begin at the first sign of tension.

"A husband and wife should try to find out what they're doing to each other and listen to the other person's side. Not listening is not giving fair respect. The main thing is to stay in your own skin and don't blame. The minute you fix blame you stop working on the problem.

"It's better to say 'I feel awful' rather than 'We're not doing it right.' The latter fixes blame.

"I saw one couple who had been married forty years and they had never really communicated with each other. They had never expressed their antagonisms toward their in-laws, they had never expressed certain mild things that annoyed them, and they never really told each other they wanted certain kinds of attention. After meeting with me two or three times, they found out these things, and they came like a revelation.

"The inhibitions people have against communicating what's really in their hearts is amazing."

Dr. Murray Straus studied how middle-class couples conduct arguments. He listed a range of actions, including: "discussed the issues relatively calmly"; "got information to back up his or her side"; "yelled or insulted"; "threw something"; and "pushed or hit."

Dr. Straus found that couples who use a lot of verbal violence are far more likely to use physical violence as well. And as the intensity of harsh words increases, the level of physical aggression rises even more rapidly. This was true for both men and women in his study. Dr. Straus concludes that as anger grows, a person is more likely to carry it to extremes. It also becomes increasingly easy, he says, to go from hurting a spouse verbally to hurting him or her physically.

Eisenberg and Micklow also found that spouse abuse often escalates from verbal to physical. In fact, they found that verbal arguments preceded physical attacks most of the time. The arguments that led to violence ranged from blame over a misplaced pack of cigarettes to more serious questions of jealousy and rejection. Often the arguments are not the real cause of violence, but because of a severe lack of communication, the couples never talk about their real problems and never have the chance to try and resolve them.

Here's an example from a police blotter.

On October 16, 1975, about 10:30 P.M. an argument between my husband and myself began about the location of the TV set. . . . As

I was getting a glass of ice water from the refrigerator, he grabbed me and hit me with his fist on the nose. Then he beat me about the head and chest. He also choked me. I was bleeding badly, and he dragged me into the bathroom and sat me on the floor and poured water over me. I knew this even though I was partially unconscious.

Is it possible that so much violence and brutality developed because of the location of a TV set? Obviously, the problems in this family go beyond the surface trouble. Could this incident have been avoided if this man and wife had established better lines of communication and were able to discuss their real problems? It's a good bet that the answer is yes.

The lack of communication in violent couples extends beyond the immediate family. Profiles repeatedly show they lack close friends and have little contact with their neighbors. Few belong to groups such as the PTA or community organizations. There is a pattern of inability to use other people to help solve problems.

Battering couples often do not communicate with their children. "There is a tendency among some parents to avoid verbal communication and rely on physical discipline," says Dr. Steinmetz. "Not only does this method restrict interpersonal communications between parents and child but sets a pattern of disciplinary process in which sanctioned limits of physical force are continually extended." As a result, problems develop with the children that are similar to the ones developed between the marriage partners.

Dr. Gelles notes that hostile and aggressive communication by the wife often provokes the husband to beat her. Examples he found included: nagging and chiding the man about something he refused to do; name calling; the use of profanity or ethnic slurs; verbal attacks aimed at specific character traits or actions.

In the Kalamazoo study, twenty out of twenty-five respondents stated that the victim had engaged the assaulter in a verbal argument. Specific examples involved nagging about finances, infidelity, and visitation rights.

Dr. Straus believes that physical aggression is caused by the things people do and say to each other and not by personality traits.

In a study, he found that the greater the amount of verbal aggression between spouses, the greater the amount of physical aggres-

sion. This finding contradicts the theory behind encounter groups
that it's best to "get it off your chest" and "let it all hang out."

It should be noted that violent verbal arguments are not considered true communication. Research shows that verbal aggression
does not lead to an examination of the real problems between a man
and wife. Instead, verbal aggression masks the real problems and is
an impediment to real communication.

Sex

"There is abundant evidence that sex and violence go together—
at least in our society," says John O'Brien.

Researcher M. Faulk suggests that marital violence may sometimes be sexually stimulating in itself. He states that some wives
report that their husbands want sexual intercourse soon after a violent outburst. Faulk goes on to report that it is uncertain whether
the violence itself is sexually stimulating or whether husbands are
trying to use sexual intercourse as a means of reconciliation.

Faulk writes: "Some wives report that their clothes were partly
torn off during the violence, and a few saw this as sexually motivated. It seems likely, however, that in many cases the clothes
were torn off to prevent the women from escaping."

Dr. Gelles adds: "The research and theoretical discussion which
focuses on the relationship between sex and violence support
Faulk's contention that sex is not an intrinsic component of marital
violence."

The question of sadomasochist relationships has been carefully
examined by O'Brien, who writes:

> There are the sadists and masochists, individuals who can only
> obtain sexual pleasure by inflicting or receiving violent acts. We
> could dismiss such people as pathological exceptions. But it seems
> better to consider sadism and masochism as simply extreme forms of
> behavior. . . . The sex act itself typically is accompanied at least by
> mild violence and often by biting and scratching.

One theory holds that the higher the level of antagonism between
men and women, the greater the tendency to use violence in sexual
acts. O'Brien observes:

It is incorrect to assume a direct connection between sexual drives and violence because such an assumption disregards the socio-cultural framework within which sexual relations are carried out. It is these social and cultural factors rather than sex drives per se which may give rise to the violent aspects of sexuality in so many societies.

Equally fundamental and equally important for their potential in reducing family violence, are changes in such basic aspects of the family as the power structure—especially the male dominance and *Machismo* values and norms which form a subtle but powerful part of our sexual and family system. . . .

There is a widespread belief that most women are masochists. Feminists argue that women have been victimized by this belief. In *The Ladies' Home Journal,* Karen Durbin writes:

The masochism theory is most popular among people who don't know much about psychology. Masochism is an element in some wife-beating cases, but it's been blown out of all proportion. It's an excuse for ignoring the problem. Our society doesn't do much about marital violence. If anything we encourage it by encouraging men to be tough and women to be submissive. Our culture holds out violence as a channel of expression for men.

In the Kalamazoo study statements by agency people—who have responsibilities to provide assistance in the community—reflected the popular theory that the couples were involved in sado masochistic relationships. This theory holds that "some women enjoy being beaten, put down and abused. They have either a psychological need to be punished or enjoy weak and passive roles."

When the Kalamazoo researchers talked to the battered spouses, they reached a different conclusion. "The characteristics of sado-masochism as mentioned by professionals in the literature do not appear to be supported in the client findings."

Kathleen Fojtik, president of the Ann Arbor NOW Chapter, is outspoken in her views on the subject. She says: "People like to think the woman who is beaten is passive or masochistic and enjoys it. I don't believe it.

"If you would read the testimony of women who attempt to

prosecute their husbands for beating them, you would find no indication that they enjoyed it or regarded it as an integral part of life.

"It was because of alcohol, or because the husband suddenly became mad with rage.

"The man experiences self-hatred, plus frustration with his life or his job.

"The woman is the victim of misplaced anger. The husband can't take it out on his boss. She is the closest and easiest to beat and batter."

The tacit approval of wife beating from society and its institutions particularly angers Mrs. Fojtik.

"A judge in Flint heard a case involving a man charged with assault to kill his wife. A policeman who had been on the scene testified against the husband. So did the wife.

"The judge threw out the case on the basis that a man's house is his castle and the police were trespassing."

The second case occurred in Detroit circuit court.

"A woman charged her husband with criminal assault. Later, she came in to withdraw the complaint, saying it was not bad enough. It turned out that the prosecutor had told her it was not a strong enough case.

"What had the man done that was not strong enough for legal action?

"He tied his wife to a bed and slashed her genitals with a knife."

Poor Self-image

Wife beaters are often men who feel they are less than they ought to be. Repeated studies point out that the male spouse abuser is a man who feels he does not measure up to society's ideal of masculinity. Part of that image involves embracing violence—real men like to hunt, fight, play football, be aggressive—and some men feel a need to engage in violence to prove their manhood.

Dr. Richard F. Lyles, director of The Crisis Center in Atlanta, Georgia, says a major reason why men beat their wives is to "compensate for his own feelings of being less than an adequate male. Violence tends to show up the idea of masculinity."

The problem, according to many observers, starts in childhood. Girls are brought up to be delicate and submissive, while boys are brought up to be rough and aggressive. As a result, boys learn that the way to demonstrate their masculinity is through violence. When they grow up and become men anxious to prove their masculinity, they naturally turn to violence.

Studies of wife beaters consistently reveal that these men feel inadequate about various aspects of their lives, particularly their jobs. Our society tends to define a person in terms of his job, and a man who is seriously dissatisfied with his job is dissatisfied with himself. Important elements of a man's job are the amount of prestige it affords him, the amount of money he is able to earn, and where it places him in relation to his friends, relatives, and neighbors. Dr. Gelles found in one of his studies that violence was more prevalent where a husband's occupational status was lower than his neighbors.

The same point can be made for education. Wife beaters are often educational dropouts. Similar feelings of inadequacy can develop as a result of dropping out at any level—grade school or law school—if the man tends to view himself as a "failure" for not completing the course, or if he tends to think of those who completed what he did not as "better." Sometimes the feeling involves proving "I'm as good as they are."

In his study *Violence in Divorce-Prone Families,* O'Brien writes:

> There is considerable evidence that the husbands who . . . display violent behavior are severely inadequate in work, as wage earners, or in family support roles.
>
> Severe dissatisfaction with one's job and being an educational dropout at one level or another were also found to contribute to a husband's use of physical violence on his wife. The frustration theory of violence would predict that with middle class educational expectations of at least one college degree, college dropouts may experience more frustration and job dissatisfaction and thus resort to physical violence as a problem-solving device more often than do individuals who have completed the amount of education they desire.
>
> Compared to those from the non-violent group, the violent men

were more often seriously dissatisfied with their job, more often educational dropouts at some level and often brought home earnings which were the source of serious or constant conflict.

These feelings of inadequacy are often intensified if the man's wife has more education, comes from a "better family," or earns more money than her husband. O'Brien notes:

> In comparison to the background of their wives, the men in the violence group were more often less educated than their wives and more often the holders of jobs with an occupational status classification lower than their wife's father.
>
> The data clearly support the hypothesis that family centered violence is associated with the occurrence of a condition in a family where the achievement ability of the husband is less than or inconsistent with his proscribed, superior status. . . .

A man who feels inadequate is easily triggered to violence when confronted by verbal assaults from his wife.

"Certainly machismo is a factor when a man feels insulted, degraded and put down by a woman's ridicule and lack of respect for his manhood," Dr. Gelles says.

As noted earlier, a number of studies have documented that verbal abuse often precedes physical abuse. In a case in which a woman has superior verbal skills and is able to punish her husband's vulnerable ego with cutting remarks, the only way the man can "get even" is to use physical force.

Since his wife has attacked his masculinity, he feels justified in proving he is masculine by making use of an acceptable masculine response—violence. "You doubt I'm a man? I'll show you I'm a man." Pow!

Men with poor self-images and deep feelings of inadequacy are naturally prone to jealousy. The studies all report that extreme jealousy is a very common cause of family violence.

Some observers feel that men are as much the victims of the macho mentality as women.

"I feel society and women demand too much of men," says Judge Oneglia. "We expect them to be strong, capable, and coping in all situations. They can't be and know it. They often feel weak, passive, and out of control like everyone else, but they can't admit it. They assert power to fill the manly idea and appear strong."

A similar opinion is voiced by Peggy Anne Hansen, a member of a Maryland wife-beating task force, who says: "We put too much pressure on men to perform in every way, as breadwinner, father, and captain of the ship."

An executive in Cincinnati, Ohio, reveals he sought a divorce rather than try to live up to the macho image, which he believes is foisted on men by women.

"I believe that behind this ghastly business of wife beating, the true cause lies in the woman's greed for fables, chief of which is the need—or felt need—for machismo, the hairy-chested brute.

"I yawn through a Clint Eastwood spaghetti Western. I find Charles Bronson about as exciting as candle drippings, but I notice females in these dismal epics are wide awake and panting.

"Women, I conclude, *love* fake men and despair of the real product. Does anyone believe Charles Bronson exists other than in female minds?

"In the real world—fearsomely complex next to Hollywood— men under stress almost invariably respond in a way other than Clark Gable's or Richard Widmark's. Women don't understand this because few American women have lived very much. Theirs is a world of shadows, of fiction, of counterfeits."

Often linked to a wife beater's distorted self-image is a distorted view of what others should be like, particularly his wife. He has an idealized vision of what a woman, a wife, a lover, a mother should be, and invariably his wife fails to measure up. Indeed, some of the idealized roles may be in contradiction with each other— "I want a saint to raise my children and a whore in the bedroom." And when this kind of man discovers that his wife isn't the sort of person she ought to be, he feels justified in "punishing her."

Dr. Lyles of Atlanta says, "Some wife beaters have a highly developed sense of what others ought to be doing. This kind of perfectionism, which expects a perfect behavior pattern from others, gives rise to the extreme violence when others violate this code. This justifies his violence."

Frustration

This cause of spouse violence is closely linked with the preceding one: poor self-image. Many of the frustrations abusive men cannot handle are related to their jobs, perceptions of themselves and their wives, and their inability to achieve their goals because of lack of education or inferior social and economic status.

Dr. Steinmetz writes: "There are many social structural conditions which tend to increase the chances of an act of brutality occurring such as frustration resulting from societal imposed boundaries."

Frustration is a major factor in family violence because aggression is an accepted response to frustration.

As one marital therapist observes: "If a man is upset, he isn't supposed to cry. It's more manly to put his fist through the wall. Only sometimes the wall is his wife."

Frustrations can develop over sexual problems, how to raise the children, crowded living conditions, almost any element of family life.

Judge Oneglia says: "I think that certain people simply can't tolerate the degree of intimacy a marriage requires. More beatings occur on holidays and weekends when the wife is making emotional demands for attention and communication which the husband can't tolerate. He responds with violence."

Dr. Judd Marmor says: "I think we have to see wife beating within the context of a society in which there is an enormous amount of frustration and tension.

"We are living in an extraordinary period where economic tensions and unemployment are very great. These kinds of pressures drift down into the family inevitably and reflect themselves in family tensions."

Eisenberg and Micklow, interviewing battered wives, found repeatedly that the attacking husband was described as being unable to tolerate the slightest frustration.

A typical comment they received is:

"His bad mood precipitated the fights. He got mad over little things like dinner not being ready when he came home from work or that I don't think before I speak.

"And I remember one night we were having dinner, and he had come home from work pretty tired and pretty cross. I knew that he was cross, so I just stayed out of his way, but suddenly at dinner he just exploded and just put his hand under the table and flipped the whole thing across the room, food, dishes . . . everything.

"He would just get so tense that if I said anything to disagree with him, he would become extremely angry and slap me or give me a push and send me flying across the room."

The critical role that the inability to handle frustration plays in family disputes is confirmed by an admitted wife beater who came to grips with his problem only after his first wife divorced him.

"I just had no skill or experience in resolving frustration in a healthy way," he relates. "I would seethe and fester. Then I would get bombed one night and blow up."

A low tolerance to frustration is a condition found among all sorts of men.

"A lot of men are under the same frustrations whether they're rich or poor," says Commander Joseph DiLeonardi, head of the homicide sex division of the Chicago Police. And regardless of economic status, these men often direct their anger toward their wives.

Feminist Del Martin observes: "A man takes his frustration out on his wife because he can't tell his boss off, he's worried about money, he's tired or bored, he suffers anxiety over his masculinity. As a man he is expected to be head of the household, the breadwinner and problem solver."

Inabilities to deal with frustration can often be traced to childhood. Dr. Leroy G. Schultz, in an article entitled "The Wife Assaulter" published in *The Journal of Social Therapy,* described the assaulter's childhood as one characterized by a domineering, rejecting mother relationship in which the child experiences primary aggression. Because expressions of this aggression would result in further rejection and punishment, the child passively submits to the mother, simultaneously preventing his anger from reaching a level of conscious expression. The child-mother relationship is later duplicated when the child turned adult enters into a marriage. At that time the dependency is transferred from mother to wife.

Dr. Schultz writes:

It is when these dependency needs are frustrated or when frustration appears, or is perceived as imminent, that aggression breaks through. In short, it is where the husband senses that his dependency gratification is being cut off that he overtly attacks the frustrating object, his wife. The conflict is one between hostility toward the wife and dependency on her. The first was held in rigid control as long as the second was satisfactorily met. The aggressive outbursts came when the husband felt that dependency gratification was being permanently cut off, as in the wife's admission of having a lover or her stating she was going to get a divorce or separation. Such a threat of both physical and psychic withdrawal of love was intolerable to the husbands, whose ordinarily rigid hostility-control system broke down.

O'Brien feels that society will have to change in order to relieve many of these situations men find frustrating.
He writes:

The male dominant ideology of our society also plays a part in producing violence. Take the norms which require male economic superiority in occupation and income for instance. These serve as powerful sources of frustration for those men who, because of social restrictions or personal characteristics, cannot meet the cultural expectations. New, less frustration, and therefore less violence-producing norms would emphasize instead how well one did a job and how much enjoyment was received from an occupation—not the prestige of selected jobs or the amount of income received relative to the wife.

Change

Men prone to batter their wives tend to see changes in their lives as threats. And when they feel threatened, they fight back by beating their wives. Common changes that often precipitate violence are when the wife becomes pregnant, obtains a job, or attends school. Changes in the wife's personality such as becoming more independent and less submissive or physical changes such as putting on weight or changing the color of her hair can also trigger violent reactions.

The Kalamazoo study reports a number of instances of violence brought about by change in the family's life.

Respondents indicated that many times the abusive situations arose suddenly when the woman tried to begin a new life of her own through a job, or began having opinions of her own. With the wife having been passive for years the husband would view this situation as a very threatening one and would resort to violence to frighten her back into a more submissive role.

In several cases, the assaulter had expectations of the victim that were not being met, i.e. that she would not change, that she would be submissive, that she would be able to cope well with difficulties. Half of the victims interviewed had been assaulted when they were pregnant.

One attorney stated that he has noted instances of spouse assault in situations where the women had returned to school. His opinion is that the husband feels threatened that his wife is becoming a different person from the woman he married. Two other professionals indicated that assaults occur in instances where the woman has ideas of her own and the man wants a submissive wife. A counsellor recalled a family in which there were unrealistic expectations. The man was an American and the woman was a war bride from an Asian country. He had expected her to easily adjust to life in this country. When she had difficulty coping, he became frustrated and beat her severely.

In their book *The Male Dilemma,* Anne Steinmann and David J. Fox developed the concept that much of the conflict in marriage can be traced to the courtship, in which both parties play roles that they plan to abandon once they are married.

The man assumes the culturally accepted dominant role and the woman the approved passive stance. Typically, they view marriage as the goal to be reached and the courtship the path that must be traveled to reach that goal. Once married, they both intend to stop playing games and settle down as their "real" selves.

During the courtship ritual, the woman might be more submissive, less argumentative, more willing to accept the man's judgments and decisions. The man might become more considerate, more understanding, more willing to do the things that please her.

It's not uncommon for engaged couples to feign interest in each other's likes. She may smile bravely through a cold, damp football game while hating every minute of it, and he might sit through a ballet to impress her.

There is a joke that illustrates this condition. A man and woman are dating, and they make it a practice to visit every modern art gallery they can find. After they are married, he says to her: "Honey, I have a confession to make. I don't know what you see in this modern art."

And she says: "Me? I thought you liked it."

The abundance of marital jokes that contain the line "I have a confession to make" is a clear indication that in our culture the practice of wearing a different face during courtship is not only accepted but widely recognized. The "I have a confession to make" jokes are only funny because the tellers and listeners can relate to them.

It's been said that on the wedding night there are six people in every honeymoon bed: the man, the person he thinks he is, and the person she thinks he is, as well as the woman, the person she thinks she is, and the person he thinks she is. The mixing of these half-dozen people can be traumatic. The perceptions of self and the misperceptions and expectation of the partners are often the causes of violent conflicts.

It's commonplace for married couples to find themselves saying: "You're not the man I married," or, "You've changed . . . you're not the same person you used to be."

"The causes of battle can be traced without much difficulty to conflicting expectations for marriage and conflicting views of the role that each sex should play in that marriage," write the authors of *The Male Dilemma*.

> Once married, once they had given up most of their other free-doms, both felt, paradoxically, that they were at last free to be themselves. And when the honeymoon was over, literally and figuratively, both woke up to the delayed realizations of just who this person was that they had married. . . .
>
> Pity the man who thought he could count on the pretty, passive deferential little thing he courted for help and support in marriage only to discover that she is a very assertive and strong-willed woman.
>
> Pity the woman, too, who thought she married a man whom she could lean on only to discover he can barely stand up, let alone support her. According to the old wives' tale, she is supposed to marry

him first and then change him. But she may not be up to the job, or if she is, neither she nor her husband may be overjoyed with the result.

Changes such as these are almost sure to produce violent reactions from certain men.

A marriage of teen-agers is one certain to be filled with change as they mature into young adulthood. The changes in expectations and perceptions between, say, 16 and 21, can be enormous. And with the other negative conditions—unemployment, poor communications, lack of self-confidence, pregnancy—all likely to converge, violence has an excellent chance to erupt.

Dr. Fogel says:

"Kids get married at 16 or 17, and by the time they're 22 they're different people . . . they've been going in completely different directions and becoming mature with different values, different interests, and it's a disaster at that point. One may be very intellectual, like to read, and want to go to school; they have three children, and they interfere with schooling; then the other just wants to watch the boxing matches and go drink beer with the boys.

"Counseling before marriage would help avoid the violence some couples exchange."

Sometimes it is marriage itself that is the foreboding change the man fears.

Judge Oneglia observes: "In the majority of cases of couples who live together without marriage, the man has never laid a hand on the woman. Within a week of the wedding he's beating hell out of her."

The authors of *The Male Dilemma* make a similar point concerning the change marriage can bring to a couple. "Men and women can be friends and lovers outside the bounds of matrimony, but they often find themselves becoming the bitterest of enemies as they assume the role of husband and wife."

Pregnancy is a change that routinely brings on spouse abuse. "Violence occurred during pregnancy in almost one-quarter of the families reporting violence . . ." writes Dr. Gelles in an article entitled "Violence and Pregnancy," published in *Family Coordinator*.

In many marriages, the pregnancy caused a change in the family routine. Often the husband did not want to change his routine of work and leisure. This led to conflict, arguments and in some instances violence.

The crucial point in bringing about violence was that the stress of pregnancy was added on to an already high level of structural stress in these families.

Husbands who marry pregnant girls may feel increasing stress as the baby approaches (or as the wife swells).

One woman related: "Our problem was getting married and having a baby so fast . . . that produced a great strain . . . I wasn't ready. I had the baby six months after we were married."

In addition to the change in family and the biochemical changes in the wife, Dr. Gelles believes there are three other reasons why pregnant wives are assaulted by their husbands.

These are: sexual frustration, defenselessness of the wife, and prenatal child abuse. This latter reason centers around the idea that the husband is trying to hurt the unborn child more than the wife.

"If our assumption about violence toward a pregnant wife being prenatal child abuse is correct, then this violence may serve as an indicator or predictor of future abuse of children in these families," Dr. Gelles says.

There are two periods of change in married life that are peak times for violence, according to Dr. Steinmetz.

One is early in the marriage, the first couple of years when the couple is trying to adjust to each other. It is also when they have the largest number of expenses. It is also when the wife is likely to become pregnant, and this puts a lot of pressure on the husband because no longer is he just half responsible for himself and the wife half responsible for herself. He's not only responsible for her, but also for this new child. This frequently means moving to a larger residence and it's a time of high frustration and high conflict. It's also the time of the highest number of divorces.

The second period when I found the most conflict occurring is when you have adolescent-age children and this also appears to be a logical time. We raise our children to be independent. We expect them to make independent decisions and then they come along as adolescent-age children and we're not always happy with the in-

dependent decisions that they want to make. Many times these decisions go contrary to our value system and the child ends up the
source of a lot of conflict and the conflict frequently ends up with the
use of physical force between husband and wife.

Violence as a Resource to Solve Problems

Studies show most beaters come from violent homes. They see
their fathers beating up their mothers, and sometimes they even
become victims.

This point was examined in an earlier chapter.

Drs. Straus, Steinmetz, and Gelles all believe that violence is
learned behavior. Spouse abusers are not born but made by their
parents in the home.

Judge Oneglia agrees. "I think violence is learned and that it's
based on a man maintaining a superior position in the family. The
wife is usually economically dependent. He knows he can hit her
and get away with it. In general, these are men who are respectable
in every other way. But they tend to come from homes where their
mothers were beaten, where the father was absolute ruler and the
mother submissive."

Not only do they learn that violence is an acceptable way to
solve problems but that it works. They learn that violence is a
resource to be used like any other resource when needed.

Dr. Steinmetz writes:

> Social learning theory would predict that if a particular method of
> resolving conflict is perceived to be successful, this method is likely
> to become part of an individual's behavior repertoire. Therefore if
> physical force is perceived as successful in resolving conflicts, even
> if this success is temporary, physical force is likely to be used for
> resolving the next problem.

The Kalamazoo study reports:

> Assaulters are usually under some stress and they often lack re-
> sources such as finances, job satisfaction, health or other means to
> help establish themselves as a person. An individual lacking re-
> sources for coping with stress might turn to violence as an alterna-
> tive. Violence, therefore, can be viewed as a resource. . . .

At least five professional respondents report that they believe that men view it as their masculine right to dominate their wives through either verbal or physical abuse. Men cannot handle verbal assaults from their wives and must assert themselves physically to retain their dominant position in the relationship. Husbands therefore do not view this as a problem which requires attention, but simply as an effective method for handling conflict.

This point is illustrated by a wife beater from the Boston area, who says: "I always thought a man should take care of a woman, you know . . . protect her and treat her right. But sometimes when I was drunk my wife would just say something that would tick me off, and I'd hit her, then I would black out.

"When I came to, I always felt guilty and ashamed. I would swear I wouldn't do it again, and I meant it. But I just couldn't help myself. I learned very early that using my hands was a good way to get what I wanted."

Studies show that when a person is encouraged to unleash aggression, he is increasingly likely to continue such behavior. A University of Wisconsin psychologist, Leonard Berkowitz, says: "The feeling of well-being that comes from the release of tension is an immediate emotional reward that tends to strengthen aggressive response."

What this boils down to is that if something makes us feel good, we repeat it. The combination of successful resolution of a problem plus the reinforcement of feeling good act as powerful motivators for the continued use of violence.

There is a great deal of talk about harmony in the family, but in practice there is a great deal of acceptance of violence.

"In fact, the family is pre-eminent in every type of violence from slaps to torture and murder," says Dr. Straus. "There's an informal norm that makes a marriage license also a hitting license."

To summarize, these are the nine fundamental reasons why men beat their spouses: Mental illness, alcohol and drugs, public acceptance of violence, lack of communication, sex, poor self-image, frustration, change, and because they have learned to use violence and regard it as a resource for solving problems.

The act of turning a complex sociopsychological condition into a list is always an arbitrary exercise. It is done here to facilitate examination and discussion. In reality, these nine points are interwoven and interrelated in ways that make it difficult, if not impossible, to separate them into neat little boxes.

CHAPTER SEVEN

Karen's Story—
A Case History

Some women should be struck regularly—
like gongs!

Noel Coward

The doctor studied the dark purple bruise—about the size of a saucer—on Karen's stomach.

"What happened?"

"I fell," she lied.

"You fell?"

"Yeah . . . I get klutzy when I'm pregnant. I'm always bumping into things and falling."

"Well, you better be careful. From the size of this bruise, it must have been a severe . . . a severe fall. You could injure your baby. Severe blows like this could cause mental retardation or even death to the baby."

"I know. I don't want to hurt him. It wasn't my fault. He . . . I just fell. . . . My baby's not hurt, is he?"

"It is hard to tell, but I don't think so. . . . But, Mrs. Kryzeck? Please be careful . . . and tell your husband you can't take any more *falls* like this one."

The doctor turned and walked out the door and into an adjacent examining room in which another pregnant woman waited to be examined.

Karen was glad he was gone. She felt ashamed and didn't want to talk about her bruise. She was embarrassed. She knew the doctor knew she didn't get the bruise from a fall. She knew he knew her husband had hit her, and this made her feel ashamed and nervous. She dressed as quickly as she could and left.

Across town in the Ford assembly plant, Karen's husband Chet stood first in line at the time clock. His time card was already inserted halfway into the slot as he waited impatiently for four o'clock to arrive. When it did, he pushed his card in all the way to get it stamped, then dropped it into the ''out'' rack as he bolted out the door.

He moved briskly across the street and then down the block; he entered the Crystal Tavern. The first shift at the plant was filling up the bar, but the bartender was ready for the burst of business. He had lined the bar with shot glasses filled to the brim with amber-colored rye whiskey. Behind each shot glass was a bigger glass filled with draught beer.

Chet stationed himself at his regular spot, and the bartender automatically set a shot and a beer in front of him. Chet downed the shot with a quick jerk of his wrist, then drained about half of the beer.

''Again!'' he gasped as he slid a five-dollar bill on the bar.

He finished off the rest of the beer while the bartender handed him two more glasses, took his money, and turned to the cash register.

Chet lined up his drinks, the beer close to his right hand, the shot slightly behind it and off to the right. He took his change and placed it in front of him on the bar between him and the beer glass.

Within minutes the bar was filled, and several of Chet's regular drinking buddies assembled near him in their familiar spots. Each followed Chet's ritual: a fast first drink immediately followed by a second, the on-deck drink, which stood untouched for the next few minutes. Each new arrival offered to buy a round for those who had arrived ahead of him. The drinks were accepted or refused depending on the amount of time that had elapsed since the last round. The ritual was well known to all the participants. Each man kept a mental scorecard, and each knew when it was time to buy and time to be bought. The tally was extended from one day to the next when necessary.

The routine seldom varied. Each man allotted himself so much time to drink, and then he would rush out to make a bus or get his car from the parking lot.

Chet had exactly twenty-eight minutes of drinking before he would have to leave for his bus. If he missed it, he could get another in fifteen minutes and another in fifteen more minutes. But after that, it would be forty-five minutes to an hour until the next one.

Nearly always, Chet made the first one. But tonight he decided to drink a little longer because he didn't have to work the next day. It was Thanksgiving.

Karen had done most of the holiday shopping earlier in the week, but she had waited until late Wednesday to pick up the turkey because it took up too much room in the refrigerator. The bird was resting in the sink, all 24 pounds of it.

Karen was planning a quick, simple supper, and after the kids were ready for bed, she would begin the preparations for the next day's feast.

Chet was due home at 5:20 if he caught the first bus. When he didn't show up, Karen waited until 5:35, the time the second bus got him home. When there was still no Chet, she kept things hot until 5:50, the time the third bus got him home. When he didn't arrive, Karen fed the kids and cleaned up the dishes.

Chet had missed all of his regular buses. Karen knew he must be drinking. She was not surprised because it was not unusual when he had the next day off.

"Please, God," she said in her mind. "Don't let him get hurt, and please, God, don't let him get too drunk."

Karen spent the evening peeling vegetables, stuffing celery, and making turkey dressing. She also fixed up a Thanksgiving center-piece for the table. She took a cardboard pilgrim's hat she had bought in a dime store and arranged it like a cornucopia overflowing with fruits, nuts, and green and golden gourds.

At about 9:30 she decided to go to bed. She planned to be up early to pop the turkey in the oven.

As she started for the stairs, she heard a car drive up and stop in front of the house. It was Chet and his friends, and they were singing loudly—and badly.

"Aaaaaaand we'll send the echoes to the heavaaaans. . . ."

She smiled. It was their old school song. They were having fun tonight. He wouldn't be in a nasty mood.

Karen watched as he climbed out of the back seat of the car. There were four of them—all old friends from the neighborhood—and they were laughing and shouting.

Chet stood teetering on the sidewalk, watching the car roar off down the street. He turned and staggered up the front steps, still slurring the old school song.

Karen met him at the door.

"Hi, beautiful," he shouted.

"Hi."

"Aaaaaaand then we'll send . . ."

"Not so loud. You'll wake up the kids."

Chet was glassy-eyed and grinning. He dropped his voice down to a whisper and sang: "And then we'll send the eeeechoes to the . . ."

He was laughing so hard he couldn't continue. He draped an arm around his wife's shoulder and laughed some more.

"Ooooh boy! We don't make much money, but we have a lot of fun. Hi, beautiful . . . You got the cutest little baby face . . . Hi, beautiful. . . . You got the baby face. . . ."

"Boy, you got some load on. You'd better go right to bed."

"Bed? The night is young, and you are sooo beautiful. . . . I can't go to bed yet."

"Come on. I'll make you a cup of coffee."

They walked into the kitchen. He bumped into the table and knocked off a glass. It smashed on the floor.

"Oooops."

"Come on, Chet. Watch what you're doing."

"Sorry about that . . . sorry."

"Sit down before you break something else."

He sunk into the chair. Karen began scooping the coffee grounds into the percolator.

"Baby face! You got the cutest baby face!"

"Not so loud. You'll wake the kids."

"Say, what do we have here?"

He got up. Walked across the room and grabbed the paper hat from the centerpiece and jammed it on his head. The nuts, fruit, and gourds splattered all over the floor.

"Hey! What the hell you doing?"

Chet tilted the hat rakishly on his head and sang: "Swaaaaneeee, Swaaaaaanneeee. How I love . . .

"Goddamn you! I had that all fixed up for the centerpiece. You drunken bastard."

"Hey . . . what the hell's the matter with you?"

"I spent all night working getting ready for tomorrow, and you come home and wreck it all in two minutes."

"What'd I wreck? Goddamn glass . . . fuckin' paper hat? You know what your trouble is? You don't know how to have any fun anymore."

"You call this fun? Picking up after some drunk?"

"You can't stand to see anybody happy. Every time you get pregnant, you turn into a regular bitch. Nobody can have any fun. Just bitch, bitch, bitch."

He swung his hand across the table and sent the rest of the fruits and nuts flying to the floor.

Karen stood by and watched in silence.

"You know something? When you're pregnant, you're no more fun. You worry about a goddamn paper hat, and you bitch. . . ."

"When you're through, you can clean up this mess. I'm going to bed."

"Mess!" Chet shouted. "What mess? I'll show you what a mess is." He picked up the turkey and threw it on the floor. Then he opened the refrigerator and began pulling out the contents and throwing them on the floor. He took the newly peeled potatoes, bobbing in water, and dumped them on the floor. He threw the celery, the milk, the pickles—everything that Karen had spent the night preparing—and threw them all on the kitchen floor.

She watched in stunned disbelief, then shouted: "You bastard!" She ran across the room and punched him on his arms and chest.

Chet backhanded her, and she moved away.

"You're not supposed to hit me. . . . The doctor said you're not supposed to hit me anymore."

"What did you say?" He spoke very slowly and very deliberately.

"The doctor said you're not supposed to hit me. I could kill the baby."

"You *told* the doctor I hit you?"

"No. I didn't tell him. He saw the bruise on my stomach. . . ."

"You told the doctor I hit you?" He exaggerated every syllable of every word. While he spoke, he slowly unbuckled his belt and slipped it off. He wrapped one end around his right hand several times and began slapping the heavy metal buckle—embossed with the word love—against his left hand. Slowly he inched closer and closer to his wife. His words and the slaps of the belt established a terrifying cadence.

"You . . ."
slap
"told . . ."
slap
"him . . ."
slap
"I . . ."

When he was close enough, he finished the sentence by whipping the belt across her face. The buckle smashed against her teeth, and they rang with pain.

Karen turned away, and the second blow stung her shoulder. She darted across the room, and the third blow missed. When she was out of range, she turned and watched him from a safe distance.

Even pregnant, she was too fast for him when he was drunk. He couldn't catch her. He didn't try. He began slapping the belt against his hand again.

"Come here, baby," he slurred. "I want to give you something."

Karen didn't speak. She watched, intensely searching for any sign of sudden movement.

Chet stood there, swinging his belt, patiently stalking his wife. The tension-filled silence was broken with:

"Hey, Mom. . . . What's all the noise?"

It was Bradley, their eight-year-old boy.

"Hi, Dad. What you doing?"

"Go to bed. What are you doing up?"

"It's okay, Brad," said Karen. Quickly she moved across the room and slipped past her husband.

"What's all the mess?" the boy asked. "What happened?"

"Never mind, Daddy will explain it to you tomorrow." She took the child's hand and hurried upstairs.

"I'll explain *you* tomorrow," Chet shouted. "We're not finished here."

He stumbled back into the kitchen. He stood for a minute, looked at the floor, covered with what was meant to be a festive meal, and mumbled something about teaching her a lesson.

He dropped into a chair and put his head on the kitchen table. In less than a minute he was asleep and snoring loudly.

When Karen heard the snores, she knew it was safe for her to go to bed.

The morning sun was magnified through the kitchen window, and it bathed Chet—still slumped on the table—with hot rays. His neck burned, and his body ran with sweat. His mouth was completely dry. He found himself half awake, staring at the jacket fabric on his arm on which his head rested. He was confused. It was some time before he decided to lift his head. He was surprised to find himself in his kitchen. He saw the food strewn all around him. He dropped his head back down on his arms. He couldn't remember what had happened, and he didn't want to think about it now.

He tried to return to oblivion, but he couldn't. He heard the kids playing and watching TV in the next room. Then he heard his five-year-old daughter Kim say: "Hey, Dad. What's the turkey doing on the floor?"

He didn't answer. His daughter tugged his sleeve. "Why is the food on the floor?"

"I don't know," he mumbled.

He got up. His knees were weak, and he steadied himself on the table, then left the kitchen and headed upstairs. He found Karen in the bedroom. She was dressed and watching the Macy's parade on TV. She didn't speak.

Chet walked into the bathroom. He began to brush his teeth, but he had to throw up. Karen turned up the sound on the TV set so the noise from the bathroom wouldn't spoil the show.

After he had showered, shaved, and put on clean clothes, Chet approached his wife.

"What happened?"

"What do you mean, what happened?"

"Last night . . ."

"You were here. . . . What the hell you asking me what happened for?"

"I don't remember. . . ."

"Crap!"

"No . . . I can't remember what happened. I saw the stuff all over the kitchen . . ."

"You're not going to get away with that crap. You know damn well what happened."

He grew irritated. "If I knew, I wouldn't ask."

"What do you think happened?"

"I don't know. I can't remember anything. I was out drinking with Marty and Bill. I don't remember coming home."

"How come you never remember any of this stuff?"

"I don't know."

"Let me refresh your memory. You came home drunk as a skunk, broke a glass, ripped up the decorations, threw the turkey on the floor, and threw all the food I worked all night getting ready all over the kitchen; then you beat me with your goddamn belt and passed out! That's what happened."

"Christ . . . I didn't do that?"

"Well, somebody came in here and beat me up. He looked just like you. If Brad hadn't come downstairs, you probably would have killed the baby and me."

"Oh, God, I feel awful."

"I feel awful, too. It hurts when you beat me with your belt buckle in case you don't know it. The doctor told me yesterday you're going to kill our baby if you don't stop hitting me in the stomach."

"Oh, God, I'm sorry . . ."

"Are you trying to kill me? Don't you want this baby?"

"Sure I want it. I don't know what happens to me when I get drunk. . . ."

"Well, I know. You come home and beat the hell out of me and call me names because I'm pregnant, and it's your fault I'm pregnant to begin with."

"I'm sorry, honey. God, I'm sorry."

"The doctor saw the bruise on my stomach from the last time and said you could kill the baby. Never mind me. I know you don't give a shit for me, but you want to kill the baby or wreck his brains before he's born?"

"No, I don't want to hurt nobody. I lose my head when I get drunk."

"You lose your head . . . the next day you're hung over . . . I'm black and blue. I can't go out anymore because everybody knows you're always beating me, and I'm too ashamed to walk around with a cut lip or a black eye."

"I'm sorry, honey. I'll never do it again . . . honest . . . I'm really sorry. I feel so ashamed. . . . I'll never do it again."

"You're sorry now, but what about the next time you get drunk?"

"I'll never hit you again. I swear to God on a stack of Bibles . . . I'll never hit you again."

Karen began to cry.

"Don't cry, honey . . . I'll be good . . . I promise."

"You always say that, but the next thing I know I'm flat on my back, and you're punching the hell out of me for nothing."

"I won't do it again. I swear. So help me. May God strike me dead and send my soul to hell forever. I'll never do it again."

She continued to cry, and he held her hand and stared at the floor. On TV, the hundredth band blared by, and the announcer ranted on about the floats and some big balloon of the Disney characters. After a while Chet said, "I'll go down and clean up the mess. What do you want me to do with the turkey?"

"Stick it up your ass!"

In the weeks that followed, Chet was a model husband. He always made the first bus. He drank, but he didn't get drunk. He was affectionate and considerate. On Tuesdays—Chet's bowling night—Karen went to bed early. She wanted to be asleep when he got home to avoid the risk of another incident following a night out with the boys.

On the surface, things were going well, but she felt nervous and apprehensive. She was under a constant strain. She wanted to be happy, but she was afraid to let herself relax.

They had been married for nine years but had known each other all of their lives. They went to the same church, attended the same schools, shared many of the same friends. They began dating in high school and married right after graduation. Chet got a job, and she began having babies. They owned a house with a big mortgage, a car with twenty-six payments, a couple of TV sets, and their kids were healthy. Karen had everything she had ever wanted—except happiness.

She lived in a world of shifting extremes. Sober, Chet was a quiet and benign husband. Drunk, he was a snarling, violent animal. She was never sure which one she would have to face. Fear was a permanent boarder in her home.

As Christmas neared, she tried to get into the spirit of things, but the songs of joy and merriment mocked her. She was tired and lonely. She was in her seventh month and, as she always did, had swelled up to the point at which she looked as if she would burst. As always, Chet had stopped showing any sexual interest in her the moment her body had begun to change. Now when he touched her, it was to inflict pain.

She considered Christmas as an obstacle to be overcome. Christmas cheer meant lots of drinking, and drinking meant trouble.

The Saturday before Christmas, Chet's gun club held its annual Christmas party. As usual, it was a stag affair. It started in the afternoon and went on through until everyone got too drunk to stay any longer.

Karen always worried about drinking at the gun club despite Chet's assurances that the club enforced its strict rule that all weapons had to be under lock and key before the bar could open.

He left about noontime, saying that he would be home early. As the day dragged by, she nervously watched the telephone and waited for it to ring.

She fixed supper and sent the kids to bed early. She paced around the house, waiting for him to get home. She couldn't stop thinking that something terrible was going to happen. Finally, to take her mind off things, she began furiously to clean her kitchen. She worked on the stove, and when it was sparkling, she turned her attention to the refrigerator.

At about 8:00 P.M., she heard footsteps on the porch and the front door rattle. Elated, she ran to open the door.

She saw him through the window. He was drunk, but at least he was in one piece. She pulled open the door to let him in. She stood there, her eyes dancing and her face beaming.

"Get out of my way, bitch," he snapped.

She closed her eyes and felt her happiness seep out of her like milk from a leaky carton.

Later that night she called the police. She was hysterical, and the house was in shambles. The children were crying, and the neighbors from both sides came over to see what was going on.

The cops arrested Chet and took him away. After questioning Karen, the officers wrote the following report.

> Victim stated the first argument started over a pack of cigarettes. Victim stated accused [her husband] held her against the bathroom wall by the hair and continued to beat victim with his right hand. Victim is seven months pregnant at the time. Victim stated accused kept telling victim, "Bitch, you are going to lose that baby," and then accused would beat victim in the stomach again. After the assault in the bathroom, accused told victim to cook dinner. Victim stated the accused picked up a butcher knife and put it to the victim's throat and told victim, "I am going to kill you and you know I can do it too, don't you?" Victim answered, "Yes," and accused laid the butcher knife down on the table and turned around and hit the victim in the face with his fist and knocked victim to the floor. Then the accused sat down on victim's stomach and put his knees on victim's arms so victim could not block any licks from accused. Then accused started beating victim in the head, face, and stomach. The accused got to his feet and told victim to get up. Victim stated

she tried but was unable to do so and fell back to the floor. The accused started beating and kicking the victim and kicked a kitchen chair over on victim's stomach. Victim stated she blacked out. Victim stated when she regained consciousness the accused was still beating her.

Chet's dad posted bail for him and accompanied him home. Karen was not there, she was in the hospital. Karen's mother was staying with the kids. When Chet and his father walked into the house, she flew into a rage.

"You're crazy! You tried to kill my daughter," she screamed. "That no good son of yours ought to be locked up forever. . . ."

"I told him the same thing," said Chet's father. "I told him he's got no business hitting a pregnant woman. . . . I told him . . ."

"Look at him," chided the mother. "Big man who hurts his wife. If I was a man, I'd kill you!"

Chet said nothing. He took it and stared at the carpet.

"How's Karen today?" asked the father.

"What do you think? She's black and blue, that's what. . . . She almost lost the baby, thanks to your hero son here."

"Well, don't blame me for him. I never raised him to beat up girls. I'm disgusted with him myself."

Finally, Chet said, "Can she have visitors?"

"She can have visitors, but she don't want you!" shouted the mother. "You stay the hell away from her, or you'll be back in jail. . . ."

"I'm sorry," said Chet. His voice was barely audible.

"Sorry? Listen to him! Now he's sorry!"

Chet couldn't stand the humiliation, the deep sense of shame that enveloped him. "I'm going out," he said. "I've had enough of this shit."

"Where you going?" asked the father.

"Good riddance," shouted the mother.

Chet hopped in his car and drove to the other side of town. He stopped near a neighborhood bar in which no one knew him, went in, took a corner stool, and got quietly drunk.

The next day, when he returned home from work, Chet found Father Grabowski waiting for him in the house. If he'd known he was there, he wouldn't have gone in. He still couldn't face people.

The priest smiled warmly and shook Chet's hand. Karen's mother said nothing. She pretended she didn't notice him and kept busy preparing supper for the children.

Father Grabowski put his arm around Chet's shoulder and motioned with his head to walk into the living room. There the two men sat, and Father Grabowski gently lectured Chet and explained the seriousness of the situation. He told him that Karen didn't want to return but that he was trying to convince her that she should for the good of the children and to preserve the holy state of matrimony.

He extracted a promise from Chet that he would not drink anymore and that he would never raise his hand to his wife again. Chet solemnly promised. He told the priest he was sincerely sorry, that he loved his wife, and that he wanted her home again so he could make things up to her.

Satisfied with Chet's sincerity, the priest heard his confession, gave him absolution, and promised he would talk to Karen that night and try to convince her to come home.

"You want to eat, Father?" asked the mother.

Father Grabowski declined politely and made his farewells.

When he was gone, Chet sat down with the kids to eat.

His mother-in-law glared at him for a moment, then muttered, "What ya want to drink?"

"Beer," he said.

That evening, Father Grabowski telephoned Chet. After he was on the line, the priest got Karen to talk to him.

The conversation was strained and guarded.

"Honey, I'm awfully sorry for what I did. I really am," he said.

"You always say that, but then you get drunk and do the same thing. Do you realize you tried to *kill* me and kill our baby?"

"I don't remember . . . Christ, I don't remember any of it. . . ."

"Well, I do. I'll never forget it. I'll never forget the look on your face and the way you kept punching me and punching the baby. . . ."

She began to cry.

"Don't cry, honey. I feel bad enough already . . . don't cry
. . . I love you . . . I love the kids. . . ."

"I don't think I'll ever be able to trust you again."

"Don't say that, honey. I feel awful . . . I feel like killing
myself . . . I'm so ashamed."

"Oh, God, I don't know what to do. I want to die. I don't want
to ever see anybody again. I feel so dirty and hurt. I just want to
disappear and die."

They talked for almost an hour. Karen agreed to come home
when she was able. She didn't know what else to do. She knew she
could never love Chet again, but she was Catholic, and she was
married, and there were the kids to consider, and Father Grabowski
was insistent. The resistance had been beaten out of her. She was
confused and terribly alone.

The doctors thought it would be good for her if she went home
for Christmas. So two days before, she was checked out right after
the morning hospital rounds. She had told Chet he shouldn't miss
work, that it would be fine if just her mother came to get her.

That night Chet got the first bus and arrived home with a bouquet
of roses.

"Hi."

"Hi."

"Here. These are for you."

"Thanks. I'll put them in water."

"How ya feel?"

"Sore."

"Well . . . yeah. . . . Your mother here?"

"Yes! I'm here. What did you expect?"

"Ah, nothing. I just wondered if you was here."

"Well, I'm here. Somebody's got to keep an eye on . . . an eye
on the kids."

"Yeah, yeah . . . good idea."

Chet sat down. He was nervous and tense. Karen walked away
into another room, but her mother remained behind.

"You got a lot of making up to do."

"Yeah . . . I know, Mom."

"Did you get a good look at her? She's black and blue from head to foot. I got no respect for you anymore, Chet. How any man could do what you did I just don't know.''

"I know, Mom. I'm sorry. Christ, nobody wishes it didn't happen more than me.''

The front door flew open, and young Brad came in.

"Hi, Dad.''

"Hi.''

"Hey, Dad? Did you hit Mom and make all those marks?''

"Who told you that?''

"I did,'' said Karen as she walked back into the living room.

"What'd you do that for?''

"He asked me. Don't you think he wondered what I was doing in the hospital, and why I'm covered with bruises?''

"Did ya, Dad?''

"Your mom and I had an argument. Go away for a while, will ya?''

"No, it's all right. You might as well tell him the truth. He already knows. He's not dumb. He's got two eyes, and besides, everybody in the neighborhood is talking about it.''

"Dad? Did you beat up Mom?''

"Well, I guess I hit her a couple of times.''

"You bastard!''

"Hey, what kind of way is that to talk to your father?''

"You're not my father. I hate you, you bastard.''

"What you tell this kid?''

"The truth.''

"Jesus. You're turning my own kids on me.''

"I didn't do it, Chet. You did.''

"Listen, kid. Don't give me any of your lip.''

"You gonna beat me up? When I grow up, I'm gonna kill you!''

"Christ, what is this?''

"I hate you!'' the boy shouted as he ran back out on to the street.

"Why'd you have to tell him?''

"Because I wanted him to know the truth.''

"Jesus. What for?''

"So he can call the cops the next time.''

"Ah, honey. There ain't gonna be a next time. I told you that."

"I know."

"Well, can't you forgive and forget? Can't we make a fresh start?"

"No." She said it with such finality that it ended the conversation. She left the room again, and Chet picked up the newspaper.

The next day—Christmas eve—Chet was once again first in line at the time clock. When it struck four, he was off for the Crystal Tavern. He followed his routine, and when it came time to leave for the first bus, he finished his drink and started to leave.

"Hey! Where you going?"

"I got to get home."

"Wait—I didn't buy you a Christmas drink."

"I can't."

"Come on. Christmas comes but once a year."

"I'd like to, but I got to go."

"Wait a minute. Your house isn't going to blow away. Hey, give him a little Christmas schnaps."

"I shouldn't. I ought to go."

"Ahhh, you missed that bus already. Here—Merry Christmas."

"Well, okay. But just one."

"Merry Christmas."

"Merry Christmas."

"Hey! Give us another round here."

"What the hell. It's Christmas! Right?"

"Right!"

Karen and the kids were watching a special on TV when Chet lurched in the front door, covered with snow.

"Christ! Why don't somebody sweep off the porch."

Every muscle in Karen's body grew taut.

The children all stared with open mouths.

"What's the matter with all of you? What the hell you staring at?"

"Oh, God, Chet. Not on Christmas eve. You promised."

"I promised what? Who do you think you are? You always have to bitch. That's all you are—a nagging bitch."

"Don't you hit Mom," shouted Brad.

"Shut up, you little bastard, or I'll knock *you* across the room."

"Get out of here!" Karen shouted. "Get the hell out of here. You're not going to ruin our Christmas. Get out of here!"

She began pounding him with her fists.

Chet punched her in the stomach. She gasped, her knees buckled, and as she tried to catch her balance, she wobbled, suspended for a second like a stop-action movie.

At precisely that frozen instant, Chet's right fist exploded in her face. The blood rushed out her nose as she fell to the floor. The children screamed, and Brad ran into his father and hit him with his tiny fists.

Chet grabbed the boy's arms and in one continuous sweep swung him in the air and threw him across the room.

The boy flew into the gaily decorated Christmas tree and sent it crashing to the floor.

Karen had raised herself to all fours when Chet hammered his heel into her hip and knocked her flat again.

"Run, Brad! Run!" she cried.

The boy picked himself out of the rubble of the Christmas tree and ran past his father, through the kitchen, and out the back door.

"Come back, you little bastard," Chet shouted.

He ran out after him, but the boy had disappeared.

Chet stumbled through the snow, cursing. Then he saw his son. He was in the house next door, and he was motioning furiously toward his home.

"Better get your ass out of here," he said out loud. "They'll be calling the cops again."

He moved around to the front of his house where his car was parked. He fished out his keys, started the auto, and drove off.

When Chet woke up, he was shivering from the cold. He looked around and realized he had been sleeping in his car. It was light out. He tried to collect his thoughts. He'd been drinking. His car was parked behind one of the bars he often visited. He must have gotten drunk and slept it off.

"Christ," he said to himself. "It's Christmas, and I'm out here sleepin' off a load in the car."

He tried to start the car, but it resisted. "Must be the battery," he mumbled.

He got out of the car and walked over to the bar and tried the door. It was locked. He shuffled through the snow down the street to a corner pay phone.

He was shaking from the cold and his hangover. He pulled out some change from his pocket, picked up the phone, and paused. He couldn't remember his number. He began trying out combinations of numbers until he hit one that sounded right. When he was sure he had it, he deposited a quarter—he didn't have anything smaller—and dialed it.

The phone rang several times before it was answered.

He heard Karen's voice say, "Hello."

"Hello, honey," he said. "I just wanted to let you know I'm all right. Is everything okay at home? About last night . . . I'm sorry. . . ."

CHAPTER EIGHT

Why Does a Woman Take It?

> Those whom we marry are those whom we fight.
> *African Proverb*

Why do battered wives stay with their husbands?

A simple question, but one with a complex answer.

Almost all of the research has centered on battered wives who have decided to end their marriages and not on those who stay and take it. Our own research shows that women reach the decision to end their marriage only after a history of beatings and reconciliations. They act when they reach a point at which they can take no more, and this point is different for each woman.

We found that many spouses will suffer a series of severe attacks, some with weapons, without so much as calling for help, while many call the authorities after a threatening gesture from the husband.

The decision to break up the marriage comes about after there is a change in the woman's attitude toward her husband. The decision to seek legal assistance is the result of a change in the wife's behavior not the husband's, studies show.

A victim of spouse abuse for seventeen years relates: "After you live so many years, and you wake up one day, and your body has just about had it, you say, 'My God, I just can't take another punch.' That's what happened to me. I just reached a point where I said, 'No more. Nothing is worth it.' I decided I would rather struggle and see if I couldn't make it, so I just up and left, and that's been it."

One of the major reasons a battered woman remains with her husband involves her attitude and the attitudes of her family, her peers, and society in general. The combination of these attitudes forms what could be called the *zeitgeist* of violence. The stronger the *zeitgeist,* the harder it is to break out of her situation. When the *zeitgeist* of violence is strong, the woman sees her violent world as "normal." If she thinks her life is no different than anyone else's, she is not apt to take steps to change it even though it is painful and unpleasant.

We find that among the factors that create the *zeitgeist* of violence and determine how inclined a woman is to end a battering relationship are:

Was there spouse abuse in her parent's home? Are her friends and relatives also battered? In her social circle is it expected that men will occasionally beat their wives? Does her husband feel that he has the right to beat her? Does he feel she needs to be beaten from time to time? Does the battered wife share his attitude? What do other people expect of her? Is divorce unacceptable? Is "sticking it out" regarded as a virtue? What is the level of marital violence in the community? What is the wife's subjective meaning of violence? Are there any external constraints put on by others living in the house?

Childhood is a critical stage. Some females are literally trained by their parents to become battered wives.

Sixty-six percent of the women who saw their parents exchange blows were later victims of violent attacks by their husbands, according to a study by Dr. Steinmetz.

Witnessing such activity teaches the child how to be violent and also instills a subconscious approval of the use of violence.

Young girls may grow up thinking that men are supposed to hit their wives, and such role expectation may become the incentive for their husbands to use violence on them. And women who have been raised in violent homes are more likely to marry men who are prone to the use of violence.

The more often a girl is struck by her parents, the more likely is she to grow up and be hit by her husband.

The less a girl experienced violence in her family, the more apt she is to view intrafamilial violence as deviant—thus, the more she is willing to seek assistance or a divorce when assaulted.

Dr. Gelles writes: "Our research on marital violence suggests that many victims of family violence do not view these acts as violence or as problems. Women who have been beaten severely by their husbands often state that they 'deserved to be hit,' that they 'needed to be hit' or that 'husbands are supposed to hit their wives.' "

B. L. Daley, a counseling psychologist of Columbia, South Carolina, says: "It appears to be a social phenomenon in many cases where the wife expects to be treated this way because 'men get frustrated, get drunk and beat their women.' Probably some wives want to be beaten. For some it may be the only attention they get."

Elaine Weiner, a psychiatric nurse who counsels battered wives in Montgomery County, Maryland, observes: "Some women really believe they deserve the beatings."

The Kalamazoo study concludes:

> Evidence seems to point towards a cultural theory as an explanation for the prevalence of spouse assault as a means of coping with stress. A cultural theory might also explain society's tolerance of spouse assault and would point out that hitting one's spouse is a tacitly approved cultural norm.
>
> Not surprisingly, because of community attitudes that approve of spouse assault, or at best view it as a private family matter, there are few sanctions that can be brought to bear in dealing with the assaulter. The few sanctions that are available, are rarely applied.

A battered wife, Betsy Warrior of Boston, says: "I was seventeen when my husband first beat me. I was accustomed to seeing a certain amount of male hostility expressed towards women, so I took it for granted."

The battered wife living in an atmosphere of acceptance of marital violence weighs her options in terms of the amount of punishment she receives compared to the rewards of her marriage—security, companionship, sexual satisfaction, etc.

When violence is the norm, it is much more difficult for a battered wife to take steps to end a marriage than it is for a woman used to more placid conditions. Since violence is accepted to some degree on all levels of our society, the decision to terminate a marriage because of the husband's violent behavior is relative. It's also difficult.

Andrea Dworkin, in her book *Woman Hating,* writes: "When we women find the courage to defend ourselves, to take a stand against brutality and abuse, we are violating every notion of womanhood we have been taught."

Jodi McNeel, executive director of the Fort Worth, Texas, Bay Area Committee on Drug Abuse, relates: "We have found that many of the battered wives calling in choose to stay in their present situation. We have tried giving them many different options and talking over alternatives with them, but again the callers prefer to remain in their homes."

Researcher Elizabeth Truninger lists seven reasons why some women stay with husbands who beat them. They are: (1) poor self-image; (2) belief their husbands will reform; (3) economic hardships; (4) the need of their children for the father's economic support; (5) doubt they can get along alone; (6) belief that divorces are stigmatized; and (7) the fact that it is difficult for women with children to find work.

Other reasons that are often mentioned include: She is too afraid to take action; she is too ashamed to tell anyone; she feels trapped in the marriage, totally dependent on her husband, and has no place to go.

A surprising number of women have a very simple answer for why they stay with a man who abuses them. "I love him."

A victim of three decades of abuse relates: "I loved him, and it took me thirty years to get over it. I knew in 1964 I didn't need him, but I couldn't get over wanting him. He beat me, he knocked me around ever since we were married, but I still loved him."

Mixed up with love is hope and loyalty. Ms. Warrior, who had a stillborn child after being beaten, says: "When we were young, I thought things would change, and I stayed with him."

Nurse Weiner explains what often happens in her counseling sessions with battered wives. "They always enumerate the good qualities, the marvelous attributes of the men, and they downplay the beatings.''

Many battered wives are ambivalent about their husbands, feeling both love and hate. Dr. Richard F. Lyles, director of an Atlanta, Georgia, crisis center, observes: "It's interesting that people can feel almost simultaneously directly opposite feelings. It seems possible for people to feel love and hate almost simultaneously even though they appear to be opposite emotions.''

Women who feel such mixed emotions are often confused about what they should do. Unsure of what action to take, they most often take no action and simply remain with their violent mates. Many wives refuse to call police after repeated beatings. Helen L. Andrews of Washington, D.C., appeared on a neighbor's porch one wet, rainy night, saying she needed help because her husband had beaten her.

The neighbors offered to call the police, but Mrs. Andrews said no. The reason: "My husband has been arrested on a drug charge. He's in so much trouble with the police with this other business they'd just lock him up again,'' she said.

Two weeks later Mrs. Andrews was found dead. Her husband killed her and then committed suicide.

A woman in Boston relates: "I actually thought if I only learned to cook better or keep a cleaner house, everything would be okay. I put up with the beatings for five years before I got desperate enough to get help.''

A co-ed at Howard University told police she had been beaten dozens of times during the previous year and that her husband had tried to kill her. "I didn't press charges because I was afraid he'd be expelled from college and his career would be ruined. I didn't leave because I couldn't afford to move out, and I have no friends or relatives here to move in with.

"He came into the bedroom waving a broomstick. He turned off the lights so I couldn't see him, and he started calling me dirty names. Then he began hitting me all over my body with the stick. We struggled, and he dropped the broomstick. Then he tackled me and dragged me to the washing machine. There was water in it, and he tried to drown me.''

Only then did she decide to take action.

Concern for her children is another reason battered wives give for staying with their tormentors. The remarks of a suburban Maryland woman are typical.

"You have to think of the children first. How will the kids handle it? Will I be making them neurotic? Will I ruin the kids' lives?

"It's a hard decision to make—it really is. But then I realized that fighting is not a good thing for the children, so we left."

Jodi McNeel adds: "We have found that our callers will take some action if the husband has threatened to harm the children. It seems that the wives are more concerned for the health and welfare of their children than for themselves."

Georgene Noffsinger, a former battered wife who is now a counselor says: "We still cling to the fallacy of keeping the family together for the sake of the children, whereas in reality for the sake of the children, the couple should separate."

It is a perverse quirk of nature that the abused woman often takes on greater feelings of guilt than her abuser. Typically, a battered woman attributes her beatings to some personal inadequacy—something she's doing wrong. It's a common experience for psychiatric professionals to hear the most pathetic victims blaming themselves for their broken limbs, swollen faces, blackened eyes, broken teeth—even critical knife and gunshot wounds—inflicted by their mates.

"Being beaten up is the most degrading, humiliating, crushing kind of thing that could ever happen to a person," says Norma Jean Redwine, a 34-year-old battered wife from Kensington, Maryland. "You feel physically limp. You feel like your whole world has just absolutely been split in two, shattered in pieces. . . . I don't give up easily, and yet I really wanted to give up . . . to go out into the snowbanks and die."

Another battered wife put it this way: "When I came to, I wanted to die, the guilt and depression were so bad. Your whole sense of worth is tied up with being a successful wife and having a happy marriage.

"If your husband beats you, then your marriage is a failure, and you're a failure. It's so horribly the opposite of how it's supposed to be.''

The task force studying battered women in Montgomery County, Maryland reports the following:

> For those who have suffered abuse at the hands of a spouse, the behavior often may have started early—sometimes within days of the marriage—and continued for decades. . . . Women tend to blame themselves without knowing why. They voice embarrassment, shame and guilt and will go to extraordinary lengths to hide the crime. There also seems to be a pattern on the part of abused wives to seek counseling help. On the part of the husbands there is a pattern of resistance to counseling help unless they become really frightened about the damage they might inflict.

Stewart Oneglia observes: ''Many women find it shameful to admit they don't have a good marriage. The battered wife wraps her bloody head in a towel, goes to the hospital, and explains to the doctor she fell down the stairs. After a few years of the husband telling her he beats her because she is ugly, stupid, or incompetent, she is so psychologically destroyed that she believes it. Many simply won't recognize that the marriage is a failure.''

A victim in Massachusetts described her situation in almost the same words: ''My husband always told me, 'You're stupid, you don't know how to do anything. You're so dependent on me you could never make it on your own.' After listening to this over and over, I really believed it. That belief kept me at home suffering until I thought I was going crazy.''

In her counseling sessions, Ms. Weiner observes:

''They usually say I love him and apologize. They feel responsible for what's going on . . . very guilty . . . very ashamed and get into this subordinate role of 'I must have done something to deserve it. I must have done something wrong.' ''

Maria Roy shares this view. She says: ''A basic problem is that society still makes women feel that if they have failed at marriage, they've failed as women. So, somehow, if their husbands are beating them, they really believe they have done something wrong.''

Battered wives themselves confirm this paradox. ''It took me five years to get over the shame and embarrassment of being beaten. I figured there had to be something wrong with me.''

Typically, it takes years before a woman can face the problem and seek outside help.

Enid Keljik, a Wall Street administrative assistant who divorced her husband after three years of beatings, says: ''I never dared to admit it. It was just something nice people don't do.''

Another battered wife relates: ''I think the main thing nobody really understands is what you go through. It's the after feelings of, like, trying to hide everything that you could and playing down the rest. That hurts. You don't need to have to tell your friend, 'My husband hits me, and that's why the black eye.' If the beatings don't hurt that much, that does. That tears you apart.''

Georgene Noffsinger says: ''Women often fail to tell even their closest friends and relatives if attacked. Shame is the big thing. Women are ashamed to admit that it happened to them. They're ashamed to admit their husbands did it to them.''

A word repeated over and over by battered wives is ''trapped.'' To many, the forces of society seem to conspire against them to trap them in their marriage and to block every avenue of escape.

''If you take out an assault and battery warrant against your husband, he may lose his job,'' explains Mrs. Noffsinger. ''This simply makes economic matters worse for her and the children. If you go the divorce route, your standard of living drops. A lot of women, especially if they've been housewives all of their lives, don't like to face that. They ask themselves: 'What can I do? Where do I go? What do I do for money?' ''

Maria Roy makes the same point:

''Women are often economic prisoners. They fear they'll lose their house, their savings account, and almost everything else if they leave their brutal husbands.''

Other battered wives have little or no access to money.

They are unemployed, and the only money they have is given to them by their husbands. It is not uncommon that there is precious little left over from the household allowance for the wife to use to help herself escape. A woman in Detroit relates it took her two years to save $1.75. When she got $5.00 from her grandmother at

Christmas, she was able to buy bus tickets for herself and her daughter and flee her husband.

Judge Oneglia says: "Wives tolerate beatings because of their dependency. My typical client is thirty-five to forty years old, married at least ten years, with several children and without marketable skills. She has no place to go, no job, money, or credit of her own."

Mrs. Noffsinger adds: "As an over-thirty wife with children, rarely if ever employed, how do you take the first step?

"Where do you go? What do you do with the kids? When you leave, you can be guilty of desertion.

"Do you run out the front door and stand on the front lawn waiting for someone to rescue you? Often women go out and sleep in a car. That first step is very inhibiting. It's darn scary to run out of the house in the middle of the night and not know where you're going to be twelve hours from now.

"You don't always get much sympathy. Close relatives, even parents say: 'You made your bed, now lie in it.'"

The fewer resources a battered wife has—education, job skills, access to money, a car, friends—the fewer alternatives she has to staying married. Or to put it another way, the more entrapped she is by marriage, the more reluctant she is to end it. The less dependent a wife is on her husband, the more apt she is to call an outside agency for assistance. Many people theorize that housewives with little education will not do anything when attacked. But we find that the lower-class wife may find it easier to break up her marriage than wives who economically are better off.

Maria Roy states: "It is often harder for middle-class women to get themselves out of the situation because of economic fears. The lower-class woman may be on welfare already, so she has nothing to lose by leaving. But the middle- and upper-class woman who hasn't worked in a while and has a low image of herself has more problems getting out of the situation. She doesn't want to give up her home and car in the suburbs. But she must reach that turning point where she gets so angry she'll do anything to get out. Some women never reach that. We hope through AWAIC that more will."

What generally happens is described by Ms. Weiner. "After they sit there at the meeting and talk about how they're going to do this or that . . . save a little money to be independent, how they're going to find their own place or stand on their own feet . . . they look at their watches and say they've got to go home to cook dinner."

Mrs. Redwine recalls being asked by a psychotherapist why she had not separated from her husband earlier than she did. Her answer was: "The biggest thing was fear of being alone, of not being able to handle things, of having to take total responsibility."

Her worry is not an isolated example—in fact, it's commonplace.

"Even though you have all that argument and all that physical abuse, you're never really sure if you can make it outside by yourself. Another big thing is you don't know if society will accept you. What will your friends say?" is a typical remark by a battered wife.

But a major concern for many battered women is that they literally have no place to go. "If the bars are closed, one's parents do not live nearby, and the family has few, if any, close friends, where does she flee?" asks Dr. Gelles.

"The problem is this whole thing comes down on them, and there is no retreat," says Police Commander George Bannon, who did a study on social-conflict assaults in Detroit. "There is no way to run home to mother because mother probably has the same kind of problems or maybe even lives in the same flat. There is no ability to go out and hire a motel for the night."

And even when a woman does decide to take action, she can find the road full of blocks and pitfalls. In general, family violence is considered a private affair by the police, the courts, and a large segment of the population. Because of this, the battered wife can face a discouraging array of obstacles when she seeks relief.

Among the most salient problems battered wives face are the following: First, almost all assaults take place over weekends, holidays, or evenings. During such periods, assistance is usually difficult to secure; neighbors are away, police forces are often extremely busy, legal-aid offices are closed, and banks are not open for the quick withdrawal of money. A wife who has to escape the home without sufficient money will not only have a hard time employing legal counsel, but room and board will also be difficult to get. While it is inexpensive to hire a lawyer for a thirty-minute consultation, she will not be able to engage long-term legal services without money, and in order to qualify for public assistance, she must remain separated from her mate. However, staying away may put her in legal jeopardy if her husband decides to counter with a suit for desertion and she is not able to prove "constructive desertion."

Second, if the wife leaves with her children, chances are there will be no shelter for them. Very few shelters today offer this type of group accommodation. And if she leaves without the children and opts to remain separated·from her husband, when the case comes before a judge in formal litigation, it is possible that she will lose her children for failing to provide for them. As long as the husband is providing room and board for a wife, the court does not like to order a husband to pay additional maintenance. The wife's only avenue is to return or else suffer the possible consequences. The only way to force the wife beater out of the house is by injunction, and it is almost impossible to get a court to issue this.

Third, fear motivates many battered women to remain with their violent men. Many are afraid to go and afraid to stay. They know after a series of beatings that if they stay, they can expect more of the same and that there is little they can do to prevent the beatings.

Many battering husbands are extremely possessive and filled with infantile jealousy. Wives of such men fear that even if they leave, their husbands will hunt them, find them, and beat them for leaving. With little or no expectation of help from the police or the courts, many are too terrified of what their husband might do to them to try leaving.

In the University of Michigan study *The Assaulted Wife: Catch 22 Revisited,* the authors state:

> Fear accounted for the lack of self defense. Nineteen of the 20 victims identified fear as their initial reaction to having been beaten.
> . . . Some women were so shocked and frightened by the violence that they were totally unable to respond.

For example, one battered wife explains:
"I would cover my head with my arms and crouch in the corner. I was too afraid to fight back."

Typical were comments such as: "When he hit me of course I was afraid. Anybody would be if somebody larger than you decided to take out their anger on you. I really couldn't do anything about it. I felt as if I was completely helpless in that situation."

According to this study, "Thirty percent of the victims attempted to defend themselves. They unanimously agreed that the severity of the beating increased proportionately with their amount of resistance. Fear was coupled with a strong sense of humiliation."

Some sample comments were:

"He used to kick me when I was down, like a dog."

"If my clothes got ripped during the fight, he would make me sit and sew them right after the beating."

A woman's decision to stay or go to seek help or suffer in silence is often determined by the frequency of her beatings. Women who are severely beaten often are more liable to take action than those who are beaten less frequently, recent research shows.

"Interviews with abused women who remained with violent spouses and with women who sought outside intervention indicate . . . the less severe and less frequent the violence, the more likely a wife is to remain with her husband," reports the study *Violence in the Family*.

Women who are beaten more than once a month are the best candidates to end their marriage.

Dr. Gelles, in his study of eighty families, reports:

> Only 42 percent of the women who had been struck once in the marriage had sought some type of intervention. 100 percent of the women who had been hit at least once a month . . . either obtained a divorce or separation, called the police or went to a social agency. . . .
>
> Women hit from weekly to daily are most likely to call the police, while women hit less often (at least once a month) are more inclined to get a divorce or legal separation.

On the other hand, many women endure years, even lifetimes of abuse, from men.

The popular notion that a battered wife is as sick as her husband is illustrated in a recent newspaper article by Ann Landers, the most widely read advice columnist in the U.S.

> Dear Ann: My husband bruises me during quarrels. Yes I mean physically. Divorce or separation: No, most of the time he is good to me. Joint counseling? Several years didn't stop the hitting. Karate? It's an invitation to escalation. Besides, he's stronger than I am. Police? NG in a small city where people talk.
>
> Meanwhile, is there some quiet legal device to restrain or penalize him short of being so badly beaten up that I have to go to the hospital?
>
> Black and Blue

> Dear Black and Blue: If you've had several years of counseling and your husband is still beating you and you're still living with him, he is kinky beyond hope and you, my dear, have a deep-seated need for punishment. Obviously you two feed on each other's neurosis.
>
> According to the experts, a man who gets his jollies beating up women can always find someone who will tolerate it and they are both sick.

Even some feminists partially share this view. Maria Roy says: "It may very well be that the woman who marries a wife beater and endures his assaults year after year has psychological problems equal to his. To be roughly handled has been considered by many women, especially women of the working classes, as indispensable evidence of love."

Dr. Marguerite Fogel observes: "There is a pattern I have noticed. Certain women seem to attract violence in men. They report over and over again, with different men, the same pattern. Eventually, they end up being beaten. There is the aspect of sexual excitation for masochists."

The assumption that many—if not all—women are masochists is more than a folk belief. Sigmund Freud concluded that all women were masochists because it was a natural condition for them. He believed, and taught his followers, that women hate themselves because they don't want to be women—they want to be men.

"The repudiation of femininity must surely be a biological fact, part of the great riddle of sex," he wrote. As a result of his belief, Freud believed masochism was normal in women and abnormal in men. "Masochism is a female trait," he taught.

Dr. Karen Horney, in her book *Feminine Psychology,* presents a summary of psychoanalytic views on feminine masochism. She writes:

> The specific satisfactions sought and found in female sex life and motherhood are of a masochistic nature. The content of the early sexual wishes and fantasies concerning the father is the desire to be mutilated, that is, castrated by him. Menstruation has the hidden connotation of a masochistic experience. What the woman secretly desires in intercourse is rape and violence or in the mental sphere, humiliation. The process of childbirth gives her unconscious masochistic satisfaction, as is also the case with the maternal relation to the child. Furthermore, as far as men indulge in masochistic fantasies or performances, these represent an expression of their desire to play the female role.

Later in the same work, Dr. Horney attacks many of the long-held notions concerning the nature of woman.

> To such doctrines that woman is innately weak, emotional, enjoys dependence, is limited in capacities for independent work and autonomous thinking, one is tempted to include the psychoanalytic belief that woman is masochistic by nature. It is fairly obvious that these ideologies function not only to reconcile women to their subordinate role by presenting it as an unalterable one, but also to plant the belief that it represents a fulfillment they crave, or an ideal for which it is commendable and desirable to strive.

Modern feminists do not buy the Freudian argument as a justification for violence against women.

"One of the major outgrowths of the Women's Movement in the 1970s has been to increase the sensitivity of women and society to two major crimes which women fall victim to: sexual assault and physical assault at the hands of their husbands," says Dr. Gelles. "Battered wives and rape victims are often accused of 'asking for it' deserving it or 'enjoying' their victimization."

Susan Jackson takes strong exception to the willing-victim theory.

"The accusations by psychologists and others against battered wives, like the accusations against rape victims, that they invite or even need to be violently abused, if not murdered, cannot be ignored. . . .

"The argument that women invite and somehow need to be beaten and therefore no wife beaters should be arrested is like arguing that since everyone has a Freudian death wish, no one should be arrested for murder."

Another feminist writer, Letty Cottin Pogrebin, in *Ms.* magazine writes: "The claim that women provoke the violence of which they are so often victim is to argue that Jewish passivity invited genocide or that the exploited poor are to blame for the corruption of the rich."

Professionals who work daily with battered wives don't believe that the victims want to be beaten.

Andrew B. Loman says: "The victim does not actively or passively encourage this abuse as some behavioral scientists could contend. Rather, she is a victim of a sick man and a society that does little to encourage his treatment and/or punishment."

Maryland counselor Noffsinger concludes: "You can't drive somebody to violence if his head's screwed on straight."

CHAPTER NINE

Tracy's Story—
A Case History

A wife may love a husband who never beats her,
but she does not respect him.

Russian Proverb

"Arrest him!" screamed Tracy Mitchell. "Arrest the bastard! See what he has done to me?"

She stood there, her body shaking in an emotional upheaval brought on by the effects of anger and fear. Her upper lip was twisted into an obscene knot that distorted her speech, making her sound like a drunk or an inarticulate idiot. She was neither.

Seconds before, her husband Tom had opened their apartment door, and now two police officers were standing in their living room.

"Arrest him," she said once more.

"In a minute, ma'am," said the taller of the uniformed pair. "First we got to get some information. Please . . . sit down . . . try and compose yourself. We're here to help you."

As he spoke, he walked across the room and motioned to her to be seated.

The other officer said to Tom: "Sir? Let's go out to the kitchen and talk this over."

"Certainly," said Tom. "Anything you say."

Not until they were both out of the room did Tracy relax a bit. She sat down on the edge of a chair.

The police officer stood in front of her. His face was expressionless. He paused a moment, then softly asked: "Do you mind if I sit down?"

"No . . . of course not . . . please do."

Tracy was in an overstuffed chair. The police officer, who was about the same age as Tracy, sat down on a footstool directly in front of her. He carefully placed his nightstick on the floor.

Then, slowly and deliberately, he reached up and took off his hat and set it on the floor between his feet. He stared at it briefly, took a deep breath, then exhaled noisily. It was a rehearsed, practiced ritual designed to calm down the emotionally charged atmosphere.

His black curly hair fell down on his forehead, and he pushed it back with his hand and smiled.

Tracy was in no mood to be charmed.

"I want you to arrest him. He beat me up. I want him arrested."

The police officer, still smiling, said: "Now, now let's take it easy on arresting him for now. First tell me how it happened."

Tracy explained that she had met her husband in a bar after work as they had planned. He was there first, and she found him in a bad mood. Tracy arrived with one of the girls from her office, and they were both laughing and acting silly. Her husband was nasty and insulting. He made a remark about her "queer" friend that she let pass. Tracy had a drink with Tom, and they left. While driving home, Tom accused her of having a homosexual affair with the girl from the office.

"At first, I thought he was making a bad joke, but he said it several times, and I knew he was serious. I tried to laugh it off, but he called me a lesbian again, so I slapped his face. We didn't say anything more all the way home, and I thought that was the end of it. When we got into the apartment, he punched me and sent me flying over the coffee table.

"He punched me in the face and breast and stomach, and I started to scream. He kept calling me a lesbian and punching me. I screamed, and the guy next door kept banging on the wall yelling at me to shut up. He yelled he was going to call the cops, and I screamed back, 'Please do!' All the while, Tom kept punching me and calling me names. I don't know what made him stop . . . I guess he got tired. When he went into the kitchen, I got up and ran out of the apartment to a pay phone and called you."

"You hit him first?" asked the officer.

"I slapped him after he kept insisting I was having an affair with a girl I work with."

"Does he have any reason to think that?"

"No."

"You shouldn't of hit him first. A lot of guys are okay and never lay a hand on a woman until she hits him first. Have you had this kind of trouble before?"

"Yes, but he would only hit me once or twice—not like tonight. I thought he was going to kill me."

They talked a few minutes more, and then the officer picked up his hat and stick and told Tracy to wait there, that he wanted to talk to his partner. He went into the kitchen, and the other officer came out and sat down next to her.

"How are you feeling now?"

"Look," she answered. "I don't want to sit here and chit chat. I want my husband arrested."

"Well, now, I'm not sure you want to do that."

"Well, I am."

"Look at it this way, honey. If he gets arrested, it could get into the papers, and he could lose his job. You don't want that to happen do you?"

"I don't care what happens to his job. I'm not going to be a punching bag for some crazy man."

"Now, now, dear. That sort of talk leads to more trouble. Let's all stay calm and try to work this out like adults."

"I don't want to work things out. I want him put in jail."

"Well, now, I don't know about that. We can't just go putting people in jail. We have to have a crime committed before we do something like that."

"But he beat me up."

"Lots of people have scraps. If we put them all in jail, we'd have half the city in there."

"You mean you're not going to arrest him?"

"Well, I don't see how we can arrest him. After all, the alleged incident took place in the privacy of a home between a man and wife. Don't you think it would be better all around if we didn't try to make too much of this?"

"No, I don't."

"Well, lady, we can't arrest him without a warrant."

"How do I get one?"

"It's very complicated . . . very involved . . . you don't want to go through all that red tape."

"What do I have to do?"

"Well, you have to get a judge to issue a warrant, and none of them are working this time of day. You have to find a judge and get him to come down to the courthouse and sign a warrant, and they don't like being called at home, and he probably wouldn't come, anyway. Besides, the courthouse is locked up. He would tell you to go down to the complaint center at the precinct, and I think it would be better for everyone if you two kiss and make up."

"I don't want . . ."

"There, there now, honey, don't feel so bad. It happens all the time. People get mad at each' other and fly off the handle, but they patch it up afterwards."

The other cop came back into the room, followed by her husband.

"Now I've had a nice talk with Mr. Mitchell, and he realizes that he shouldn't of hit you, and he's willing to forget the whole thing if you are."

"I'm sorry, Tracy," said Tom.

"There now!" shouted the cop. "He's willin.' Come on now, Tracy, give a little, too. Let's settle the whole thing nice and quietly."

Tracy was dumbfounded. It was all too bizarre. A few minutes ago she was getting the hell beat out of her, and now everyone was standing around, smiling and shaking hands. It was a Fellini movie—all distorted and twisted. The only thing missing was a dwarf in a clown suit.

"All right now, folks, take it easy."

"Thank you, Officer," said Tom. "Sorry to have bothered you."

"No bother. Just try and settle things peaceable now."

They were gone. Tom stood by the window looking out at the night. When he saw the two policemen get into their car and drive off, he turned and walked back toward Tracy. When he was close to her, he grabbed her chin with the palm of his hand and squeezed her jaw. He forced her up on her tiptoes, then smashed her head against the wall.

"Don't ever try that trick again," he said through gritted teeth. "Do you hear me? Don't ever try that again!"

Tracy struggled, and he threw the weight of his body against her and pinned her to the wall.

"You little son of a bitch," he growled.

Then he tightened his grip on her jaw until she thought it was going to crack like a dry walnut. The pressure forced her mouth open, and she couldn't speak. She was pulling with both of her hands at one of his but to no avail. He was an incredibly strong man. He squeezed a little harder and moved her head so that her face was directly opposite his but tilted slightly to the left. Then, with the lightening strike of a reptile, he bit her on the tip of her nose. He clamped his jaws onto her soft flesh and shook his head like a crazed wolverine. Tracy fell to the floor in a heap, her hand cupped over her nose.

He left her there, and she curled up in the fetal position and cried her way through the night.

In the morning, neither spoke. She watched him dress and fix himself a cup of instant coffee. She watched every move, and she stayed as far away from him as she could.

His only words were: "You going to work?"

And her only word was: "No."

When he left, she locked the door after him and ran to the bathroom mirror. She was covered with bruises from her hips to her hairline. Her lip protruded and was the color of fresh liver. Her eyes were surrounded by raised purple islands, and her nose bore a ring of red teeth marks.

She gently touched her face almost to test it to see if it was really her reflection.

"Oh, God . . . look at you. I'll never be able to go out like this."

She turned away and cried. She didn't know what to do. She

turned on the TV, hoping it would distract her so she wouldn't have to think about what to do. She watched an assortment of talk shows and game shows, and finally she decided to take a shower and change her clothes from the day before.

When she was dressed, she put a scarf over her head and pulled it forward to cover as much of her battered cheek as possible. She called a cab and waited in the window until she saw it drive up outside. Putting on her sunglasses, she ran out and got in, giving the driver the address of the citizen's complaint center.

She followed the signs at the center and found herself standing before a police sergeant seated imperially at his high desk.

"Gee, lady, what'd you do to deserve that?"

"I want to file a complaint."

"Well you come to the right place."

Neither spoke, and finally Tracy asked: "What am I supposed to do?"

"You want to file a complaint?"

"Yes."

"Are you sure about this, lady? You know an awful lot of women come down here and say they want to swear out a complaint and make us fill out all the paperwork, and the next thing you know they change their mind, and they don't want to make a complaint no more, and all of us has wasted a lot of time. Why don't you think about it for a couple of days, and if you still want to do it, come on in again."

"I don't need to think about it. Look at me. You think I want to be beaten like this?"

"Well, lady, you can never tell nowadays. Why don't you take a seat over there, think things over some more, and make sure you know what you're doing."

"I know what I'm doing. I don't want to think about it. I want to press charges of assault."

"Well, okay, lady. If you're sure you know what you're doing. This could cause a lot of trouble for your husband."

"I know."

The sergeant eventually took her name and address and told her to go upstairs to another room and wait. She found a large room filled with battered desks and chairs and file cabinets. A dozen or so people were walking about, but all of them ignored her.

A long wooden bench stretched out against one wall with several women sitting on it.

Tracy was confused. She looked around for someone to acknowledge her presence. No one did. She walked over to the bench to ask a question of one of the women seated there. Before she could speak, one said: "You're in the right place, honey. Take a load off your feet. They'll call you when they're ready for you."

Tracy sat down. Another woman looked at her closely for a few minutes and said: "Well you certainly got a good one, didn't you?"

Tracy didn't know how to respond, so she just sat there.

"Don't feel bad, kid. You'll get used to it. My man's been beating me for twenty years. Every once in a while I have to get him thrown in the can, or he'll kill me."

Tracy could hardly believe her ears. "How long did you say?"

"About twenty years. What happened to your nose?"

"Nothing."

"Nothing! That's a laugh. It looks like he bit you. You married to one of them biters? Old Harry never done nothing like that to me. He likes to punch me around, but he never tried to bite me. I bit him on the finger once. He knocked out my tooth for that."

"Why do you take it?"

"Well, you know how it is. That's the way men are. You can't live with 'em, and you can't live without 'em. But believe me, kid, you're doing the right thing. You have to throw a scare into them sometimes, or they go too wild. It don't pay to take too much shit. But you know, to tell the truth, sometimes I deserve what I get. I can be a real bitch at times. When I get too far out of line, old Harry gives me a few punches and straightens me out. Sometimes a woman needs it."

"Well, I don't need it, and I don't want it. I don't know how you can say the things you just said."

"Well, you know it takes all kinds . . . excuse me, honey, he's calling my name."

Tracy spent the rest of the afternoon sitting on the hard bench, staring at the cigarette butts on the floor and at the water streaks on the walls. At nine minutes to five she heard her name.

"Mrs. Mitchell?"

"Yes . . ."

"Sorry to keep you waiting so long. We had a lot of action here today. Say, you got quite a treatment there. What did the other guy look like?"

"Can we get on with this?"

"Well, that's what I wanted to talk to you about. We don't have enough time to do it all today. I leave here at five. I'm sorry you had to wait so long, but there's nothing I can do about it. I suggest that you come back at nine A.M., and we'll try to get you in first thing."

"But I've been waiting all day . . ."

"Well, I know, but there were a lot of people here today."

"You don't seem to understand . . . I want to report a crime. I've been severely beaten. I should think you could see that. I want to swear out an arrest for my husband."

"Well, yes, Mrs. Mitchell, I know. But perhaps it would be better for all concerned if you thought about it for one more night. You know, it's a long drawn-out process, and most women end up dropping charges. It's much better if you try to settle your marital problems outside of the criminal system. It's rather messy, and it causes a lot of problems for everyone."

"I don't care if it causes you problems or not. I want some protection. My husband's out of work now, and he'll be coming home, and he might beat me up again. I want the police to stop him."

"Well we can't do that, ma'am. We can't stop him from beating you up. We can only prosecute him afterwards."

"What?"

"That's right. Look now, it's almost five, and I have to go. Come back in the morning if you still want to file a complaint."

"But what if he beats me again?"

"Well, in that case, call the police. Good-by now. I have to run."

Tracy felt drained of strength. She walked out of the building and stood in the cement courtyard outside and watched the flights of pigeons while she tried to decide what to do next. The whole thrust of her action had been parried by an indifferent bureaucracy. Her efforts for the day had accomplished nothing. Without ever making the decision to return home, she found herself hailing a cab and heading back toward the apartment.

She let herself in, not knowing what to expect once inside. It was empty. She searched about for some indication that Tom had been there. Eventually, she saw a note taped to the refrigerator.

> Tracy,
>   I had to get away for a few days to get time to think about us.
> You probably need some time, too. Right?
> I'll call you later.
> Tom.

She was elated. She collapsed in the overstuffed chair and kicked off her shoes. For the first time that day, she was able to relax.

During the next four days, she remained cloistered in the apartment. On the second day, Tom called. He told her he was staying with friends and that he felt it would do them both some good to spend some time apart. She agreed.

Tracy spent a lot of time looking at her battered face in the bathroom mirror. On the second day, she thought it looked worse than the first. It helped to convince her that it was not a good idea to try and fight the bureaucracy at the complaint center two days in a row. It was best to take a day off.

The following day she began to look a little better, but she convinced herself it was not time to go back downtown again. Each day she looked a bit better, and each day she felt less like reporting the incident.

Finally, on the fifth day, she began to feel apprehensive. She started to worry that Tom would be back soon, and she was terrified that he might beat her up again. She mentally scolded herself for wasting so much time. She dressed and took a bus downtown.

Tracy went to the desk sergeant, but it was a different man there. She explained that she had been there earlier to file a complaint, but the sergeant told her in a dry monotone: "Sorry, lady, there's no record of a prior appearance here."

"But I was here."

"I'm sorry. There's still no record of your being here."

"Well, never mind. I still want to file a complaint."

She found herself back upstairs, once again sitting on the same hard wooden bench against the wall. An hour passed before an assistant prosecutor called her name. It wasn't the same man she had spoken to before. He motioned to her to come over and sit in a wooden straightback chair set alongside his battered, paper-cluttered desk.

He introduced himself and asked what he could do for Tracy.

"I want to sign a warrant against my husband."

"Well, I'm afraid *you* can't sign a warrant."

"But I was told that to get my husband arrested, I'd have to come down here and sign a warrant."

"Who told you that?"

"Two cops . . . the two that came to my house when I called."

"Yes . . . I see . . . Well, I'm afraid that's not quite right. You can't sign a warrant. A warrant must be signed by a judge, and then an arrest can be made. A citizen doesn't sign the warrant."

"I don't know. Maybe I got the words mixed up. I was told to come down here and sign *something.*"

"Did you want to come down here?"

"Yes. I want to file a complaint against my husband."

"You want to sign a complaint?"

"Yes."

"I see . . . well that can be arranged, but first would you like to explain the circumstance of your complaint?"

Tracy told him the story of meeting her husband and the beating that followed.

"When did this alleged beating take place?"

"It's no alleged beating. Look at my face. Does that look like an alleged beating?"

"Well, it's merely a legalism . . . When did the alleged beating take place?"

"Five days ago."

"Five?"

"Yes."

"Why did you wait so long to report it?"

"I didn't wait. I tried to report it to the cops, and they told me to come down here. I came down the next day, and they made me wait around all day, and then I was told it was too late to do anything that day. I haven't been able to get back until today."

"Who told you it was too late to file a complaint?"

"One of the men here."

"One of the assistant prosecutors?"

"Yes."

"What was his name?"

"I don't know . . . he didn't tell me."

"How do you know he was an assistant prosecutor?"

"Well, I don't know what he was. He was dressed in a shirt and tie, and he came over and told me it was too late."

"And you don't remember his name."

"No . . . Is it important?"

"No, except he shouldn't have told you that. He should have remained and taken your information."

"I didn't know."

"It's all right. You say that the incident took place five days ago. Was that on the seventeenth?"

"Last Wednesday. I don't know the date."

"Here. Look at this calendar. Was it the seventeenth?"

"Yes."

"What time?"

"At night."

"Are you sure it was Wednesday the seventeenth and not early the morning of Thursday the eighteenth?"

"I'm not sure of the exact time, but we met after work for a drink and came home. It couldn't have been too late. Certainly no later than 10 o'clock on the seventeenth."

"Did the police officers file a report of the incident?"

"Yes . . . I guess so . . . I told them I wanted my husband arrested."

"Did you see them write anything down?"

"No."

"In that case, I doubt if there was a report filed. Do you know the names of the officers who investigated?"

"No . . . They didn't say."

"They wear nametags. Did you notice the names on the tags?"

"No. I was too upset."

"Did you see their shield numbers?"

"No. Like I said, I was very upset. I'd just been beaten up."

"Did you see a doctor?"

"No."

"Why not?"

"Well, I wasn't bleeding, and I didn't think a doctor could do much for me. I know enough to put an icepack on."

"What about internal injuries?"

"I didn't think about that."

"Did you ask the police officers to take you to a hospital or to your family doctor for treatment?"

"No."

"Have you been to a doctor yet?"

"No."

"Are you still living with your husband?"

"Yes and no. He hasn't been home since that night."

"He left on the seventeenth and hasn't returned?"

"No, he left the next morning to go to work. I couldn't go to work looking like I did, so I stayed home. Then, after spending all day down here, I went back to the apartment, and he wasn't there. He left me a note saying he was going someplace to think."

"Do you have that note?"

"No. I threw it away."

"Has he returned?"

"No . . . not yet."

"Do you expect him to come back?"

"Yes . . . I don't know . . . I guess so."

For a long minute the prosecutor looked at Tracy as if he were rehearsing in his head what he was going to say next. When he spoke, he said:

"Now let me see if I understand all this. You say you had an argument with your husband five days ago. The argument led to some blows. You called the police, the officers investigated and determined that there wasn't sufficient evidence to make an arrest, but they informed you of the procedure to follow if you wanted to pursue the matter.

"By your own admission, the injuries you received were superficial."

Tracy interrupted: "Superficial . . . who said they were superficial? Look at my face. I was beaten five days ago, and you can still see the bruises and his teeth marks on my nose. I don't call that superficial."

"Well, Mrs. Mitchell, you told me that you did not seek medical treatment either in a hospital or from your doctor."

"Yes."

"Well if you were seriously injured, wouldn't you go to the doctor?"

"Sure, but . . ."

"And you didn't go. Right?"

"Yes."

"You *did* seek medical treatment?"

"No."

"You did not. Well, if you did not seek treatment, then obviously you didn't think your injuries were serious."

"Well, I didn't think they were serious enough to go to the hospital, but that doesn't mean I felt they were superficial."

"Now we're playing word games, Mrs. Mitchell. You weren't hurt badly enough to see a doctor, were you?"

"No."

"Okay. Five days after your husband walked out on you, you came down here and wanted to press charges."

"Yes, but I was here the next day, too."

"Un huh . . . But you can't remember who you talked to?"

"No."

"You know what this sounds like to me?"

"What?"

"It sounds like you and your husband had a fight. He walked out on you, and now you want us to go and find him and drag him back home for you. After he's back, you'll have a change of heart and drop the charges.''

"That's not what I want at all. I'm afraid he *will* come back and beat me again.''

"And you wouldn't *like* that?''

"No. I wouldn't.''

"How long have you been married, Mrs. Mitchell?''

"Five years.''

"Has he beaten you before?''

"Yes.''

"Have you ever reported it?''

"No . . . no, I haven't.''

"You've been getting beaten for five years, and you never did anything about it?''

"No . . . I thought he would stop.''

"Mrs. Mitchell. I always say the first time the dog bites you, it's the dog's fault. The second time it's yours.''

"What's that supposed to mean?''

"Nothing, Mrs. Mitchell, but lots of women enjoy getting pushed around. They enjoy punishment. They like to be dominated.''

"Are you calling me a masochist?''

"I'm not calling you anything . . . I'm a lawyer not a psychiatrist. You used *that* word, not me. You seem to be familiar with the term and what it means.''

"That's great! I'm familiar with the word murder, and I know what it means, too. Why don't you accuse me of murder?''

"The law doesn't work that way. You have to have evidence, which brings me to your situation, Mrs. Mitchell . . . What evidence do you have?''

"Evidence?''

"Yes, evidence.''

"Have you looked at my face lately?''

"How do we know it was your husband who beat you?''

"Ask the cops.''

"That will be hard to do since you don't know the names of the investigating officers.''

"Well, you could get their names."

"I suppose it might be possible, but from what you said, it doesn't appear like a report was filed. Now that was five days ago, and we have hundreds of calls to answer. It means going through hundreds of reports, and if there was no report filed in the first place, then we will have to try and locate the officers who were on duty that night and if we find them hope they can remember your case out of the hundreds they have investigated. Now with no police record and no hospital records it will be extremely difficult to establish. Were there any witnesses?"

"No . . . except the guy next door."

"Did he see your husband beat you?"

"No, he didn't see him, but he heard me screaming, and he yelled at us to be quiet."

"Does he yell this way often?"

"All the time."

"Then he probably would have trouble remembering a particular time and date which took place some days ago."

"I guess . . ."

"Mrs. Mitchell, would you like to be put in jail on the testimony of an uncertain neighbor who didn't witness the crime?"

"Well . . . no."

"There you are. No judge and no jury would accept this as adequate testimony to prove—beyond all reasonable doubt—that a crime has been committed."

"I guess not."

"Well, Mrs. Mitchell. You're a smart woman. With no evidence, no witness to an alleged crime five days old, I think you can understand the situation. I'm not going to ask a busy judge to issue a warrant for a flimsy case like this, first of all, because I don't want to bother him with a lot of nonsense and secondly, even if I did believe you, this is not prosecutable. We have more work than we can handle now, and I see no point in taking on a case that will, I feel, be called off, anyway. And if it isn't called off, it will be thrown out of court."

"You're telling me there's nothing I can do when my husband decides to beat me up?"

"I suggest you call a minister or a priest or the both of you go to see a marriage counselor and try to work your problems out between yourselves and leave the criminal justice system out of your private affairs."

"But I don't want to see a marriage counselor . . . I want him arrested!"

"Sorry. I just don't think there is sufficient evidence here to ask a judge for a warrant."

"So he can beat me up anytime he pleases?"

"No. I didn't say that. I said there is insufficient evidence in this case to prosecute."

"That's it?"

"As far as I'm concerned, it is. You have the right to sign a complaint if you wish, but I'm telling you ahead of time I won't recommend that the judge issue a warrant, and unless I do, he won't sign it."

"The judges do what you tell them?"

"Well, they generally take our recommendations in these matters."

"Then there's nothing I can do."

"Nothing here. I suggest you contact a marriage counselor."

"But I don't want one!"

"Well maybe you ought to hire yourself a lawyer and settle your differences in civil court."

"I don't suppose there's any point in my insisting on signing a complaint?"

"No. Not much point."

Tracy went home, and Tom was there ahead of her. At first, neither one said much. As the night wore on, they began to talk, then to argue, and eventually he hit her, and she called the police.

A scene reminiscent of the first investigation by the police occurred. The officers—different ones—were like actors in a rerun. They were polite, smiled a lot, and refused to make an arrest. Then they left.

The next beating was even worse.

When Tracy regained consciousness, she was in a white room with a rubber tube up her nose. The nurse smiled and said:

"Hi . . . everything is okay. You're in St. Mary's Hospital. You've been hurt, but you're going to be okay now."

Tracy was confused. She knew she was in a hospital, but she couldn't remember how she got there. She then gradually began to remember the fists in the face, the punches in the body, the kicking, the blackout.

She cried softly. Then she heard a familiar voice.

"My poor baby . . . What's happened to you, my poor baby?"

It was her mother. The two women cried openly in each other's arms.

When Tracy left the hospital, she went to live with her mother. She also returned to the complaint center and went through the same routine with the desk sergeant but met with a different prosecutor in the big room upstairs.

This time she had copies of her hospital records, which described her injuries in specific detail.

The prosecutor listened carefully to her, then asked:

"Are you still living with your husband?"

"No."

"Do you plan to go back to him?"

"No."

"Well, in a case like this, I don't think it will be necessary to issue a warrant."

"Why not?"

"Since you're no longer living with him, you probably are more concerned that he stays away from you than you are that charges be pressed. Isn't that right?"

"I want protection, but I also want him arrested."

"I see. Mrs. Mitchell, you realize that an incident like this could cost your husband his job and will do you no good. In fact, he might just become madder if you threaten him with prosecution."

"I want him punished for what he did to me."

"There's no doubt that you sustained severe injuries, but to be perfectly frank, Mrs. Mitchell, judges are reluctant to issue arrest warrants after only one incident."

"It's not the first time. He's beaten me up before."

"Did you report it to the police?"

"Yes, the last time I did."

She explained the incident and how she had tried to get a warrant.

"I see. Was a warrant issued then?"

"No."

"Did you sign a complaint?"

"Well . . . no. I didn't actually sign the complaint because the prosecutor said he wouldn't get the warrant."

"Then there's no record of this incident here."

"I don't know. Don't they keep some record of who they talked to?"

"No. If the matter is being dropped, as most of these family matters are, then there's no point in making more paper work. We've got enough here already."

"Then that beating doesn't count. He gets away with that one?"

"With no way to prove anything, I'm afraid it won't do much good. But we are going to help you. Now if you'll just take a seat over there, I'll get the paper work started and call you when it's ready."

Tracy returned to the hard wooden bench against the wall and waited. She sat there for a little over an hour before the prosecutor called her back.

He handed her a manila envelope with some papers inside.

"Take this over to Room 1014 at the courthouse."

"What about my husband's arrest?"

"That's out of my hands now. I suggest you take these papers over to 1014, and they'll explain everything to you."

"But I want my rights . . ."

"You'll get them. You can be sure of that, Mrs. Mitchell. Take these papers over to 1014, and they'll explain the next step to you. We have to follow procedures."

Tracy left the complaint center and took a bus to the courthouse. She found the right room and entered. It was a large room filled with office furniture. There was a high counter just inside the door, and next to it was a low railing that marked off an area about 4 by 15 feet in which people waited before being ushered through a swinging gate and into the larger part of the room.

Tracy handed the envelope to the clerk who looked at it and asked: "You here to get a peace bond?"

"I was told by the prosecutor at the complaint center to come over here."

"Yeah . . . to get a peace bond."

"I'm not sure what the legal terms are . . . Is there something wrong?"

"No. But you want a peace bond, and the man who takes care of that isn't here right now."

"Isn't there someone else?"

"No, just Mr. Kent, and he's not here."

"When will he be here? This afternoon?"

"Well, I don't know for sure. Sometimes he doesn't come back, but he's in here every morning. Why don't you come back then."

The next morning about 10 o'clock, Tracy returned to the office with the papers in hand and asked for Mr. Kent.

"He's not here. He's in court in the morning."

"But you told me yesterday to come back this morning."

"Yeah . . . well, you have to catch him early before he leaves for court. If you want to wait for him, you're welcome."

Tracy sat down and waited. She waited for two hours and went up to the clerk and asked: "Do you have any idea at all when Mr. Kent will be back?"

The clerk, a different one than the person she had spoken to earlier, answered: "That's him over there."

"Why didn't someone tell me? I've been waiting here all morning to see him."

"He knows you're here. He'll get to you as soon as he can. Please be patient."

Tracy sat down and waited another half hour. Then she noticed that the man who had been pointed out as Mr. Kent was walking out of the office. She jumped to her feet and called after him.

He seemed surprised.

"Yes, what is it?"

"Mr. Kent, I've been waiting to see you for two days, and now I see you leaving the office. Can't you do me the courtesy of least giving me an appointment? I can't sit around and wait for an audience for days on end."

"Sorry. I didn't know you were here to see me."

"What?"

"No one said anything to me about your being here."

"But I asked that woman a half an hour ago when you were coming in, and she said you knew I was here and would get to me."

Kent looked confused. "Mary . . . Mary, did you tell this lady that I knew she was waiting for me?"

"Yeah . . . I just assumed that Alice had told you. She's been here all morning."

"I'm sorry. I really am. But I'm just on the way out to a lunch engagement that can't be broken. What is it you want—a peace bond?"

"I'm trying to get a man arrested for assaulting me."

"Well, we issue peace bonds up here."

"They told me at the complaint center to come over here."

"They did?"

"Yes."

"Well, okay. Tell you what. Leave those papers here, and I'll take a look at them and call you."

"But . . ."

"Be sure and write your phone number on the envelope . . . Mary, this lady is going to give you this envelope. Please put it on my desk . . . Thanks . . . good-by now, I have to run . . . I'll call you after I've looked them over."

Tracy turned in the envelope and returned home. For the next two days she waited and then decided to telephone Mr. Kent to see what was happening. She called several times, but Kent was never in to take her calls. Finally, on the fourth day she called and got through to him. He seemed confused again, apologized, and said they were very busy. Tracy had the feeling he was rummaging through a pile of papers on his desk trying to find hers. Eventually, he said he had the papers and told her that she should come to his office at 2 P.M. the next day.

Tracy arrived, and after only fifteen minutes of waiting she was allowed through the swinging gate and taken over to Kent's desk. He smiled weakly and motioned to a chair.

He explained that a peace bond was being issued for her. Her husband would be ordered to "cease and desist" from attacking her.

"But what if he ignores this?"

"Then he can be brought before a judge."

"What will happen to him then?"

"It's hard to say. He might put him in jail. Most likely he'll give him a warning."

"But I want him arrested now. I don't want to wait for another beating. He's liable to kill me."

"I don't know about that. A lot of women ask for what they get."

"What's that supposed to mean?"

"Nothing. Nothing at all, just an observation. Our job here is to issue peace bonds. If that's not what you want, then you've come to the wrong place."

"But I was sent here by the complaint center."

"If you don't want a peace bond, then you had better go back to the center and talk to them."

"All right. Give me the peace bond. I'm tired of this run-around."

Tracy left the office frustrated and mad. She had spent five days fighting the bureaucracy and wasn't sure she had accomplished a thing.

About five days later Tracy received a telephone call. It was from Tom.

"What's this paper you had sent to me by the judge?"

"It's a peace bond. Read it and you'll see what it means."

"I have read it. I think it's a rotten thing to do."

"Too bad."

"Just because you want to run around with your lesbian friends is no reason to get me involved with the courts and cops and stuff. You don't need any peace bond . . . I wouldn't touch you or your queer friends with a ten-foot pole."

"That's fine with me . . . just leave me alone."

"I don't know what happened to you . . . you used to be normal . . ."

"Look. I don't know where you got this idea about my sexual preferences, but it's something that's all in *your* head."

"Well, perhaps you'd like to explain . . ."

"No, I wouldn't. I don't want to explain anything to you. I don't want to see you or talk to you or have anything to do with you."

"That goes double for me."

"Fine. I want to come over to the apartment and pick up my things."

"What things?"

"My clothes, and cosmetics, my records . . . my belongings."

"I threw them all out."

"You *what?*"

"I threw them all out."

"You threw out my records?"

"Naah . . . I'm keeping them as payment for the trouble you caused me."

"You are like hell."

"What do you think you're going to do about it."

"I'm coming right over and get my stuff. . . . You better not have thrown anything out."

Tracy hopped in a cab and went over to the old apartment. Tom was there. They argued. He refused to let her take her records, and once again she was savagely beaten.

Tracy went to her doctor. She had learned that much. She wanted a medical record of the incident. Then she went to the complaint center, followed the by-now familiar routine, and eventually sat down with yet another assistant prosecutor. She told him her story from the beginning and said she wanted to sign a complaint and have her husband arrested for violating the peace bond.

"Well, we don't usually make an arrest in a case like this."

"What?"

"What we normally do is notify your husband to appear on a certain date to discuss the matter. It's sort of an informal hearing. We try to get matters like these settled without going to court."

"But I was told that the peace bond would protect me. Now I want it enforced. What good is it if he can beat me up when he wants to?"

"Well, Mrs. Mitchell, the circumstances here are a little different. After all, you went to his apartment, he didn't come after you."

"What difference does that make?"

"A man has a right to be in his own apartment. He pays the rent. It's his home. You're the one who barged in on him."

"I didn't barge in. I told him I was coming, and I wanted all my own things."

"You said you wanted to take some LPs . . ."

"Yes, they were my records. I bought them before I was married. They're my collection."

"Do you have receipts showing you bought them?"

"Of course not."

"Then it really comes down to your word against his, right?"

"Well, ask our friends. They'll tell you, they are my records."

"I'm afraid the court would regard them as community property, Mrs. Mitchell. Your husband has as much right to custody as you do, and since you deserted the domicile, I don't think the court would feel that you have any right to remove them prior to a just settlement agreed to by both parties."

"But they were mine . . . I love those records . . . I want to keep them."

"I can understand that, but we're talking now strictly in terms of the application of the law."

"I want to sign a complaint."

"Very well. I'll have the papers filled out."

"What about his breaking the peace bond?"

"You better take that up with the people over at 1014 at the courthouse."

Tracy signed the complaint, and the following day she went to the courthouse. She got the usual run-around there, and finally she was told to go to another office. There she told the whole story over again, and the counselor said he would send a letter to Tom notifying him of an informal hearing after he checked with the police and the doctor to make sure the necessary records were on file.

Several days later, Tracy received a notification in the mail setting the date for the hearing. She was still with her mother. She had not returned to her job after the last beating. She couldn't face anyone there. She had a new job but had to give it up because she was asking for so much time off to attend to her problems with Tom.

On the day of the hearing, Tracy arrived at the designated place and sat nervously at a table. The hearing officer came in and sat at the end of the table. He arranged a file and a yellow legal pad by his chair and chatted with Tracy about inconsequential matters.

The appointed time came and went, and after waiting another half hour, the hearing officer said: "It looks like he's not going to show."

"What happens now?"

"We'll send him another notification—a much stronger one."

"And what if he ignores that one?"

"We'll cross that bridge when we come to it."

The next day Tracy took her mother's car and drove to Tom's apartment. She went to a pay phone in the lobby of the building and dialed his number. It rang a number of times, and she decided he wasn't home. She went upstairs and let herself in with her key.

Once inside, she looked around and found, as she had suspected, that Tom had not thrown her things out. She began to work quickly. She found her suitcases and packed her clothes and personal things as quickly as she could. She took them down and locked them in the back seat of her car. Next she found a box and packed up her records and was careful to take only the ones that were hers before she was married. She carried them down and loaded them in the car. She looked around the apartment to see if there was anything else she wanted and decided there wasn't, locked up, and drove to her mother's house. She was well pleased with her afternoon caper.

That evening, Tom telephoned her. They argued about what she had done, and Tom said he was going to call the police.

"Good luck," she said. "But don't hold your breath while you wait for them to do anything."

Later that night, Tom came over, and Tracy's mother let him in the apartment. They argued some more, and Tom explained to Tracy's mother that he suspected her daughter was engaged in a homosexual affair.

Tracy slapped his face, and Tom punched her in the stomach and breast, and while she was doubled up in pain, he punched her in the mouth and sent her to the floor.

Tracy's mother screamed and began flaying him with delicate punches. Tom raised his shoulder to ward off the punches and shouted: "She started it."

Tom retreated from the house, and the mother went to comfort Tracy. She told her mother to call the police.

This time when the police arrived, Tracy got their names. She told them calmly she wanted to file a complaint. This time she had a witness, and the police took down the information.

Next she asked the police to take her to the hospital emergency room.

"You don't look hurt, lady," protested one of the cops.

"I have internal injuries," she said. "I may be bleeding internally. Are you refusing to take me?"

"No, ma'am. Not at all. We'll take you right over."

When Tracy returned to the complaint center, the police were a bit more courteous than they had been in the past. When she got to the prosecuting attorney, she explained she had the officers' names, that a report had been filed, that she had a witness to the crime, that she had been treated for injuries in the hospital. She had all the times and dates memorized. She told him that a peace bond had been issued against her husband, that he had violated it and failed to show up at a hearing, and now this latest incident was the second violation of the bond.

The attorney listened and made detailed notes.

"You seem to know what you're doing," he remarked.

"It comes from experience," Tracy answered.

The assistant prosecutor agreed that there was enough evidence to believe that a crime had been committed, and he said he would request the judge to issue a warrant for Tom's arrest.

The warrant was issued, but Tom was not arrested. She called the police and the prosecutor several times, but they said they had not been able to locate him.

Tracy realized that the police were not looking for Tom and that they would probably never arrest him. Both she and her mother worried that he would find out and come over and attack them. The two women talked it over, and finally they decided that they should buy a gun.

Tracy went to a gun shop and purchased a hand gun and a box of bullets for $35.00. The man in the shop showed her how to fire it. She put it in a drawer by her bed. She had planned that both she and her mother would go out to a shooting range someday and practice firing, but they never got around to it.

The next week Tom was picked up on a traffic ticket, and after a routine check, the officer discovered that there was a warrant pending against him and arrested him.

He was indicted and then released without bail on his own recognizance.

Tracy learned of these events much later.

She and her mother were watching television when they heard a knock at the door. Tracy's mother opened it, and Tom quickly pushed it open. Tracy's mother pushed her body against the door on her side, and both women screamed at him to stay out. Tracy ran toward the bedroom.

The older woman was no match for Tom, and he was able to push the door open and race into the apartment.

Tracy was loading the gun when he walked into the room.

"Put that down," he ordered. "You don't know how to use that thing."

She clicked the barrel into place and released the safety catch as the man in the store had demonstrated.

"Stay back, Tom. I'm warning you. I'm not taking any more beatings from you."

Tom smiled and began walking toward her.

"Now give me that before you hurt yourself."

"I'm not kidding. Stop or I'll shoot."

"Be reasonable now, Tracy," he said as he took another step toward her.

She pulled the trigger, and the noise was deafening, the flash blinding, and the smell overpowering.

Tom died instantly—shot in the face.

The police arrived in force, and took pictures and wrapped up the body, tried to question Tracy's mother—who was hysterical—and Tracy, who sat impassively on the bed in a state of shock.

Finally, the body was removed and the evidence collected and marked, and a police officer put handcuffs on Tracy and took her out of the apartment.

By coincidence, one of the cops, the young one, was the same officer who had investigated the first incident months before.

He was visibly shaken. As he escorted Tracy toward the black and white police car he said to her: "Lady, you know you can't go around shooting people. What made you do it?"

Tracy stopped walking and turned and looked the young officer in the eye. "You did," she said softly. "You did."

CHAPTER TEN

The Law, Police, and the Courts

There are no rewards for refereeing a family fight.
A Detroit Cop

When a battered woman comes to the end of her endurance, she reaches outside of her home for help. For most women, it is an act of desperation—one taken with reluctance. Typically, it has taken her a long, long time to work up her courage. Finally, she does it. She calls for help, hoping for compassion and understanding. What she will most likely get is hostility and cynicism.

Usually, the police, attorneys, prosecutors, public defenders, and even judges feel they should not get involved in so-called "family problems."

Confusion develops because wife beating can be a criminal offense, a civil matter, or both. Most battered women don't realize this, and many fail to understand the distinctions. It is common practice for the police and lawyers to actively try to discourage a woman from taking criminal action. They try to get her to drop the matter or persuade her to pursue it through the civil channels.

These official roadblocks can be confusing even for a well-educated woman, and they become incomprehensible for the less fortunate on the lowest end of the spectrum.

The battered woman, searching for a path out of her violent world, finds instead a circular obstacle course leading nowhere.

"The system is cumbersome, misleading, inconsistent, confusing, and often inadequate," says feminist Mindy Resnik.

Most states have shown little interest in passing laws that deal specifically with wife beating. Only three—California, Hawaii, and

153

Texas—have such laws that make it an automatic felony for a husband to beat his wife. In most of the other states, when such laws are introduced—often at the prodding of NOW or other feminist groups—they get scant support in the male-dominated legislatures. Last year, when the Maryland legislature was debating a wife-beating bill, a woman called a crisis line to pass on a piece of ironic information. The caller revealed that one of the legislators leading the fight against the proposed law was her husband. She also said she was divorcing him—for wife beating.

Although male chauvinism is often displayed in these debates, it is not the only reason for opposition. Many people are sincerely convinced that no new laws are needed, that the ones already on the books are adequate to do the job.

Susan Jackson argues: "The problem is not a lack of laws . . . the problem is that existing laws are systematically unenforced . . . the problem, which is much the same nationwide, is that women whose husbands beat them—often on a regular basis—have no effective remedy within the system as it now operates."

The system operates on the basis of selective enforcement of the law. Assault is a crime in every state. Since wife beating is a form of assault, then wife beating is a crime in every state. In practice, however, wife beating is not treated as a crime but as a civil matter. Prosecutors deliberately look the other way even when a man admits he beats his wife. For example, divorces are routinely granted on the grounds of cruelty and physical abuse. Yet it is almost unheard of that a husband—even one who admits in court that he has beaten his wife—is prosecuted for the crime.

Selective and arbitrary enforcement of the law is a major obstacle to the battered woman's chances of obtaining her rights or equal treatment.

Emily Jane Goodman, co-author of *Women, Money and Power,* observes:

> A woman passenger in an auto accident may sue the driver for damages, whether they are married or legal strangers. But if she's punched in the nose, her legal options depend on her marital status. A wife hit by her husband loses access to courts and laws available to others.

The problem is that the laws and courts are supposedly acting in the interests of the family unit, though at the expense of married women. The attitude of the legislature, police and judges is that they are dealing not with a public crime, but signs of a troubled marriage. . . .

Official indifference to the cries for help from battered wives is documented in a study completed by Sue Eisenberg and Pat Micklow.

Eighty percent of the victims sought out immediate professional aid from police. In approximately one-half of these cases, the police responded with a house call. In only one case were arrest procedures utilized. In that instance the assault was not characterized as a severe felonious assault until a day later, yet the police arrested the husband on the basis of outstanding traffic warrants.

When the police fail to help, the abused woman has to turn elsewhere—to crisis centers, churches, or shelters. But in many places there are no such organizations available. Then she must depend on her friends or relatives. Even in places in which social agencies exist to help the battered wife, they are often inadequate. The situation discovered in Kalamazoo is fairly typical. This study concludes:

The community resources are not mobilized to deal with spouse assault as a problem. Victims of assault often find themselves in a double bind, in that the help that is available does little or nothing to solve the problem. At the same time, victims are blamed by many professionals for not wanting to solve the problem and for staying in the situation. The system has no adequate measures for dealing with spouse assault and possibly because of the frustration of being unable to solve the problem the blame is often placed squarely on the victim.

The implications of the findings suggest that victims of spouse assault often have few if any acceptable alternatives to staying in the situation. Should the victim decide to prosecute and should the assaulter be incarcerated, it may mean the loss of needed income for the family.

Women are trapped in a situation in which they become virtually powerless to help themselves. They find themselves in an irrational world in which no one will listen, no one cares.

This desperate, frustrating predicament is vividly recounted in a report published on May 27, 1976, in a Maryland weekly newspaper, *The Montgomery County Journal.*

He came down the stairs and picked her up, she said. "He had his fist doubled up, and went like this"—she swung her fist across in front of her in a backhand motion—"and like this"—she swung it back. "I can still feel that. It really hurt. I thought for sure I was going to die."

She said he continued to hit her around the head and she tried to get away, but "When someone is in a rage like that it's a little difficult to get away from them, when he weighs 175 pounds and you weigh 125."

She said he pulled her into a bathroom and shoved her up to a mirror and insisted she look at herself, although her eyes were nearly swollen shut, and said, "Aren't you lovely, I'll teach you."

Then she said, he took her to the front door, opened it, said "Get out," and pushed her out, naked and bleeding.

She tried hysterically to get back in, she said, tearing the screen, and when she was unsuccessful, she broke four panes of glass out of the window beside the door to try to get in that way.

"I'm standing out there with no clothes on when he opened the door and pulled me in by the hair on my head," she said. She said he told her "I've got your mother on the phone, in Arizona."

She said her mother suffers from a grave heart condition. "I tried to sit down and talk to her. She wanted to know what was going on. I said, 'Mommie, he is beating me.' She said, 'Oh my God.' I got hysterical. I was crying and this man was looming over me. I ran into the bathroom and grabbed a shawl, that was all there was, and ran out the door. My mother was still on the phone."

The woman said she ran to a neighbor's house. "As I was going up the steps I think I fell or something. I was on my knees. I had the shawl wrapped around my waist." She said she banged on the door and a man came and opened an inside door, but not the screen door.

"I don't know whether I told him I needed help or not," she said. "I think it was pretty obvious I did. He said, 'Go away, or I'll call the police.' I said, 'Please do.'" She said the man, who she didn't know, shut the inside door.

He did call the police, and she stayed on the porch until they arrived. She said a policeman or an ambulance attendant put a raincoat over her, and they took her to the hospital.

Officers went back to her house and picked up clothing for her, she said, and took her husband to the Bethesda police station. She was treated at the hospital emergency room and then the officers took her to Commissioner Anthony Cain, to swear out a warrant against her husband. Cain declined to issue the warrant.

By that time, it was early Saturday morning. Cain, she said, told her he would not issue a warrant because the incident was a domestic matter and suggested she go to the county prosecutor Monday if she wished to pursue the matter.

This incident took place in Bethesda, Maryland, but it could have happened in any town in the U.S. It graphically illustrates two of the problems encountered by the battered wife. One, the reluctance of people to get involved in problems between a man and a wife—even in extreme situations such as this one when a woman crawls naked and bleeding onto a neighbor's porch. The second is the official indifference to her plight. The police were helpful, but the commissioner, a minor official empowered to act in place of a judge to set bonds and issue warrants, clearly didn't feel that a crime had been committed.

The indifferent response of this woman's neighbor is not unusual. Besides unwillingness to become involved in problems that do not immediately affect you, there is the firm belief that what happens in the privacy of an individual's home is no one else's business, including the police and the legal establishment.

This concept that a ''man's home is his castle'' has great appeal. Home is the refuge from the problems and pressures of the outside world. It's a place we can all escape to. The outside world should not intrude. This view is generally held by private citizens and endorsed by police, lawyers, legislators, and judges. Attitudes have changed little in the more than 100 years since a judge in North Carolina ruled: ''If no permanent injury has been inflicted, nor malice, cruelty nor dangerous violence shown by the husband, it is better to draw the curtain, shut out the public gaze and leave the parties to forget and forgive.''

Essentially, the same argument is still advanced today by Washtensaw County, Michigan, chief prosecutor, William Delhey, who says: "I think the sanctity of the marriage is more sacred than the criminal law and the one-punch fight . . . it overrides the criminal code."

He is not alone in this opinion that the law should tread lightly when it enters the threshold of an individual's home. A police officer in Washington, D.C., Thomas Hoffman, observes: "There isn't a lot we can do in these cases. We can't physically throw a husband out. We just don't have that right under the law. You can advise them that there are county agencies that will counsel them . . . you can advise them that they can secure warrants and take it through the courts, and after that there's just nothing you can do but just turn around and walk away because it is their home, and if they want to fight in it, there's really not much we can do about it."

The police officer's reasoning is based on the general public's attitude toward the problem. Judges today are still handing down decisions not much different from the 1874 ruling cited earlier. The courts consistently rule on the side of the citizen and uphold his rights in his home. An example was presented in the Kalamazoo research, which reports:

> An attorney related the following incident as an example of the legal community's interest in the area of family disputes. A policeman accompanied a woman back to her home to pick up her belongings. The husband told the policeman to leave and later assaulted him.
>
> The policeman brought assault charges against the man. When the case was brought to court, the judge dropped the charges because the man had told the policeman to leave and he stayed.

This may be good law, and it may reflect the public consensus regarding the sanctity of the home, but it does almost nothing to protect the battered woman. The rights of personal privacy come in conflict with the rights to life and the freedom from attack. Once she enters her home, a woman has some of her rights suspended. Society's attitude seems to be that the bigger issue—the right of privacy in the home—is more important than a few black eyes and broken noses. No one, however, has asked the battered wife which of her Constitutional rights—privacy or equal protection under the law—she wants enforced and which she wants suspended.

It is not an easy question for society to deal with, and there has been no great rush to clarify the issue. As Eisenberg and Micklow observe: "This question confuses police, judges, and lawyers. For the most part the solution today seems to be ignore it."

Some first tentative steps to addressing this question were taken in the new spouse-abuse law recently enacted in Hawaii. If the investigating police officer feels that the wife is in danger of further physical harm, he can order the husband out of his own home for a cooling-off period of at least three hours. If the husband refuses, he can be arrested.

Despite the good motives of the legislature, there are strong feelings in legal circles that this law would be declared unconstitutional if tested in the Supreme Court.

Those who have investigated this area of conflicts of rights are divided on solutions but generally in agreement with the views of Detroit Police Commander James Bannon, who says: "We must begin to view domestic violence as a public issue rather than a private problem. As distasteful as it may be, society must recognize the role it has played in creating an ideal of the sanctity of the home behind whose doors anything goes."

Their first cry for help by most battered women is to the police. Many expect a modern version of the white knight in shining armor to arrive, sweep her up, and defend her from her tormentor. What she gets falls drastically short of this romantic notion. A battered woman's first experience with the police is likely to put her in a state of stunned disbelief.

Alice Johnston of Albany, New York, relates her experience: "The first time he beat me, I just took it. I cried and tried not to let anyone know. Then it happened the second time and lots of times after that. One night I finally called the police.

"They came and asked me if I wanted my husband arrested. They wanted to know how I would survive with the kids and no money. So I told them to go away, and my husband beat me worse than ever for calling the police. I didn't call the cops again."

A Michigan battered wife described her experience: "Yesterday, my husband came and knifed my car, ripped the tires, slashed the roof, grabbed me, and told me the next time I was going to get it like the car. . . . After he left, I called the police. I was put on hold . . . they didn't even ask me my name."

Dee Zurbrium of Laurel, Maryland, says she called the police for help and was told, "We can't get involved in a domestic quarrel, lady. The best thing you can do is get out of there because next time you may be dead."

One victim describes her predicament this way: "I have been to the police many times and had pictures taken. But by the time they get around to doing anything, everything is cooled down, which I think is really bad news. Because, you know, they can't do anything right away for me, and that's bad. I mean when you've got someone beating on you, the main thing you want to do is just get him out of there. And as the police say, there is nothing we can do. They just won't intervene in family arguments without a restraining order or something."

Women who expect the police to come rushing at breakneck speed to their aid are usually disappointed. In the Michigan University study, researchers found it took between twenty minutes and four hours for the police to respond to a call. In some cases the police refused to come at all.

The Detroit Free Press, in an article headlined "Emergency Number Still Has Kinks," reports:

"A near-breathless woman, beaten by her husband, dialed 911 to ask for police assistance. 'Does he have a weapon?' the operator asked.

"She answered he did not.

" 'Then I am sorry. We won't be able to help you,' the operator said to the dismayed woman."

In Washington, D.C., Yvonne Barrow relates:

"My husband and I had been separated a short while. One night at about four A.M., he returned drunk to my apartment. He tore the door off its hinges when I wouldn't let him in. A neighbor called the police, but they didn't arrive until about seven A.M. They forced him to leave.

"About an hour later, I went out to do the laundry, and he was still there. . . . He wouldn't let me get in my car. He tried to kick me, and I hit him with a piece of iron. He threatened to kill me. Neighbors called the police for me, but the policewoman wouldn't do anything because he is my husband."

The current approach to family calls is in effect stacked in favor of the attacker. The police come, and nothing happens to help the battered woman. The cops tell her of the perils of the legal machinery, the trouble it will cause, quiet her down, and leave. The net effect is that the woman's cry for help has been rejected. She's been told it's not a real problem. The husband's position has been reinforced. The inaction by police says to him, "We're here because we were called, but we don't think this is serious. We're here to patronize your wife." This conveys an official stamp of approval on the husband's behavior—it's okay to beat your wife. He knows that if he were really breaking the law—stealing a car or attacking property—then the cops would arrest him.

In police agencies in every part of the country, there are records to show that the wife beater is a repeat offender. Repeated lectures and gentle advice have no effect on the problem. When the cops leave, the husband often resumes the beating. This situation leaves the wife frustrated and defenseless. Often she is driven to murder as the only means by which she can defend herself. When the man is bigger and stronger, and after the police have repeatedly indicated that they will not intervene in her behalf, then she is faced with one of three choices: (1) submit to another beating, (2) flee her home, or (3) defend herself as best she can. Driven to the brink of despair, it's not uncommon for a woman to take a gun or a butcher knife to her husband. In Washington, a battered wife with no weapon available attacked her husband while he slept—by pouring boiling water in his ear.

The accumulation of frustration and fear drives many other women to take the law into their own hands. Eisenberg and Micklow note:

> Faced with a violent husband and no alternatives, she may equal-
> ize the situation herself by using a deadly weapon such as a gun or

knife. The wife killing her husband is not a rare crime. The United States Crime Reports indicate that 31 percent of homicides occur in the family and of those approximately one-half are between spouses.

James Bannon makes a similar point: "The woman feels, legitimately, I maintain, that she has no other recourse but to deal with the situation in the best way she can. And feeling that way, her response is to get the shotgun out of the closet and blow the aggressor away."

Judy Hartwell, a 28-year-old housewife from Belleville, Michigan, found herself in such a situation. In court she admitted stabbing her husband Fred in the chest five times while trying to escape from him.

"I didn't mean to do it," she testified. "I didn't want to hurt him. There was nobody I could call for help. The police wouldn't come. I was very much afraid."

Her defense attorney told the jury the killing was the result of a "moment of sheer desperation" after having endured beatings with sledgehammers and rubber hoses.

Judge Susan Borman of the Detroit recorder's court says: "In my court I see a lot of wives killing husbands after many years of beatings. . . . The gun will be there, and they'll reach for it, and then the husband will be dead. And it will be this mild-mannered, passive-aggressive woman, as they call it in the probation reports."

The victim and the police view the immediate problem of the battered wife in entirely different ways. For this reason, it is almost certain that the experience will prove frustrating and disillusioning to the woman. When the victim calls the police, her essential concern is protection. She wants the law to stop her husband from beating her. She is demanding her rights as a citizen to protection from violent force. She is also demanding justice. She wants the person who has committed an assault on her body taken away, punished, and prevented from assaulting her again.

The police, on the other hand, view the matter from an entirely different perspective. From their point of view, their job is to quiet things down and leave, to avoid making an arrest, to keep the matter unreported, and to settle the problem without resorting to criminal charges, the courts, or lawyers.

"The traditional police response has been to separate the combatants, attempt to restore order, tell them if they really want to, they can take out a warrant and then get back in service," explains Jared D. Stout, director of planning and research for Fairfax County, Virginia, Police Department.

The police officer considers his job to be to talk the angry woman out of causing unnecessary problems. The woman, who typically has endured previous beatings before becoming desperate enough to even call the police, has her ace in the hole ripped up and tossed in her face.

Implicit in the police's action or inaction is the assumption that the matter is not important. The police also reflect the implied attitude that wife beating is a normal, everyday thing that all men do at least once in a while. The battered wife is told in effect, "Your safety is not serious. Don't cause a lot of trouble for all of us."

Susan Jackson says: "The police tend to believe, at least as much as any man does, that men have the right to beat their wives. The effect of their arrest-avoidance policy is to discriminate against women."

Some feminists suggest that a high proportion of police officers are themselves wife beaters and have no sympathy or understanding for the victim's problem.

Part of the problem lies in the fact there is no glory in making a record in wife-beating cases. Prosecuting attorney, arresting officers, police officials, politicians, all anxious to further their careers, tend to concentrate on the types of crimes that will result in the most "credit" and earn them the "best publicity" to improve their public image. Wife beating and family assaults are viewed as no-win situations. They are dangerous, dirty, and of little use to anyone's career.

Most police officers do not consider handling wife-beating cases as an essential part of their work. "Police have long looked on the problem as an unwarranted part of their job," says Dr. Morton Bard. "If police work is crook-catching, this certainly isn't it."

This police reluctance to consider spouse abuse as an important part of their job was demonstrated in Columbus, Ohio, where officers were surveyed about participating in a family crisis intervention training program. About half indicated that they were not only uninterested in taking the course but were actually *opposed* to it.

Even the language used by police officers indicates their low regard for wife-beating investigations. The possible felony is muted by euphemisms such as "domestic disturbance," "family squabble," "family trouble," "lover's quarrel," and "family spat."

An accurate description of the present situation is given by Circuit Court Judge Blair Moody of Wayne County, Michigan, who says: "The law-enforcement agencies feel, well, that's just a domestic problem, and you should see your lawyer and handle it in civil court. A domestic call is not serious in their view. They view other calls as more serious."

James Bannon concurs: "It is always the attitude, get rid of the complaint. Get it out without absorbing it into the system, without messing up someone's docket, because nothing is going to happen when they get into court, anyway."

This attitude, however, runs counter to the intent of our laws. The Handbook on Criminal Law states:

> The broad aim of the criminal law is, of course, to prevent harm to society—more specifically, to prevent injury to the health, safety, morals and welfare of the public. This is accomplished by punishing those who have done harm and by threatening with punishment those who would do harm to others. Sometimes the harm to be prevented is physical: death or bodily injury to a human being in criminal homicide or battery.

When this legal concept gets translated into police procedure, something gets lost in the translation. Even the written rules of police forces endorse the attitude that wife assault is not a crime. A typical example comes from the Detroit Police Department's General Orders, which flatly state:

> Family trouble is basically a civil matter. It is not a police function to arbitrate or undertake negotiations in marital difficulties. . . . Where there is no injury or there is an injury, but immediate medical attention is not required; if it appears reasonable that no fur-

ther assault is imminent; the identity of the assailant is known to the victim; the complainant shall be advised to report the incident to any precinct station. If he wishes to prosecute, he shall apply in person to the detectives in the precinct where the assault took place at 8:00 A.M. weekdays.

Police admit they put a low priority on answering "family disturbance" calls. Micklow and Eisenberg asked a police lieutenant this question:

"If there was a robbery or an attempted rape and some other criminal activity going on and simultaneously you received a family dispute call, how would these offenses be rated in terms of emergency?"

The police official answered:

> Well, there is no real set policy defining how the calls will be screened or answered. . . . If there is one car free and available for calls, and if he had an armed robbery in progress or say a serious auto accident call, and at the same time had an assault and battery or a family disturbance call, of course, the armed robbery would probably take the first priority, the accident second and the family disturbance third.

Ironically, however, police are well aware of the dangers they often face in answering less important "family trouble" calls. The FBI study for an eight-year period showed that 20 percent of the total number of police officers killed in the line of duty died while answering family-disturbance calls.

The standard arrest-avoidance policy was also outlined for researchers Eisenberg and Micklow in an interview with Lt. Casmir Kurek, who teaches the domestic-complaints course at two police academies.

> Q. When a police officer answers a domestic call are arrest procedures utilized at all?
> A. No. We try to avoid that.
> Q. And why is that?
> A. Well, because it's usually a basic family problem. Unless there

is a serious infraction of the law. We stress that we try to avoid arrest if at all possible.

Q. If, for instance, the woman has been punched by her husband, has a split lip or a bloody nose, would that be considered a serious infraction of the law?

A. No.

Q. If a husband kicks or punches his wife in front of the officer, will an arrest occur?

A. It has occurred quite often where the husband will haul off and punch her right in the mouth in the officer's presence. As far as the State is concerned, he can make an arrest. He can be the complainant, according to law, but it's not followed generally. Prosecutors and the judges take into consideration that this is a family dispute. The officer—he feels it is up to the individual. It kind of puts the police in the middle. Damned if you do and damned if you don't.

Q. And if the woman still requests some type of protection? She says "Oh my God, don't leave, he might become more furious at me since I called the police." Are there any protective measures which the police give?

A. There are no protective measures that the police can give and the reason is fairly obvious. There just aren't enough police to go around to protect people. What people usually want is for the police officer to stay right there and protect them. And it is physically impossible.

Many law-enforcement experts frankly admit that the police don't know what they're doing when it comes to investigating wife-abuse cases.

Tim Crowe, a senior consultant at Westinghouse Justice Institute who conducts crisis seminars for law-enforcement officers, says:

"Policemen answer these calls, but they don't know quite what to do. So they de-emphasize them. Yet it is one of the most important things they do."

James Bannon also feels police are not qualified to do the job. "Traditionally, trained policemen are the worst possible choice to attempt to intervene in domestic violence.

"The real reason that police avoid domestic-violence situations to the greatest possible extent is because we do not know how to cope with them.''

Dr. Bard adds:

> A family crisis which has deteriorated to the point of threatening violence is in critically delicate balance and requires a high level of skill on the part of the intervening authority who is expected to mollify the situation. Regretfully, the police officer, if he is unprepared for this function and left to draw upon his own often biased notions of family dynamics and upon his skill as a law enforcer, may actually behave in ways to induce tragic outcome. . . .
>
> There is evidence then that police officers in today's society are realistically involved in many interpersonal service functions for which traditional police training leaves them unprepared. It is further suggested that intervention in family disturbances is one such function in which unskilled police performance may in fact endanger the policeman and may fail to prevent eventual commission of capital crimes or assault.

Police departments across the country have begun special training both for new recruits and older officers in crisis intervention. Most police officers claim they would rather answer an armed-robbery call than intervene in a family dispute. As the FBI statistics cited earlier point out, more police officers are killed in family disputes than in any other type of call. So police aversion to responding is understandable.

Like it or not, the family disturbance is a severe problem for the police, one that occupies a great deal of their time.

Some departments have created special units to handle family-crisis calls. For example, in Hayward, California, Project Outreach teams a family counselor with police officers for domestic calls. The system has reduced these calls from 50 to 20 percent. Fairfax County, Virginia, is planning a mobile crisis team to respond to all calls involving mental health problems, including suicide and wife abuse. Myra C. Wesley, director of the Woodburn Mental Health Center, who wrote the proposal for the unit, says: ''It will be staffed by a specially trained team to counsel husbands and wives and to try to show them there are other ways to deal with problems other than beating your wife over the head.''

Most police departments feel that since so much time is spent on family dispute calls, it is impractical to train specialists. Instead, they have adopted the approach that it is better to give all officers some training in how to handle the problem.

The emphasis in all such courses is to teach the officer to defuse the situation and get the battling couple off the criminal track and onto one leading to either counseling or civil action. The San Jose, California Police crisis-intervention training course is considered an excellent one both by the trainees and other police agencies. An evaluation by more than 400 officers who completed the course showed more than 95 percent rated their training highly favorable. According to Chief Robert B. Murphy, there are six objectives to this training. They are: (1) to increase officer safety in disputes; (2) to decrease the amount of time spent on disputes; (3) to reduce repeat calls; (4) to decrease citizen injuries in disputes after the police arrive; (5) to increase referrals out of the criminal justice system; and (6) to provide superior service to citizens in crisis.

A similar course conducted by the Columbus, Ohio, police is also considered highly successful. Officers were interviewed ninety days after completing their training, and 80 percent said they were more effective in their work as a result of the course (a complete reversal of their opinion *before* they took it). Twenty-seven percent said there was a decrease in the need for force in handling family disputes, and 39 percent said there was a decrease in the number of arrests resulting from family-trouble calls.

Probably more typical is the much less extensive training police cadets receive in family-crisis intervention in Montgomery County, Maryland. A cadet receives 865 hours of classroom training, 6 of which deal with crisis intervention.

In many cities, the real lessons come on the job where new men learn from old officers. It is common practice for two officers to respond to domestic calls. The procedures a new man actually learns in the field can vary widely, depending on the knowledge and experience of his partner.

Dr. Bard, one of the nation's leading experts on family-crisis intervention and a former police officer, has drawn up a 19-point outline to be used by police for effective intervention in family disputes. His steps are:

1. Prevent violence by separating the disputants.
2. Allow only one person to talk at a time.
3. Take the disputants into separate rooms.
4. Switch officers so that the stories check out.
5. In listening to the stories, try to find out in each case what each individual contributed to the conflict.
6. If one of the disputants holds himself to blame, find out in what ways the other shares the blame.
7. Ask questions so as to get the details as clear as possible.
8. Find out if there has been a previous history of this kind of behavior.
9. See if the history goes back to before the marriage to other relationships or similar relationships in the present.
10. Give each person the opportunity to speak in detail.
11. Bring the couple together to tell their stories to each other. Again make sure only one person speaks at a time.
12. Point out similarities and discrepancies in the stories.
13. Point out the part that each is playing.
14. Get a reaction from both about what the officers say they see is going on.
15. Ask what the couple plan to do in response to what has transpired and to the officers' reactions. If they seem to understand and say they want to try to work it out, accept it.
16. If you disagree with their response, suggest that they seek other help. If necessary, make the referral.
17. Tell them that if there is another dispute, and they see that they are coming close to violence or to repeating the same pattern, they should go again for counseling.
18. While noting there will be further difficulties, assure them that if they sit down and talk, at least they can come out in the open and try to resolve their differences.
19. If not in the beginning, then before you leave, make sure that they know your name.

Throughout the country, all police departments emphasize this concept of avoiding arrest. It is the accepted police theory that wife beating is a noncriminal, nonpolice problem. It's treated as a social problem. This practice is helpful to some women. Counseling and better communications will solve her problem. But what about the battered wife who does not want to preserve her marriage at all costs? What about the woman who is filled with fear and pain?

"Police don't seem able to differentiate between a woman in danger and a woman just trying to put a scare into her spouse," says Brooklyn divorce attorney Marjory D. Fields, who estimated that about 40 percent of her 700 clients have been beaten.

Under the present arrangement, a battered wife has to do a selling job on the cop to convince him that she wants her rights. Furthermore, she is confronted with a policeman who has been trained to talk her *out of* obtaining her rights. The methods used are revealed in a course taught at the Wayne County Sheriff's Academy and the Washtenaw County Sheriff's Academy, both in Michigan.

A verbatim outline used by instructors to teach officers how to convince a woman not to press charges follows:

> Avoid arrest if possible.
> a. Appeal to their vanity.
> b. Explain the procedure of obtaining a warrant.
>   1. Complainant must sign complaint.
>   2. Must appear in court.
>   3. Consider the loss of time.
>   4. Cost of court.
> c. State that your only interest is to prevent a breach of the peace.
> d. Explain that attitudes usually change by court time.
> e. Recommend a postponement.
>   1. Court not in session.
>   2. No judge available.
> f. Don't be too harsh or critical.

The procedures used in Michigan are representative of the official police tactics used in all states. The recommended procedure is to make an arrest only as a last resort. Policemen are often officially advised: "Never create a police problem where only a family problem exists."

The assumption here is that the problems are mutually exclusive. The fact is, it is not a question of choosing one *or* the other. The police have two distinct responsibilities to the couple. The first is to restore order, prevent further violence, give advice, and offer alternatives. The second is to make sure the rights of the victim are not being abridged.

The police, and most of the social service organizations, are concentrating on the first and doing very little about the second.

Any citizen has the right to expect that if he or she is criminally assaulted, he or she can bring a charge against the assaulter and have the matter proceed through the criminal system.

Susan Jackson makes the point: "A reduction in the number of arrests without statistics to indicate a corresponding reduction in the number of attacks can hardly be considered a victory for the victims."

An attitude pervades the judicial system that the woman doesn't know what's best for her, that she is incompetent and must be treated in a condescending, "Papa knows best" manner. She is talked down to like a child. It's assumed legal matters are beyond her comprehension and that it's best if she listen to older and wiser men who will set her straight and advise her in her own best interest.

Typically, the battered wife is put on the defensive when she seeks help from the police, who are predominantly male. Instead of assistance, she is confronted with questions such as:

"Who will support you if he's locked up?"

"Do you realize he could lose his job?"

"Do you want to spend days in court?"

"Why don't you kiss and make up?"

"Why did you make him slug you?"

"Why do you want to make trouble? Think of what he'll do to you next time."

Karen Durbin, writing in *The Ladies' Home Journal*, reports:

> One woman called the police after her husband broke her nose. They took her to the hospital, bleeding and with both eyes swelling shut, but they refused to arrest her husband. "You don't want to do

that, honey,'' said the cop, reassuringly. ''It's something that happens in every man's life.''

Invariably, the police try to shift the blame. ''I have spoken to many women who told me that they called the police after a beating,'' says Carolyn Chrisman, a volunteer for AWAIC in New York. ''And when they arrived, they say: 'Well, what did you do to make him hit you?' Then the woman begins to feel that it really is her fault.''

Georgene Noffsinger says: ''I don't believe every policeman, judge, or attorney is a male chauvinist pig, but I don't think they are sensitive to the problem. I think it's a question of well-intended ignorance.

''The first thing anyone asks is, 'What did she do to deserve it?' After that they say, 'If she stuck around and took it so long, she must have liked it.' ''

We discovered a chilling example of police indifference to a battered wife's complaints, revealed not by the victim but by the husband, an admitted wife beater.

''The children were at school, and most homes near us were emptied while their occupants were at work. I got her to the ground, grabbed a belt, pulled her pants down, and gave her bottom a beautiful workout. She cried and whimpered and screamed, but I finished the job properly. She was unable to sit or lie on her back for about a week.

''Years later I was to find out that the following day when I went back to work, she went to the local police station in the little upstate New York town where we were living and demanded my arrest for wife beating. She said I had been systematically beating her for the last eight years! The chief of police, who knew me well, laughed her off with: 'Go home, Lena. You're a liar and you know it.' ''

In most states, police cannot arrest a battering husband unless they witness the crime or have a warrant issued by a judge. As noted earlier, police often refuse to make an arrest when they witness a man assaulting a woman, and women often find that magistrates are reluctant to issue warrants. Usually, they are not available late at night, and when they are, they are often less than sympathetic. A Washington, D.C., battered wife reveals: "It took me eleven years to get up enough nerve to get to one of them, and when I got there, they were insulting and sarcastic. I was made to count backwards and generally prove I wasn't crazy or drunk."

One family court judge, who presides over hundreds of wife-abuse cases every year, after refusing a woman a warrant said: "Any woman dumb enough to marry such a jerk deserves what she gets." Similar biases have been expressed by other judges, police officers, lawyers, and even psychologists.

Such treatment of a victim is unheard of in connection with any other crime except rape. For the victims there are great similarities between rape and wife beating.

Indeed, some feminists describe woman beating as another form of rape but with a frightening difference.

"You don't ask a rape victim to go back and fraternize with the rapist," says Gladys Kessler, an attorney on the board of directors of the Women's Legal Defense Fund." Rape is a completed act, over and done with, while wife beating is an ongoing situation for many women trying to hold their families together."

The vast majority of wife beaters are never prosecuted. In fact, they are seldom even charged. The battered wife has to overcome an incredible array of roadblocks and detours built into the legal system before she can prosecute her husband.

There are many loopholes used by the police to avoid making arrests. For example, many cities like Topeka, Kansas, no longer have laws outlawing drunkenness. As a result, if the police investigate a wife-abuse call and find the husband drunk, they don't arrest him on any charge.

In some states, a five-day cooling-off period must pass between the incident and the filing of charges. Battered women complain that this gives their violent husbands five full days to intimidate them into not pressing charges.

The red tape is time consuming. In Washington, D.C., for example, when a woman goes to the complaint center, she is first interviewed by an assistant district attorney. Then she is referred to a social worker who decides if counseling services would help. The last stop is an interview with an assistant corporation counsel. The process usually takes a full day.

The system is designed to wear her down. Commander Bannon, describing the typical run-around in his city, says:

"Maybe the first couple of times she doesn't pursue the prosecution. She's worried, she would lose support, the children would starve, and maybe he would beat her up worse. If she does follow through and presents herself for lodging a complaint, the attrition process continues to function. The detective may feel that there is insufficient proof for a write-up. They usually insist on medical evidence of the injury. She is sent back. She has to get a doctor. Through all this process, she is being run all over town. Quite often she doesn't have any money . . . she doesn't have anybody to stay with the kids, and she's hauling the babies along with her, and they're riding busses or bumming rides and that kind of thing. So she finally gets down here, and then some prosecutor says to her, well, now I'm not going to issue a warrant, but I'll give you a peace bond. . . . She's got an eye like this—you don't need an M.D. degree to know that she has been batted in the eye."

Another booby trap, says Peggy Anne Hansen, coordinator of the Montgomery County Task Force, occurs when the wife actually swears out the warrant. She relates:

"You have to be emotionally stable to swear out a warrant for the arrest of someone. So if a woman is terrified and has just been beaten, she's not in a very stable, calm mood, so she waits until she is.

"If the same woman is calm and has pulled herself together, and is able to say exactly what she wants, that fact can be held against her because they figure the beating wasn't as severe as she claimed.

"Then, of course, there's constructive desertion, a term most women who have gone to court know. It's a joke, according to some of the victims. To prove it—the legally justified flight of a woman from her home while in fear for her life or dignity—is very difficult."

There are other Catch 22 situations along the way. Mrs. Noffsinger relates: "You can go to the police and swear out an assault and battery charge against your husband. But as long as the man has a fixed address and a job, he'll be released on his own recognizance. The husband then becomes smarter and a whole lot angrier.''

It takes a persistent woman to get a charge filed against her husband. Even after she has conquered the official indifference, she has still more obstacles to overcome.

One is how most judges and lawyers define the crime. If a man hits his wife once, is it enough for an arrest? If not, how many punches are needed? Are ten punches enough and nine too few?

In California, the Penal Code states that if a wife is charging her husband, she must suffer more injuries than commonly needed for battery. Even in states in which it's not stated in the law, the same criterion seems to apply.

In order to decide how much is too much, the legal profession has developed many ingenious rules of thumb that vary from one location to another.

One test is frequency. Generally speaking, once is not enough. There aren't many judges who will issue a warrant or convict a man on the evidence of just one beating. The woman must show a history of being beaten, and the ones she endured before calling the police don't count. Judges and prosecutors also consider the length of time between beatings. Beatings administered no more frequently than once or twice a year do not excite the legal profession. Some jurisdictions have the rule that a woman must have at least four beatings in six months to qualify for criminal assault.

In one case history, a victim said that she was told that one beating wasn't enough. She later called her attorney to tell him that she had been beaten again and that she would try for at least one more. ''Would that be enough?'' she asked.

Another common test is the severity of the beating. Presumably, if the beating is bad enough, a woman doesn't need as many. A female attorney in Oxon Hill, Maryland, says: ''Judges are generally not sympathetic to battered wives unless the beating has been obvious and the spouse has sought medical treatment immediately and has pressed charges immediately.''

One battered wife complained after losing her case that the judge told her: ''I don't believe that a nice, professional man like your husband would do such a terrible thing. And since you went back into the house with him, that proves that the beating wasn't severe."

If a battered wife has children, she is often confronted with the choice of getting herself out of the house to safety and leaving her kids home alone with her violent husband or staying at home and enduring more beatings but being able to look after her kids.

Beatings that do not require medical treatment are generally discounted by the legal establishment. "Some police departments practice a *stitch rule* where a wound must require a certain number of sutures before an officer will make any arrests," reports Dr. Richard Gelles. "Many jurisdictions still follow the rule of *spousal immunity,* which prevents a wife from suing her husband for assault and battery. In the case of violent sexual assault, wives are also denied the right to bring actions against their husbands.

"At the moment, women and children who are the victims of violence and who do not require medical attention have few legal rights."

Some judges require the *divorce test* before granting legal relief to a battered woman. Robert Gold, a public defender in Detroit, explains: "When the lady shows that she has filed for a divorce or she is divorced, and she can convince the judge that she has really done everything possible to rid herself of this man, that's the kind of situation where the judge is more apt to take it seriously and treat it as a *real* criminal matter."

James N. Owens, chief of the misdemeanor trial section of the United States Attorney's office, candidly says: "It's very difficult for a prosecutor to believe a married woman is serious about prosecuting when she is living in the same household with a man and has not filed for divorce.

"If a wife wants to assert her right not to be beaten, she should leave home. If the woman doesn't assert her right to leave her bed and board, we're just not going to do anything to help her. Otherwise, the woman may be using us as leverage over the man's head to bring him to heel.

"I know of no abuse cases prosecuted by the United States Attorney when man and wife still were living together. These cases are usually referred to the court social worker.

"We would overburden the system if we issued a warrant for every assault case coming through the Citizen Complaint Center in which there definitely is a criminal offense. Generally, we prosecute assaults by one spouse on another only if there is a gun involved or severe injury."

In many cases, if the police find out there is a divorce pending, or if an injunction has been served, they refuse to respond. Their feeling is: This is no longer a matter for the police—it's being handled in civil court.

"This is totally and completely wrong," says Judge Horace Gilmore of the Wayne County Michigan Circuit Court. "These are assaults and batteries, and they should be dealt with criminally as well as civilly."

Eisenberg and Micklow observe:

> If a wife has had such an order served on her estranged spouse, she is still denied protection because of three inherent weaknesses in the process of enforcing these orders. First, if a wife during a pending divorce calls for police protection she is generally told to contact her attorney. Police feel they do not have the authority to enforce a civil order.
>
> Secondly, it takes several days for a preliminary injunctive order to be acted upon by the circuit court judge. The victim must contact her attorney, sign an affidavit describing the violation, process must be served on the assailant and the court must be notified. In Michigan this procedure will take an absolute minimum of four days—more often it will take between 10 and 20 days. . . .
>
> Finally, if the wife during divorce has an injunctive order, and succeeds in having her husband brought before the court to show cause why he should not be held in violation of the order, immediate relief may not be forthcoming. Judges are reluctant to impose a prison sentence for the first violation of an order.

Battered wives with no divorce action pending are also denied their rights. They are often forced to accept intermediate legal steps rather than prosecution. These intermediary steps include warning letters, peace bonds, civil protection order, and restraining orders. Procedures vary from state to state, but in general these documents serve to warn a husband—order him to "cease to molest, assault or

in any manner threaten or physically abuse'' his wife. It is hoped
that the notice will scare the husband, but peace bonds and warning
letters are usually meaningless pieces of paper.

The Kalamazoo study flatly reports: ''Peace bonds and restraining orders are usually ineffective.''

Washington assistant corporation counsel Cary D. Pollak admits:
''Obviously it doesn't act as much of a deterrent if a man is determined to beat his wife. We have to rely on the fact that he'll be in-
timidated by the order and that he'll think twice before he does the
same thing again. And it normally takes five weeks to get a hearing
to seek an order.''

Restraining orders have more teeth than peace bonds or warning
letters, but feminist Jackson finds them all equally ineffective.

''In general, it is the policy of district attorneys that no arrests
should be made pursuant to a civil restraining order, and the police
comply.''

This policy clearly goes against the law as Ms. Jackson points
out: ''Violation of a civil restraining order is a misdemeanor in and
of itself under California penal code. . . .

''When the victimized wife produces her restraining order, the
police response today is to tell her that she should call her attorney,
even when the acts restrained are detailed clearly on the face of the
order. . .''

This situation is not unique to San Francisco.

''I've never run into a contempt charge for a violation of a restraining order during the five years that I have been practicing,''
said Attorney David Goldstein of Ann Arbor. ''I've never once
seen a husband put in jail. Never once. That's what I tell my clients
when they come in . . . judges won't do anything. Secondly, if a
woman calls me at 12:00 o'clock at night and says: 'My husband
is beating the hell out of me, what should I do?' the only protection
that I, as a lawyer, can offer her is to tell her to come in, in the
morning and sign a complaint. So what protection does that offer
her? You know, if you call the cops, they'll say, 'We can't do anything. You've got a restraining order. Use it.' ''

Boston Attorney Ann Kauffman, who works at the Cambridge-
Somerville Legal Services, agrees with the contention that restraining orders are meaningless pieces of paper. ''Still we advise a

woman to take one out,'' she says. ''It's something she can do. It's an active step toward making decisions and attempting to get control over her own life instead of sitting home cowering in a corner.''

The justification for not acting on wife-beating cases most often given by police, attorneys, and judges is that most women do not prosecute after they have made the charge. From all the evidence this is certainly true.

Harold Hepler, director of magistrates in Fairfax County, Virginia, says: ''You'd be surprised to see how many women come in here at night and want to take out a warrant and are back the next morning saying they don't want one because they've kissed and made up.''

Police Chief James Levleit of Saline, Michigan, estimates: ''Out of every hundred domestic altercations we get, ninety-nine of them don't prosecute. That just makes more paper and book work for us.''

Although these figures are higher than most, it is certainly fair to say that in the overwhelming majority of cases, women who swear out complaints do not follow through with the prosecution. If she doesn't testify against her husband, then there is no case.

Detroit Judge Borman says: ''One of the first things that I learned when I worked for the defender's office is when you have an assault between friends or family members, which is very often the case, do not hold the examination, do not perpetuate the testimony, because nine times out of ten, the complainant is going to come in later and want to drop charges. So we never held examinations because when it came right down to it, the women did not want to see their husbands go to jail. . . .''

The failure to prosecute may be more of an indictment of the system than the woman. Ms. Jackson argues:

''It is simply unfair, in light of the systematic discouragement that victims receive from the police and the time-consuming and almost insuperable hurdles to prosecution erected by the district attorney's office, to blame the women for failing to follow through against their attackers and to use this failure as a primary excuse for nonenforcement of the law. . . .

''In many cases the reason a victimized woman drops charges or refuses to testify is not that she needs to be violently abused but the opposite need, to avoid a violent retaliation.

"Recently, in San Francisco, a twenty-two-year-old woman whose husband had been arrested the previous week for a vicious attack in which he had knocked out several of her front teeth and cracked her skull with the butt of a gun, called the Women's Litigation Unit to complain that her husband, out on bail, was threatening to kill her unless she refused to drop the charges against him. When she appealed to the district attorney's office to arrest her husband, she was told that nothing could be done. She was forced to go into hiding until the trial. A threat, when coupled with a just reason to believe the one who threatens will follow through, is a crime. . . .

"It should be assumed that a woman whose husband is beating her wants, first of all, an immediate end to the beatings; she wants some assurance that the beatings will not recur, and if they do, she wants an effective remedy.

"Officials should not assume that the woman is not serious, that she will later change her mind. This is a flagrant denial of her rights."

Another catch women encounter in the legal process is that they have trouble hiring lawyers. Many lawyers don't want to become involved in domestic cases. Others are reluctant to take on a female client for fear they won't get paid since few married women have independent sources of income. Women who turn to legal aid organizations are also frequently stymied.

"A woman coming to the legal aid clinic can see a lawyer if she qualifies for assistance. She must earn less than eighty dollars a week net salary and have assets of less than five hundred dollars," states a memo by a lawyer serving on the Montgomery County spouse-abuse task force.

Since many women don't work outside the home, a battered wife may easily qualify for help on the salary provision. But if she and her husband jointly own their home—the common practice—then she automatically has more than $500.00 in assets and is disqualified from free legal aid. She may be terrified to re-enter her home and literally have only the clothes on her back and the possessions she could carry to her name. Often she has no access to her husband's savings or checking accounts and is destitute in the literal sense, but since she owns half of a home, she is disqualified for free legal help.

In a criminal case, a woman should not need her own attorney. Her case should be handled by the prosecutor. Many women don't realize this, and typically it takes them a long time to find out. In a civil matter, she needs to hire her own lawyer.

Even when battered women are successful in obtaining the services of a lawyer, the experience is not always positive.

Battered women often reserve their greatest outrage for lawyers whom they claim treat them arrogantly, overcharge them, mislead them, and are difficult to contact at crucial moments.

One Washington woman said she was billed $3,900.00 for two brief court appearances, one routine legal brief, and a series of un-itemized phone calls.

Another battered wife complained that her lawyer signed without her consent a court order waiving her rights to income from rental property she and her husband jointly owned. Then the lawyer sent her an altered copy of the order that said he had done just the opposite.

The attorney of another battered wife became frightened at threats from her husband and asked her to find another lawyer. "I don't want a dead client," he told her. "I don't want to see your name splashed all over the newspapers."

Battered wives also have a problem selecting an attorney who knows the law and who is sympathetic to a woman's rights. The Kalamazoo study reports:

> . . . attorneys in the community interpret the law differently. The task force couldn't get a consensus about the meaning of the law and the legal implications of certain actions. For example, there is disagreement about the consequences of a person's leaving his or her children or home in order to separate from the situation.

Many battered wives find themselves mistreated by judges with blatant male chauvinist attitudes. For example, a Boston woman was powerless when her husband's lawyer hinted in court that she was running around with another man. When her lawyer objected, he was cut off by the judge, who said: "I've heard enough. You know you can't go around beating up your wife anymore, but if I was in your position, I probably would have done the same thing." He gave the man a two-month suspended sentence.

Most of the time wife beating is diverted out of the criminal process. This can take the form of counseling, psychiatric care, or enforceable warnings.

Susan Jackson took a detailed look at the criminal diversion system in her city. In many ways, it is typical.

She writes:

> If the police do not arrest John Doe, which they probably do not, they may refer John and his wife to any of a number of local counseling agencies such as the San Francisco Family Service Agency, the Jewish Family Service, the Catholic Family Service, to ministers, or even to friends, but more likely, if they make any referral at all, police will refer the Does to the Family Bureau of the San Francisco District Attorney's Office.
>
> The Family Bureau, which is not authorized by any California statute, consists of four investigators, none of whom are trained lawyers or phychologists. Qualifications for the job include a bachelor's degree in psychology, police science, criminal law or some related field and two years of experience in some field such as counseling, probate work or insurance investigation.
>
> And yet, the Family Bureau is the district attorney's primary tool in dealing with family violence. Unless the alleged crime is particularly heinous, complaint calls that reach the General Works Department of the district attorney's office, which handles routine cases of assault and battery, are routed to the Family Bureau as soon as it is discovered that a family relationship is involved in the complaint. The Family Bureau then applies its procedures of investigation, referral, counseling and quasi-adjudication to the problem, with the result that the vast majority of cases of family violence never reach the attention of a district attorney or assistant attorney, regardless of the victims' wish to press charges. . . .
>
> A citation hearing will not be set up by the Family Bureau unless the victimized woman insists, or if the injuries are particularly bad and there is a history of violence between parties.
>
> The first step is to send the accused a notice, politely requesting his appearance at the Family Bureau for a discussion of the problem.

This notice has no legal effect, as compared to a subpoena . . . and
if the accused fails to respond, the Family Bureau merely sends out
notice number two, which is worded more strongly, suggesting to
the recipient that the request has been made for his arrest, that he
should appear to discuss the reason a warrant should not be issued.
If the accused still fails to appear after the second notice the theory
is that an arrest warrant will be issued. In practice the number of
wife-beaters arrested for failure to appear at a citation hearing is almost zero, according to the head of the Family Bureau.

If the accused does appear, a Family Bureau investigator will
discuss with both parties the problem and its possible solutions. Although "friends" might be allowed to come along, no district attorney or other court officer is present, neither the accused nor the victim is provided with or encouraged to bring legal counsel, and any
evidence is admissible. Unfortunately, the citation hearing has no
binding legal effect, and any "solution" that may be reached is essentially useless to the beaten-wife. Back at home she is once again
at her husband's mercy, dependent entirely on his discretion, already
demonstrated as probably faulty, whether or not to abide by any
agreement reached at the hearing. . . . They can recommend warrant but the D.A. must approve.

In a recent interview, the head of the Family Bureau admitted
that one woman became so frustrated with the district attorney and
Family Bureau procedures that she asked: "What do I have to do to
get him arrested, wait 'til he kills me?"

The practice of diverting "family problems" out of the criminal
courts has produced disastrous results for many women. The accumulation of the various actions by the various agencies add up
for the battered women to a system of indifference—one it seems
designed to thwart justice, not achieve it.

The Montgomery County Task Force concludes:

The concept of diversion is noble in theory, humane in execution,
less expensive than incarceration and removes pressure on courts and
prisons. However, since victims of the crime of spousal assault will
be the majority of persons needing a "Haven" the particular problems arising out of the spousal relationship must be addressed. It is
the only situation in which we find the accused returning legally to
the home and bedroom of the victim, and in which the fear of the

victim may drive her/him to desert the home with or without children, belongings, food, money, clothes, transportation or legal advice. It is all very well to say the abuser has been amply warned by the police, commissioners, or State's attorney. However, warnings to the abuser do next to nothing to alleviate the fear of the victim who in effect is a sitting duck.

The medical profession generally displays an indifference to the problems of the battered wife. Most doctors assume a neutral stance. "I'm a doctor, not a cop, a social worker, or a lawyer" is a typical comment. Doctors are not obligated to report cases of wife abuse as they are when they suspect child abuse. Most are content to treat the injury and let it go at that. Some doctors and nurses are so uncomfortable with the wife-beating syndrome that they make jokes about it to mask their uncertainty.

The University of Michigan researchers, in their report, quote a physician, Dr. Benjamin Parker, who says:

> If a woman comes in with bruises—how did you get those bruises, what happened—I fell down the stairs, we accept her reason for her injuries. Upon examination, however, I may feel that she didn't sustain these bruises by falling down the stairs. Somebody may have hit her. But I do not ask her or delve any further with it. Accept the patient's theory . . . we don't have the time nor the inclination to go into sociological background as for the reason of the assault. . . . It's a personal problem between a man and wife and if she doesn't want to prefer charges, that's her privilege and her right and her business to do as she pleases. . . . As far as I'm concerned, personally, I don't care if she prefers charges or not. She was the one that was beaten not I, and if she doesn't want her husband arrested or put into jail that's her privilege.

Wives who flee from their battering husbands must find a place to go. Sometimes they can get refuge with a friend, neighbor, or relative for a day or two, but more often they find that they have no place to go. The problem is particularly acute for women with children.

One victim relates:

"You know you can go to the police, but what good is it going to do? They take some pictures, and that's about it. They say, 'In the morning, or next Monday, when the prosecutor's office is open, we'll see what we can do about getting a complaint filled out.'

"Most of the time with me it was on the weekends, which left me, you know, from Friday until Monday with no place to go. And so what choice do I have really but to come back to see if I can patch things up? You know, for the sake of having a place to put the kids and myself."

Women without money, transportation, or a job are literally trapped. The plight is particularly severe for low-income women.

Two days after Marina came home from the hospital after giving birth to her second child, her husband, an unemployed drug addict, began to beat her and kick her in the stomach. Several weeks later, he was at it again, this time pummeling her head and face with his fist. Bruised and shaken, she fled to the Washington, D.C., Citizens Complaint Center where an assistant U.S. attorney declined to press criminal charges because there was no evidence of a dangerous weapon. A sympathetic social worker and lawyer spent hours phoning local agencies trying to find temporary shelter for Marina and her children. There was no space. "We had to send her right back to the same place where she had been beaten and brutalized," said Nancy Dorsch, an assistant corporation counsel. "I felt like a rat."

CHAPTER ELEVEN

Battered Men

"Kid," he said, "never marry a girl you
can't knock out with one punch."

Pete Hamill

"The most unreported crime is not wife beating—it's husband beating," says sociologist Suzanne Steinmetz.

"It's understandable. Men are supposed to be bigger, stronger, brighter, physically superior, all these things, and it must be a terrible blow to the male's ego to think that somebody, namely, his small, petite, delicate, nonphysical wife is going to beat him up. Unless a man is battered to the degree where he requires medical attention, he is not going to report it.

"If you look at the homicide figures there is not much difference between the number of men who kill their wives and the number of wives who kill their men. You realize the battered wife syndrome exists because the men are physically stronger. Women have the same innate desires to use physical force that men do and when they have a weapon they do as much damage. When it comes to using minor amounts of physical force, slapping, hitting, pushing, there just appears to be no real differences between men and women. One of the reasons you have the battered-wife phenomenon is not that men are more aggressive, they just seem to be physically stronger and are able to do more damage."

Dr. Steinmetz has done the only spouse-abuse study conducted with a randomly selected sample. She found almost no difference in the percentage of husbands beating wives and wives beating husbands.

She selected four types of aggressive behavior and correlated the responses given by husbands and wives. Here's what she found:

Thirty-nine percent of the husbands admitted throwing things at their wives, and 37 percent of the wives admitted they threw things at their husbands.

Thirty-one percent of the men admitted to pushing, shoving, and grabbing their wives, and 21 percent of the women admitted doing the same thing to their husbands.

When questioned about hitting their spouse with their hands, the results were identical. Twenty percent of both men and women admitted striking each other.

In the most violent classification used—hitting with some hard object—once again, the results were identical. Ten percent of both men and women admitted they battered their spouses with something hard. Dr. Steinmetz labeled this group the serious abusers, and it is significant to note that in this most violent category, men and women were on a par. It also should be noted that the most violent people were not always married to each other.

"The data seem to indicate few differences between husbands and wives in the type and frequency of physically aggressive acts used," observes Dr. Steinmetz.

Dr. Richard Gelles, in his New Hampshire study of eighty families, found, in addition to husbands assaulting wives, wives assaulting husbands and husbands and wives assaulting each other. In twenty of the forty-four violent families, both husbands and wives assaulted each other, and in six families, the wives beat the husbands. "Husbands are certainly victimized, too," he observes.

Pauline H. Menes, a delegate to the Maryland legislature, says: "Battering is not limited to wives. There have been more than a dozen cases recorded in the state with husbands complaining that they have been abused and beaten."

In a study of 150 divorce applicants in a large Midwestern metropolitan area, John O'Brien found that 16 percent of those complaining of spouse attacks were men.

Other studies, using police reports, indicate that women are the victims of marital violence almost three times as often as men. But some social scientists question these figures because society's concept of masculinity discourages husband victims from reporting their abuse.

Most battered men are too ashamed to admit they've been beaten by their wives. The humiliation a battered woman suffers is multiplied enormously for a man who must stand before a police sergeant and file a complaint. Not many men have the courage to face the snickers, innuendos, and open sarcasm inherent in this situation.

Battered men have always been held up to a special kind of ridicule. The book *Women in the Middle Ages* notes: "Husbands who let themselves be beaten by their wives were publicly held up as laughing stocks." The situation has changed little since the thirteenth century.

Few men have the courage to face the humiliation necessary to file an official report. After the embarrassment of the incident has faded, some battered men will discuss their situation, but even then they want to remain anonymous.

"I reeled through twenty-seven years of marriage to a woman who wanted to be beaten or otherwise dominated, and when she didn't get it, took to beating me," exclaims a New York writer, now divorced. "Yes, Virginia, there are husband beaters, and my ex-wife was one.

"One Saturday morning, I was standing before the bedroom mirror brushing my hair. My wife came up beside me and asked what I intended to do with my day. I said I'd probably use it to finish a home-repair job. She slapped me hard, lunged and clawed four beautiful fingernail scratches down the side of my face, oozing blood.

"My reaction was more bafflement and hurt than anger. There had been no reason for this attack.

"At work, lie as I would about getting caught in the rose bushes, my associates knew fingernail marks when they saw them, and to my humiliation, let me know they understood the real cause."

Extensive interviews by Dr. Steinmetz and others indicate that many women strike the first blow in a family altercation. It appears that some women, still harboring some dim memory of idealized chivalry, feel that they can strike a male since "no gentleman would ever hit a lady." Correspondingly, many men interpret this code of conduct to mean "no gentleman should ever hit a lady *first.*" Once a woman smacks such a man, he often concludes, "I can't let her get away with that." Following this sequence, many men who think of themselves as neither wife beaters nor violent men end up battering their wives. More often than not, they explain their actions with a shrug of resignation and say: "She asked for it."

Dr. Marguerite Fogel says: "Some wives do provoke their husbands. Although this is certainly not always the case, I feel that it is usually the case. I have seen a number of couples in which the woman had hit the husband repeatedly before he finally hit back."

This again raises the question of female masochism. Do women slap their husbands to provoke their own beatings because they enjoy pain? Surely some do, but psychologists agree that this condition is not rampant, that masochistic women represent only a tiny segment of the population. It seems more reasonable to accept Dr. Steinmetz's proposition that aggressive tendencies are equally strong in both sexes.

Marriages between strong, aggressive women and weak, passive men are fertile territories for husband abuse. The comic stereotype of "Wallace Whimple" terrorized by his brutish wife, "Sweetie Face," does have a basis in fact. Judge Oneglia says that the battered husbands she has come in contact with "usually fit the same pattern. They are passive and dependent."

A case of a big, violent woman battering a small man was reported to a Washington, D.C., crisis line, and the victim—the man—was a cop.

Michael Versace relates the story:

"A man called on the phone and asked: 'Is this the place where people can call because of wife abuse?' I told him yes, and then he asked: 'Can husbands call, too?'

"He identified himself as a cop and said: 'My woman drinks, and every Friday night when I come home, she just starts pounding on me.'

"He told me he had a pretty hefty mama on his hands. He said he'd been severely beaten up by her several times and that he was big enough to fight back but that he didn't want to beat her, and he didn't know where to turn to solve his problem. He was very emotional.''

A wife need not be an Amazon to abuse her husband. Sometimes a woman is physically stronger than her husband because the man is sick, handicapped, or much older than his wife.

May and December romances that endure can pit a healthy woman against a feeble, aging man. A wealthy, elderly banker recently won a court separation in New York from his second wife, a woman thirty-one years younger than he. The testimony revealed that for fourteen years his wife had bullied and abused him both verbally and physically.

The old man displayed scars and bruises and told how his wife once shredded his ear with her teeth. Another time she blackened both eyes and on still another occasion injured one of his eyes so badly that the doctor feared it might be lost. The judge called it ''vicious, physical violence practiced on a man ill equipped for fist fights with a shrieking woman.''

Many men who find themselves involved in violent marriages feel as trapped as many women do in similar circumstances. A man faced with a battering wife must deal with disturbing psychological problems. Should he take the abuse or fight back? If he strikes his wife, she can bring social and psychological pressure to bear on him. If he takes her abuse again and again, he loses respect for himself and is overcome by guilt and self-loathing. If there are children, the husband is faced with another dilemma. Does he want his kids to view him as a brutish wife beater or as a sniveling mouse, dominated by his wife? Our society rejects both roles. There are few places a battered man can go for help. When he does reach out, or if circumstances propel the family problem into the public arena, a man can find his life bewildering and frustrating. He can conclude as easily as does the battered wife that the police, the courts, the clergy, and the social-service agencies are all stacked against him.

One battered man, a radio and television personality in Virginia, relates his experience.

''I spent all of my free time away from work—and part of work as well—contacting the Establishment for help: priests first, marriage counselors, doctors, psychiatrists, and would continue to do so for better than six years. They were all not only useless but in several cases harmful, for they encouraged her unique form of 'expression.'

"She ran off with another man, but after a short time returned home. I was told, principally by lawyers, that I must take her back, for if I pressed a divorce action, she would be seen as a poor, aggrieved, helpless woman, and she would literally clean me out. She could get eighty-five percent of my income and have our five children entrusted in her care.

"I never actually fought back, never hit her until about 1960. We had been invited to a cabin party up in the Blue Ridge Mountains, and when it was breaking up about two A.M., I went looking for Lisa. Most of the other guests had disappeared when I stumbled across her and another man lying on the lawn, necking. I got the man to his feet and hit him hard in the gut. He went down with a long "oops." Then I pulled Lisa to her feet and led and dragged her to our car. We were parked on a very high hill, very steep and winding. As I started the engine and released the emergency brake, she attacked. She liked to attack me when I was driving. It increased the odds that she would win. But having suffered this once before, I braked the car, after she had smashed my glasses and bloodied my nose, and gave her one almighty belt to the jaw. Knocked her cold.

"She remained unconscious until we pulled into our steep driveway. As I was making the turn, at about ten miles an hour, she opened her door and fell out on the cement. It made a mess of her face, and, it now being about three A.M., she raised up her usual cry of having been beaten. I got my hand over her mouth and dragged her into the house. My oldest boy, Jack, was on hand. He'd heard her yelling. Together, we got her to the kitchen and tried to calm her and clean up the blood on her face.

"She couldn't have been drunk. But now she seemed to be playing drunk or was in fact so far gone from sanity that she began to attack the boy first, then me. He loved his mother and was crying as he tried to fend her off without hurting her. It didn't work. She fell repeatedly, and once into a steam radiator.

"About dawn, we got her to bed. I slept on the downstairs sofa.

At nine, we went up to see how she was and found the room empty. Later, we heard she had climbed out the bedroom window, shinnied down a tree, and had walked into the street with nothing on but a slip and hailed a passing motorist. She had, she said, been beaten so and rendered so by her husband. 'Take me to a hospital.'

"The hospital log duly reported, 'severe case of wifebeating.'

"No one believed my story or my son's story of her jumping out of a moving car and then hurling herself at both of us as if determined to be marked. I got the wife-beater treatment. Promotions stopped coming, and I was shunned by the respectable element. My TV show was dropped with no explanation, yet not a word appeared in the press regarding our case.

"In Virginia, all they do is post a bill of particulars as stated by my wife's lawyers—she filed for divorce in the hospital and took great pains to hire a photographer to make fine color prints of her injuries. She had them hung in a prominent place in the courthouse where the locals come to satisfy their daily need for gossip. It's quite legal.

"In Virginia, any woman can go before a judge and claim her personal safety is being threatened by a husband, and bingo! the husband gets an injunction—lasting three months—which forbids him to approach his own home. The husband has no rights whatever. He must obey the injunction and wait three months to have his side heard. He cannot say good-bye to his children, he cannot enter the home for his clothes and toiletries. The law *does* permit a child to smuggle these things out of the house and drag them several blocks away from home where the father can pick them up in his car. He must not park in front of the house—his house—for that would be trespassing.

"Lisa had built her sadistic case against me with care. The judge granting the injunction did so on the basis of hospital evidence that she had been cruelly beaten by me. And he was shown the color photos she had taken of herself as the final proof.

"In the South, the woman holds all of the cards. If I insisted on filing a countersuit charging cruelty and viciousness, the children would be given over to her custody. I would effectively be denied visiting permits to see my own kids. We know the South is notorious for its transparent hypocrisy, but it is never more vivid than in this right of the male parent to see his offspring. One week, Lisa could say, 'Sorry, they're all sick.' Another she could lie and say, 'He threatened me on the telephone last week.' She did these things during the injunction period. So, I could insist on visitation rights, but in actuality, I could—did—go begging. Years later, I finally got a divorce. I was then fifty years of age and could look back on years of escalated torment, assaults, and every sort of personal abuse. My productive energies were sapped. My declining years would be spent alone, but at least free.''

Some women have skillfully manipulated the rules of our society to victimize their husbands. Women seeking divorces have been instructed by their attorneys ''on ways to anger males'' in order to provoke an attack to help establish grounds for a more favorable— to the woman—divorce settlement. One of the recommendations given to these wives is to tell her husband, as coldly and dispassionately as possible, exactly what she is doing. ''Imagine hearing this uttered in rock-cold tones from the woman you loved,'' a victimized man related.

There is no end to the stories from divorced men of how they were manipulated by their wives. Often the manipulation invokes spouse assault. A public relations man with one of the Fortune 500 companies gives this example:

''We had been settled in one of the state's larger cities for about a year when a hellish incident took place, the first of many. We had just completed the grocery shopping. She was in a vile mood, snapping out a string of insults, which I bore because I had my mind on traffic.

''When we pulled into our driveway and parked outside the garage, I got out to unlock the trunk. There were several bags, most of them large, and one small one containing nothing but a can of soup and a loaf of bread. My wife took that one while I struggled with a couple of monsters, bent over, naturally. Then I saw stars. She took the bag with the soup and bread in it and bashed me on the skull, laying open about two inches of flesh. I fell to my knees and struggled to rise in a half-conscious state. The wound was bleeding heavily, and I was trying to wipe the blood from my eyes.

''When I came in the kitchen door, still holding the groceries, she was standing up against the sink, facing me. She smiled a bit, then threw back her head and began screaming, 'Help, help! He's killing me.' Then a few moans and gurgles. Performance over, she again smiled and said, 'I called Mrs. Brown next door and told her if she heard me scream, she was to call the police. You've had it, you bastard.'

"Blood streaming down my face, the enormity of what she had said and done began to dawn on me, and I wanted to kill her. She ran from me screaming all the while for more theatrics, locking herself in the bedroom. I kicked the bolt off the door and charged her, just in time to find a policeman restraining me.

"I spent that weekend in jail, charged with assault on my wife. The evidence of my scalp wound was no evidence at all. 'Sonny,' one cop said, 'you musta done something *real* mean to rile up that woman and make her hit you. It was self-defense, the way I see it.'

"Two days later, before a judge, the true story came out. Under oath, my wife admitted abusing me in the car and then laying my head open. The judge thundered: 'Ma'am, you have the gall, the effrontery to come into this court and charge your husband with wife beating! Out of here, you baggage! and if you ever lift a finger to your man again, I personally will see you clapped in irons.' Beautifully spoken. Unfortunately, he died within the year, and I had lost my only friend in the halls of justice."

There are some who think that the violently aggressive female is a modern phenomena caused by the Woman's Liberation movement. True, today's feminists may be inspiring more women to react violently toward males, but the condition is not altogether new. History records the exploits of enough bloody, violent queens to attest that aggressive women have been with us a long time.

The book *Women in the Middle Ages* deals with spouse abuse in those violent times and explains that some wives were far from shrinking violets. "How capable some women were in defending themselves is shown by the fact that laws had to be made forbidding them to carry arms. Women were not allowed to challenge men to duel; if they nevertheless did so, they had to pay heavy fines. . . ."

In more recent history, *The Carpenter,* a magazine of the Carpenter's Union, reported in April 1901 that a woman in Allegheny, Pennsylvania, beat up her husband because he spent the money she had given him to pay his union dues on drinks for himself and his friends.

The magazine commented: "Many women are better unionists, better citizens, than the brutes, called lords of creation, to whom they are tied. Would that there were more women with this much spirit."

The woman with spirit has long been admired. The response most often heard—from both men and women—to a story of a man beaten by his wife is: "Good for her!"

If a battered man is a homosexual—or perceived to be one—he gets even less sympathy and consideration from our society.

Almost no thought has been given to any of the problems of homosexual liaisons that echo those found in heterosexual marriages. There are cases of "homosexual wife beating."

"Spouse abuse is not limited to heterosexual relationships," says Dr. B. L. Daley of Columbia, South Carolina. "In a lesbian situation, one tends to take the masculine role and one the feminine— one is submissive, soft, etc., and one is dominant, tough, etc."

The same condition often exists among male homosexual lovers where one is the wife and one is the husband, he said. " 'Wife beating,' can and often is found in such relationships." The reason appears to be that homosexuals are conditioned by the same things in society as heterosexuals. "They come from the same homes and from the same culture and have identical responses to frustration, anger, jealousy, infidelity."

There is one area of spouse assault that is never ignored by the police or courts—murder.

Because of the nature of the crime—there is always a body, and the death is always recorded—the most complete statistics are available in this category of spousal assault.

It is interesting to note that the FBI's annual compilation of nationwide crime statistics show: "In murders involving husband and wife, the wife was the victim in 52 percent of the incidents and the husband the victim in the remaining 48." (Incidentally, a breakdown by race shows 50 percent were black, 48 percent white, and 2 percent other.) The FBI's statistics have remained remarkably consistent over the years.

Other studies have yielded similar results. George Bach and Herbert Goldberg examined the data of 2,000 spouse killings and discovered that 54 percent of the victims were women and 46 percent men. A comparison to a study done fifteen years before showed no significant difference.

"Data on homicide between spouses suggests that an almost equal number of wives kill their husbands as husbands kill wives," says Dr. Steinmetz. "Thus, it appears that men and women might have equal potential toward violent marital interactions, initiate similar acts of violence, and in the extreme, when differences of physical strength are equalized by weapons, commit similar amounts of spousal homicide."

Although the statistics suggest that a man is just as apt to be killed by his wife as vice versa, there are arguments that hold that women are driven to kill by their victims.

Del Martin, former board member of NOW, says, "Since she's no match for her husband in physical combat, her only defense is to grab whatever is handy as a weapon. Homicide statistics indicate that a good number of wife-beating husbands end up in the morgue."

Sue Eisenberg and Patricia Micklow noted in their Michigan University study:

> The lack of any meaningful protective measures available to the assaulted wife, as well as a minimizing of the seriousness of her situation, often produce drastic results—homicide. Faced with a violent husband and no alternatives, she may equalize the situation herself by using a deadly weapon such as a gun or knife. The wife killing her husband is not a rare crime."

When it comes to spouse killing, there is true equality between the sexes.

In a society in which very little attention has been paid to wife beating, it's not surprising that almost none has been paid to husband abuse. But the condition is real and present as the statistical studies, case histories, and official records all prove. In fact, it is probably safe to assume that husband abuse is more widespread than most people would imagine.

Husband abuse should not be viewed as merely the opposite side of the coin to wife abuse. Both are part of the same problem, which should be described as one *person* abusing another *person*. The problem must be faced and dealt with not in terms of sex but in terms of humanity.

CHAPTER TWELVE

Liberating the
Battered Wife

> A battered-wife shelter in every city, in every
> country would help . . . but it's like putting
> a bandaid on a cancer.
>
> *Erin Pizzey*

Centuries of legal, social, and religious customs conspire against all women. These traditions defined her place in society and in general have made her the second sex.

Over the long history of civilization, women have gradually gained more rights. She has moved from being "mere property" toward full human status. She is reminded: "You've come a long way, baby," but today's woman adds the rejoinder: "But not far enough, baby, not far enough." There are still laws in the U.S. that discriminate against her, such as those that prevent her from suing her husband and those that require her to sustain more physical injury from her husband than is normally required to press an assault and battery charge.

The battered wife must overcome a general attitude that regards women as inferior, less able to make decisions, and in need of protection from their own imprudence. She is confronted with this attitude by police, judges, prosecutors, defenders, and legislators. She is patronized and ignored. She is subjected to ridicule and selective enforcement of the law.

The battered wife is surrounded by social pressures to "stick it out," to accept "what every woman has to put up with," and not to "make a stink" for the "sake of the family and kids." Regardless of her pain and suffering, she is pressured to do her part to maintain the image of an all-American family. It is commonplace for her friends and relatives to advise her against trying to change her life.

She is often advised by the clergy to pray and endure. Some religions forbid divorce, and the scriptures can be readily quoted to put God on the side of a violent bully.

These are powerful forces lined up against the battered wife. They are formidable—but not invincible.

Women across the nation are finding ways to break the battered-wife syndrome. A new attitude is capturing the minds of American women. Inspired largely by the feminist movement, women are demanding—and winning—equal rights and opportunities on a wide range of fronts. Nowhere is this new militancy of greater importance than in seeking equal rights to physical safety. Women are fighting for freedom from physical abuse. It is not melodramatic to say she is fighting for her life.

The Equal Rights Amendment (ERA), if it becomes part of the Constitution, would sweep away laws that discriminate against the battered wife. But even if ERA does become the law of the land, it will take decades of lawsuits to rid the land of discriminating laws and even longer for existing attitudes to change. The battered woman would be well advised not to pin her hopes on ERA. She needs to consider more practical, down-to-earth steps that she can take now.

Essentially, there are four options open to the battered wife. (1) She can do nothing and endure her fate. (2) She can seek help to try and salvage her marriage. (3) She can prosecute her husband in criminal court. (4) She can get a divorce.

At various stages, a battered woman might consider and try all four.

Extensive interviews with battered wives reveal that nearly all have endured many beatings before taking any action. Some women never reach the point at which they *must* seek relief, while others arrive at it relatively quickly. "What happens all too often is that the woman tends to vacillate," says Washington, D.C., attorney, Nan Huhn. "It's not that she necessarily is weak, but it's difficult.

"She wants to leave because the situation is pretty unbearable. But most of the time the abusive husband or male is not that way all of the time. It's an occasional thing. There are times when the relationship is very good, and that pulls her back."

Studies show that marital violence tends to escalate. The battered wife who hopes "things will get better" without taking some action is betting long odds against herself. A woman who wants her life to change has to become convinced that the change will only come if she takes action. Susan Steinmetz reports that research documents this point—battering husbands don't change on their own. When change occurs in a violent family, it follows some action by the wife.

Robert Willis, who deals with violent families daily as an assistant corporation counsel in Washington, D.C., advises: "The first time out that she gets belted by this man, she should take action. Get his knuckles cracked and get him back in shape, and it is less likely to happen a second time. He finds out that, by God, she won't put up with it."

Conversely, the woman who forgives and forgets can expect more violence.

Dr. Murray Straus says, "In most cases the main solution is for the wife to come to an understanding with her husband that he doesn't have the right to use physical force to have his way or to punish her. An amazing proportion of women take the view 'I deserved it.' Once there's that kind of understanding, nothing will prevent abuse."

The second option is to reach out of the family for help. It is extremely difficult for most women to admit they are battered wives, and seeking help is a degrading and humiliating experience.

"The biggest thing we can offer a battered wife is support when she asks for help because it's a very, very frightening thing for many women to do," says Marge Caswell of the Prince Georges County, Maryland Women's Commission. "It's a paradox, but many women feel mentally safe in a home where they've been physically abused. But fewer and fewer women want to put up with being beaten. The issue of wife abuse is now being openly discussed. Its time has come."

Women are seeking out social workers, religious leaders, and psychotherapists for help. Social service agencies, such as mental health centers and marriage and family counselors, are other sources of aid.

There are some who are optimistic that change in a violent husband's behavior can be brought about through therapy.

Dr. Marguerite Fogel says, "I believe wife beaters can be cured. Especially when they are concerned about it and want to change. I have worked with a number of them. When communication improves so that the wife doesn't browbeat and taunt, and the husband learns to express his feelings before they get to the violent eruption stage, then the syndrome becomes unnecessary.

"The danger signs are violence with things or animals—more helpless creatures—before the man actually hits a wife. Women often report to me that their husbands are violent with the children, with the cat, with other drivers on the street. Uncontrolled anger directed at other objects, breaking things—these are danger signals.

"All the couples I have seen have discussed it at length and worked on it by themselves. They sought help because they could not cope with the habits without outside reflection and other approaches. It helps a great deal to talk about it."

The willingness of the husband to undergo treatment or counseling is the key to success. Most of the time, violent husbands refuse, insisting "there's nothing wrong with me." Suggesting that a man needs help with "mental problems" is often enough to provoke another beating. However, some men have a Jekyll and Hyde personality and are filled with remorse and guilt after beating their wives. Sometimes such men are willing to seek help during their periods of remorse. At other times, they simply find reasons to justify their behavior and an excuse for their guilt.

When the husband is willing to cooperate with a therapist, successful changes in his behavior can be accomplished in up to 80 percent of the cases, according to Sanford Sherman, executive director of Jewish Family Services in New York. He recommends having the husband and wife visit the therapist together. The customary technique is for the therapist to prompt them into the opening rounds of a quarrel, stop the action, and point out to them how they are interacting with each other.

"The kind of therapy in which the man is designated as the patient is the least successful," Sherman says. "It is usually doomed to failure when the man is labeled as the sick one in need of therapy. The main reason the husband resorts to physical rather than verbal abuse is that it's difficult for him to express himself with words. This makes him a very poor patient in psychotherapy, which relies chiefly on words.

"The other method of teaching the man nonviolent ways of behaving when he is enraged is to get him to translate his anger into words or to take it out on objects rather than people.

"It's important for both partners to understand that he's afraid. He fears loss of status, loss of life, and, paradoxically, loss of his wife. The fear is intolerable to him. He must choose either fight or flight. With a vulnerable woman present, the tendency is to fight. And of course there may be provocative behavior on the part of the woman. The abused wife often wields a mean fist and can give a tongue lashing that can be more devastating to the spirit, the ego, the sense of self than a blow."

Women planning to seek help through counseling or therapy should use discretion when broaching the subject with their husbands. The findings of the Kalamazoo study are typical. "According to professionals and victims interviewed, assaulters commonly did not view their behavior as a problem."

The worst time to talk about treatment is during the violence. Herb Winstead, a former wife beater who is now a counselor in Montgomery County, Maryland, warns, "One of the things that I would like to bring out to wives is to try and avoid dealing with your husbands while they are drinking. Learn to wait until the next day because you are dealing with a person who is under the influence of alcohol or a drug, and he could react in any way. Wait until the next day to confront him, and I think you will avoid beatings in a lot of situations."

It is also recommended that a woman avoid arguing with an enraged husband and don't try and trade blows with him. Whenever possible, the best remedy is to get away from him—to physically leave until he has calmed down.

The critical point for a battered woman to remember is that it is up to her to initiate the action that will end her abuse. It seldom works the other way around.

B. L. Daley, a Columbia, S. C., counseling psychologist, says, "It's important that a woman do two things to break the battered-wife syndrome. One is not to accept being put down and not to accept herself as a person deserving to be beaten. This requires active, positive steps by the woman, which may include seeking professional help both psychiatric and legal, discussing her feelings with her husband and perhaps ultimately leaving him."

A number of the experts agree that a woman must establish that she will not tolerate being beaten. She must issue an ultimatum and be prepared to back up her statements with action. Only after a husband is convinced that his wife will not put up with his abusive actions can any real progress be made toward changing his violent behavior.

Dr. Richard F. Lyles says: "Escaping appears to me to be brought about by a woman's declaration that she no longer intends to put up with this kind of behavior. I think in some cases she must make it known that she absolutely will not tolerate it even if it means resorting to violence herself, including threats of killing her mate."

Dr. Gelles found that some of the nonviolent families in his study discussed hitting before they got married, and the wives said they "laid down the law" then. Other wives were able to set limits after they'd been beaten by sincerely threatening to leave if they were hit again. Of course, the wife must ultimately be willing and able to do so. In violent families, on the other hand, discussions of violence were quite limited and vague. Dr. Gelles concluded that "wives who overtly state what they will and will not accept in terms of violence are less likely to be hit. If hit, they are more likely to call the police, go to a social agency, or seek a divorce. But women who meekly try to set a limit on violence and then let their husbands go beyond the limit are likely to be struck often and not likely to do anything about it."

Sometimes a woman can gain some valuable truce time with her husband by having a friend or a relative stay with them. Studies show that men rarely commit abuse in the presence of an adult witness. Of course, the longer the "guest" stays, the less intimidating the presence becomes. The wife should use the time to try and bridge the communication gap with her husband and see if they can get outside help.

Battered wives can also seek emotional support, friendship, and help from various groups. Since alcohol is often connected with wife abuse, she should consult Alcoholics Anonymous if he has a drinking problem and go herself to Alanon to help her in dealing with her husband's drinking problem.

AA has an amazing success record in helping alcoholics solve their drinking problems and at the same time solve many of their other living problems.

Herb Winstead reveals: "It was the influence of alcohol that precipitated all of the violent situations that we had. Since the drinking ceased, we don't get into complications like that anymore. We have also learned to deal with our problems in a mature way and to handle our problems in a different manner.

"The last time that I was violent with my wife June was a rather serious thing. She did receive a couple of broken ribs, and I almost shot a couple of policemen with a shotgun, and it was after this crisis that I decided, well, you know, maybe there is something wrong. And that's one of the biggest problems in getting the individual to concede that they do have a problem. But once I had conceded that I had a problem with alcohol, and I started dealing with the primary problem, then I could work to clear up the other situation. But as long as I drank, I couldn't deal with anything."

Other women are finding help and comfort in feminist groups. For example, AWAIC in New York and a YWCA in Montgomery County, Maryland, both hold discussion groups for battered wives. Peggy Ann Hanson, director of the Maryland group, said it started as a class on law for women. "Several women who attended wanted to discuss their problem—getting beaten—and pretty soon they all started coming out of the woodwork. Soon we had one hundred and twenty women, most of whom said they had been beaten."

Church groups, schools, and colleges are offering courses, seminars, and lectures in various psychological techniques such as assertive behavior and Transactional Analysis that often lead to exploration of the problem of wife beating.

The third option open to a battered wife is to prosecute her husband in criminal court. As demonstrated in the two preceding chapters, this will not be an easy job. The names of the courts and the titles of officials dealing with the problem vary from one location to another, but the procedures are essentially the same nationwide.

The first step is calling the police. As noted earlier, police place a low priority on "domestic disturbance" calls and often take a long time responding. To help get them there faster, the San Francisco Women's Litigation Unit offers this advice: "A battered woman . . . should not mention in her call that the attacker is her husband or boy friend. . . . She should say instead that 'a man' is breaking into her apartment or that 'a man' has broken in and is beating her." Some battered wives take this a step further and advise telling the police that "the man" has a weapon—a knife, a gun, or club. Victims claim that some police forces won't bother to answer unless the attacker is armed. This seems particularly true if the woman sounds black, is Spanish speaking, or lives on the "wrong side of the tracks."

After she's called the cops, the woman must take steps to protect herself. Judge Oneglia, who as a lawyer specializes in marital problems, recommends: "She should get out of the house, go to a friend or neighbor, and cause as much disturbance as possible. The more witnesses the better."

Marge Caswell says: "Run outside and holler and scream for the neighbors. Go somewhere you can protect yourself."

When the police arrive, they will try and convince the battered wife not to press charges. She should insist that she be allowed to sign a complaint. The police may not explain that she has the right to file a complaint. Often they omit this option and concentrate on trying to persuade the woman to seek counseling or to handle her problem through civil channels.

To help convince the police officers that she means business, the San Francisco Women's Litigation Unit recommends: "Battered wives should write down the badge number and names of police officers who arrive to intervene.

"She should also write down details of the appropriate steps for making a citizen's arrest, for pressing charges with the district attorney." The reason is that the police will be more accurate in their information if they know notes are being taken. Police have been known to give wrong or inaccurate information to battered wives. Sometimes this happens because they do not understand the law, and sometimes they try to make the process seem overly complicated to discourage the woman.

"If a battered wife desires intervention by legal authorities, she must be prepared to insist that she be allowed to sign a complaint," writes Mindy Resnik in *Wife Beating: Counselor Training Manual*.

> It is her legal right to sign a complaint against an assailant. It is important that she realize that signing a complaint is only the first step in a process which may take months, and in some cases, years to complete.
>
> It should be understood that many hours of time away from children, or away from work, may be necessary before an assault charge is resolved. She should be prepared to testify—and be cross examined—at the trial and at various preliminary hearings.

If the investigating officers feel a felony has been committed, they can make an arrest on the spot. The battered wife who expects her husband to be locked in jail and the key thrown away is in for a disappointment. He will be eligible for bail and could be released without bail on his own recognizance. If he has a job and a fixed address, this will probably be the case. He will be out of circulation for only forty-eight hours at the most and more likely for only a few hours.

In order for the investigating officer to make an arrest on a less serious charge, a misdemeanor, he must witness the assault. If he didn't see it, then a warrant must be obtained from a judge before an arrest can be made. As we noted in an earlier chapter, sometimes the police refuse to make an arrest even when they witness an assault. The officers may tell her that she must go "downtown" to sign a complaint. She should ask to be taken there, and if the police tell her that it must be done on Monday or at some other time, she should take the time to make them be very explicit about the procedures. She should also insist that a report be filed stating the officers responded to the call and investigated, even if no arrest is made. As nationwide police statistics attest, only a very small percentage of the "domestic disturbance" calls ever get officially recorded.

Susan Jackson observes: "Preferably, the woman must have two witnesses to the incident, and it helps if there is a police report on file."

Some places require a five-day cooling off period before the victim can file a complaint. Police say the vast majority of battered wives decide not to prosecute during this cooling-off period. It's impossible to say whether they change their minds because of lack of resolve or out of fear. From the police point of view, the cooling-off period cuts down greatly on the paperwork. A battered wife who is determined to prosecute must wait out the cooling-off period, then report to the designated place and sign the complaint. She should also insist that a report of the police investigation on the day of the incident be filed even if it's five days late. She should explain that she plans to subpoena the records in a criminal action.

It is a good idea to write down the name and badge number of every officer she speaks to during the procedure. She should ask for both at the start of each meeting. She should be polite but firm. Check the spelling of the officer's name with him and ask for his first name, too. This reinforces the impression that the battered wife means business and may cause the police to treat her with more seriousness and respect.

On the day of her assault, the battered wife should seek immediate medical attention. Judge Oneglia says: "As soon as possible, she should go to a doctor or hospital and, if possible, have photographs taken. She should get to the nearest police station and swear out a warrant."

Because many beatings take place early in the morning or on weekends or holidays, the battered wife should go to a hospital emergency room for treatment. She should go for treatment even if she believes her injuries are not serious enough to hospitalize her. The emergency-room records can be used as evidence to establish the seriousness of her injuries. It's a good idea to keep receipts for any payments for treatment connected with the injury that can be used in a possible civil suit. Since she intends to prosecute in criminal court, she should ask the police to photograph her injuries so they can be entered in evidence at the trial. If they refuse, she should make arrangements to be photographed, preferably in color, as soon as possible after her beating. The victim should also record the date of an additional visit to her doctor or clinic for subsequent treatment of her injuries. These records can also be used to help establish the severity of her injuries.

Obviously, if a woman is unconscious, severely injured, or hospitalized, she will be unable to sign a complaint or make notes or question the police. This does not mean that she has forfeited these rights. She can pursue criminal legal action after she is released from the hospital.

A feminist attorney who has dealt with a number of spouse-abuse cases recommends: "I tell her, as soon as she's able, to go and swear out an arrest warrant without delay. To demand that one be sworn out by the district attorney. The second thing I would advise her to do is to proceed to the office of a competent attorney, knowledgeable in the field of domestic relations—which normally requires a very minimal consultation fee—and to find out what the situation is as it relates to their particular factual situation.

"Do not resume cohabitation with the husband until fully advised of the legal ramifications of what action and remedies are afforded to the wife under the state's divorce laws. After an arrest is made, *never* dismiss the charge."

If the battered wife can not afford an attorney, this should not dissuade her. In a criminal case, it is the government that is bringing action against her husband. Mindy Resnik writes: "She has no need for a private attorney except to understand the legal process. She should realize that the prosecuting attorney is on her side."

The first step is to sign a complaint, then seek the warrant for arrest. The battered wife will be interviewed by an assistant district attorney, an assistant corporation counsel, assistant public prosecutor, or a person with a similar title. This interview will determine if a warrant is issued or not. The victim should cooperate fully and supply as much detailed information as possible to back up her claim that her husband should be arrested for assault. "This may take many hours, or even days," warns Ms. Resnik. "The victim and/or a witness must sign a complaint before a warrant will be authorized and there is no guarantee that it will be authorized or that the assailant will be arrested." If the woman is still living with her assailant, the prosecutor will be hard to convince that a warrant should be issued for his arrest.

If the battered wife can convince the prosecutor that a crime has been committed, he will fill out the warrant and give it to a police officer to take to a judge to be signed. The judge can decide not to sign the warrant, but as a practical matter most judges usually accept the judgment of the prosecutor and sign it.

The police are then authorized to make an arrest and are supposed to begin looking for the named person. Very often they do not look very hard. Sometimes a battered wife can force the police to act by notifying them when she knows the location of her assailant. Again, it's a good idea to get the name and badge number of the officer to whom she reports this fact.

After her husband is arrested, the next legal step is the arraignment. The victim does not have to be present at the arraignment, but it is a good idea for her to attend so that she is fully informed about the status of the case. The accused, her husband, can plead guilty or not guilty at the arraignment. He is entitled to have his lawyer present, and if he cannot afford one, the court will appoint one free of charge. The woman does not have to pay the public prosecutor for his services. If she seeks the advice of an outside attorney concerning cohabitation requirements, divorce proceedings, clarification of the law, or any other legal matter, she is responsible for paying for these services.

The battered wife should bear in mind that she and the prosecutor are on the same side. Her husband is the accused or the defendant. He and his lawyer are on the other side. If the court appoints the lawyer, he could be chosen from a list of local practicing attorneys, and he is required to donate his time. In some areas, a public defender, whose salary is paid for by the taxpayers, is available to represent defendants who are not able to afford a private attorney. The battered wife should remember that even though the public defender is a government official, he is not on the government's side in this case.

Mindy Resnik believes a battered wife "should not speak with the public defender or the attorney representing her husband or the assailant. . . . The reason she should not speak with the public defender is that he may later use her words against her."

At the arraignment, the judge will set bail or other terms of release from arrest. He will also set a date for a preliminary hearing. The amount of time that can elapse between the arraignment and the preliminary hearing is usually set by law and is around twelve days. The accused can waive a preliminary hearing if he wants.

The victim and any witnesses must appear at the preliminary hearing. If she fails to appear the charges against her husband will be dismissed, and he will be released. The purpose of this hearing is to inform the accused what evidence and witnesses will be used against him so that an adequate defense can be planned.

The witnesses, including the battered wife, can be called to testify under oath. They can be cross-examined by the defense attorney and questioned by the judge. If the wife or the witnesses lie under oath, they can be prosecuted for perjury.

The battered wife should prepare carefully for her appearance. She should get the sequence of events straight in her mind, noting the time and the location of the event she is describing and how long each event took. She should expect the defense attorney to try and trip her up with repeated questions about precise details of her story.

She should avoid appearing uncertain about what happened when. She should speak in a firm, positive way and avoid using qualifying phrases such as "I think" when describing the crime. She must convince others that she is certain about what she is saying and at the same time avoid appearing as if she has rehearsed her testimony. She must be careful not to change details on the stand.

When she is being cross-examined by her husband's lawyer, she should answer only what she is asked and avoid volunteering additional information. She should avoid answering any question too quickly. She should pause before speaking, perhaps mentally count up to seven before saying anything. This slight delay gives her attorney a chance to object to a question he feels is improper.

After hearing all the testimony, the judge determines if a crime has been committed and if there is probable cause that the defendant committed it. If he is satisfied on these counts, he will bind the case over to another court. If the judge decides that no crime has been committed or that there is no probable cause, he will dismiss the charges and release the husband.

If the judge's decision is that a crime has been committed, another arraignment is set, and once again the defendant hears the formal charges against him, and a plea is entered into the record. He may plead guilty, not guilty, no contest, or he may stand mute. If he stands mute, an automatic plea of not guilty is entered. The defendant chooses if he wants his case heard only by a judge, or if he wants a trial by jury. Bail is set again, and since it is a different court and judge, the bail may not be the same. Next, the trial date is set.

It usually takes about two months to proceed from the first preliminary hearing to the actual trial. The woman should make use of this time.

Mindy Resnik advises:

> One of the best preparatory actions for trial is reading the transcript of the preliminary hearing. A copy is available at the Court Services of most courts. Look up the defendant's name in the standing file for the file number, and then give that number to a clerk who will allow you to read the transcript. It is important that a witness be credible. She should prepare for her courtroom experience and be honest about the crime.

It is also a good idea to attend a trial of a similar case. This gives the woman a firsthand look at what she can expect when her case comes up.

Sometimes a case never comes to trial. Sometimes the matter is settled through plea bargaining. The defense and prosecuting attorneys meet and decide if the case can be settled without going to court. A typical case might involve a man charged with felonious assault. The defense lawyer has heard the evidence and the witnesses and feels sure that his client will most likely be convicted. He will ask the prosecutor if he will accept a guilty plea to a misdemeanor and save the bother and expense of going through a trial. If the prosecutor is agreeable, and the defendant agrees, such a deal will be made. The prosecutor may agree to ask for a suspended sentence in return for the guilty plea. The victim is usually not present or consulted during plea bargaining. It is not necessary to consult her since it is the government that is prosecuting the case and not her. She is a witness to her own assault. Sometimes the lawyers don't even bother to notify her. It's not uncommon for a battered wife to call the prosecutor's office to find out some information about her case and be told that the matter has been settled.

Another problem for a battered wife is having to deal with several different prosecuting attorneys. It's not uncommon for the prosecutor's office to provide different individuals for the arraignment, preliminary hearings, and trial. The defense, under usual circumstances, will have the same attorney throughout all the proceedings.

The battered wife will be notified by the court if a trial date is set. Typically, she can expect a series of postponements, with a new date set each time. Most judges make every effort to give the defense adequate time to prepare for trial, and defense attorneys use repeated postponement as a tactic. They hope that the victim will get tired and either drop the charges or that the other witnesses will not be available when the case finally does come to trial.

If a jury trial has been selected by the defense, it will usually be picked the morning before the trial begins.

At the start of the trial, both attorneys in their opening addresses will explain what they intend to prove to the jury, what witnesses will be called, and why they think the jury should agree with their position.

The battered wife can be expected to be called to the stand several times and questioned carefully about the incident. She should take pains that her testimony is consistent with that given at the preliminary hearing. And discrepancies will be used to discredit her.

Witnesses are usually sequestered outside of the courtroom during the testimony of other witnesses so that they will not be influenced by what others say in connection with the case. After a witness is finished testifying, she can remain in the courtroom for the rest of the trial.

Near the end of the trial, both attorneys will summarize their cases and again remind the jury what they think its verdict should be.

When the case goes to the jury, all twelve members must agree that the defendant is guilty beyond all reasonable doubt. They can vote for acquittal or conviction, but it must be a unanimous decision. If the decision is not unanimous, it is called a hung jury, and the case can be retried or dropped.

If the verdict is not guilty, the defendant is set free. If the verdict is guilty, the judge will set a date for sentencing, usually in about two weeks, following a presentencing investigation.

It is possible to appeal the verdict to a higher court. If the verdict is guilty, the defendant may very well appeal. If the verdict is not guilty, no appeal is constitutionally feasible by the prosecution under the "Double Jeopardy" prohibition.

If the husband is found guilty, it is not likely that he will go to jail. A jail sentence is given only in the most severe cases and usually only after several convictions. Even then it is unlikely that the man will serve a maximum sentence.

Typically, a convicted wife beater will be put on probation, fined, or both. The judge can make it a condition of his probation that he stay away from his wife and stop beating her. The judge can also make it a condition of probation that the husband receive therapy or counseling to learn how to control his violent behavior. If a husband violates his parole, he can be put into jail. This threat of jail can be the wife's best protection. However, it is not uncommon for a husband to ignore the court order and proceed to thrash and even kill his wife while on probation, particularly if he has been drinking.

A battered wife whose husband has been convicted of criminal assault may be eligible for compensation as a victim of crime in states in which such laws exist. She should check on this with an attorney.

The fourth option open to battered wives is to get a divorce. This step is frequently recommended by feminists. There is a classic simplicity to this solution—the way to stop being beaten is to leave. But many women are extremely reluctant to take this ultimate step. Battered wives feel they must maintain their marriage for their children. Some are unwilling to accept the lowered standard of living that a divorce brings for themselves and their children. Many women are simply afraid of being alone or being responsible for their lives. But more women are beginning to assert themselves, gaining strength and confidence from groups such as AWAIC and NOW. The fear of a divorce is lessening.

"Usually, I advise battered wives to get out of the marriage," says Judge Oneglia. "There's often no way for the legal system to solve the problem. First she should consult an attorney. If she doesn't know one and is without funds, she can go to social services or legal aid. She should take the children to help establish her custody and by no means return home or contact her husband without legal advice. By staying in the house, she may be condoning his actions or diminishing their severity in the eyes of the law."

Mindy Resnik notes: "Divorce is the most recommended alternative for the battered woman. She must retain an attorney and be prepared for a battle over property rights, visitation rights or child custody and similar matters."

When a woman contacts a lawyer, she should discuss his fees, court costs, and a payment schedule at their first meeting. These matters should be clear to both parties from the start to prevent problems after the action has begun.

"Divorce cannot prevent an ex-husband from coming back and beating up his former wife," observes Ms. Resnik, "but the victim who chooses a divorce should always be encouraged to obtain a restraining order as part of her marriage settlement."

A typical restraining order would read: "And it is further ordered that each of the parties, his agents, servants, employees and any other persons in active concert or participation with them who receive actual notice of this order, do absolutely desist and refrain from beating, annoying, molesting, physically abusing or otherwise interfering with the personal liberty of the other during the pendency of this action." Stripped of the jargon, it is simply an order from the court to the husband to stop beating his wife or else.

Sue Eisenberg and Pat Micklow interviewed twenty battered women seeking divorces and found that no restraining orders had been obtained for many of them. "This failure of the divorce attorney is at best an oversight and at worse negligence," they say.

> Divorce attorneys rationalize this inaction on several grounds. Some state that the husband assailant inflicts more severe harm on his wife when such orders are served on him. Others fear less cooperation from the husband in the settlement of property or custody disputes. Interestingly enough, some attorneys view physical assault history as a diminishing influence on the bargaining power . . . in any event, divorce attorneys characterize the injunctive orders as relatively ineffectual.

Judges have broad discretionary power to decide the proper course to follow in enforcing restraining orders. Usually, the judge warns the husband against further violations. It is almost unheard of that a husband is jailed after the first violation of a court order. After a second or third violation, a judge may impose a fine or a jail sentence.

The battered wife should be aware that hospital, medical, police and criminal court records can be used to prove her claims of abuse in her divorce proceedings.

A word of caution is in order. A battered woman should regard the information in this chapter as an outline to help her understand the legal process. It is not meant to give legal advice or to do away with the need for an attorney. It is designed to help a battered woman deal with her attorney. The information is general and broad enough to apply everywhere in the U.S. Most of it was obtained from attorneys, and it has all been checked by attorneys. It's as accurate as we can make it, but it is not intended to be a substitute for a lawyer.

There are some other avenues for relief a battered wife can pursue. San Francisco attorney Mary Vail says individual victims who fail to secure relief through the criminal justice system can sue their attackers for damages in some states in small claims court. No lawyer is required. She must fill out a form, and both she and her husband appear before a judge or arbitrator who decides the case after listening to both sides.

The national center for dispute settlement of the American Arbitration Association is experimenting with a program that uses arbitration techniques to try and settle marital problems. The idea is to use the same approaches used in settling labor contracts—negotiation and compromise—with the quarreling couple. So far this technique has been tried on a very limited basis.

The battered wife has an obligation to help herself break out of the syndrome of violence in which she finds herself, but society as a whole also has an obligation to help her. The plight of the battered wife has been ignored for centuries. The time has come for the larger community to face the issue and begin to deal with it.

"If we're really not going to tolerate it, we've got to *stop* tolerating it," says Dr. Straus. But how?

What can those who are not directly involved in the problem do to demonstrate that they will no longer tolerate wife beating in the community? What can be done to bring about social change?

The most effective action is to help organize a battered-wife task force in your community. It has been tried, tested, and proved successful in a number of localities. One such successful group was formed in Ann Arbor, Michigan, and Kathleen M. Fojtik, a member of that group, has formulated a set of guidelines to help others organize similar groups.

She recommends calling a special meeting of NOW or other feminist group to discuss the problem of battered wives or arrange for a panel discussion on the problem, inviting representatives from the police, clergy, and social service agencies to participate. The meeting should be publicized to obtain the widest possible response. At this meeting, sign up volunteers interested in working on a battered-wife task force.

Organize the task force into committees. One of the first goals should be to produce a report on local wife beating that will spur further interest and action.

The task force should set up a network of volunteers who will donate their homes as emergency havens for beaten women and their children. The volunteers should agree to take in a battered woman for a maximum of three days. The pros and cons should be openly discussed, and only dedicated volunteers who will live up to their commitment should be included in the plan. Next, notify local social service agencies, clergymen, and crisis telephone lines that you have this service available.

"Be prepared for more than you can handle or house—you will be overwhelmed," predicts Ms. Fojtik. "Just remember, no one else is helping these women. Someone must point out that there are great numbers of these women out there who need help. For centuries, battered women have been told to 'grin and bear it.' It is now time to assist them."

The task force should conduct a telephone survey of local social service agencies and find out what services are available to battered women. If the results are typical, they will show agencies such as the Community Mental Health Organization, Catholic Social Services, and the welfare department all recognize the problem but have "no resources" to help.

The next job is to collect statistics to document the seriousness of the problem in your community. Police can supply some figures, as can social agencies, but most of the information will be collected by the task force. Specific information concerning the frequency of beatings, the response of the police and courts, should be obtained from the battered wives using the emergency shelters. The task force should design a standard questionnaire that will produce the data desired, and all volunteers conducting interviews should use the same form. When the results are examined, there will be some surprises and some shocks. For example, a Washington, D.C., study of 7,500 wives who attempted to bring charges against their husbands revealed that fewer than 200 actually were able to do so.

Obtain publicity for your program by contacting representatives of the news media and furnish them with data on the local situation. Arrange for interviews with battered wives if reporters agree to keep the sources anonymous.

Broaden the base of support by contacting groups such as the Women's Political Caucus, the League of Women Voters, the American Association of University Women, and the Junior League and try to get them involved in the project.

Involve the establishment. Get representatives from the city, county, or state governments to participate. Seek expert help from the bar and medical associations, Alcoholics Anonymous, and other organizations.

After the task force produces its report, it should begin to implement plans for action.

A legislative committee can draft a model spouse-abuse law or a resolution for the state legislature and then lobby for passage. Even if the effort fails, it can generate publicity and discussion of the issue.

The task force can assist in applying for a grant from the state or Federal Government to establish a shelter, crisis line, counseling services, police training, legal aid, or other programs useful to battered wives.

The task force can compile a resource manual of existing services for battered women, including psychological counseling, health services, public assistance, legal services, available emergency housing, and child-care facilities.

Efforts should be made to convince police agencies, both local and state, to begin to collect more data on the number of family-trouble calls responded to, the number of assaults on wives, the number of repeaters, and other information that will help give a more accurate description of the problem. Pressure should be applied to U.S. Senators and Congressmen to get them to require the FBI to collect this type of data from local police agencies and compile national statistics.

One of the biggest roadblocks to effective action to help battered wives is the lack of hard, reliable statistics. No one is collecting the kind of information needed to put the problem in a proper national perspective. Grassroots efforts can lead to a big payoff. A comprehensive set of statistics in one community can spur regional collection of data and eventually a statewide program. A state program could become contagious. The FBI already has the machinery established to collect these statistics from the nation's police forces. The job is to convince local agencies to begin compiling them and the Federal government to collate them. Once the facts and figures are in and the extent of the problem defined in meaningful terms, progress toward working for solutions will be greatly advanced.

An early project for a community task force is to establish a local telephone crisis line that battered wives can call. Lack of funds will be a constant problem but one that can be solved. For example, Nashville, Tennessee, provides a crisis line on a budget of $50,000 a year, which operates twenty-four hours a day, seven days a week. It has only two full-time and one part-time employee. The heart of the project is a cadre of eighty unpaid volunteers.

The group reports: "All potential volunteers are carefully screened by mental health professionals who are familiar with crisis intervention techniques. . . . A screening committee evaluates selected applicants and invites them to take a free, twenty-two-hour training course."

In the first year, this crisis line handled 1,627 "marital" and "family" crisis calls.

Crisis-line operators should refer requests for emergency shelter to a task force coordinator who knows what is available and what can be provided at the time of the request. The coordinator should contact the volunteer and arrange to get the battered wife to the home serving as an emergency shelter.

Before she is taken to the volunteer's home, the victim should have any ground rules explained to her and agree to abide by them. The most important condition is a promise to keep the volunteer home confidential. She should promise not to give out the address or phone number. This will prevent the husband from transferring the violence to the volunteer's home. The victim should also agree to fill out the task force's questionnaire.

The matter of expenses should be worked out in advance between the task force and volunteer. Questions such as who pays for food, bus fare, and other expenses have to be arranged in advance to everyone's satisfaction. The battered wife should not be confronted with these financial questions when she cries out for help, but after a few days it should be determined how much financial support she can provide for herself and family. It's possible that the victim may be better off financially than the volunteer.

The experts all agree that the greatest need in every community is a permanent emergency shelter run by professionals rather than volunteers.

"We desperately need some kind of emergency facility for the beaten wife," says Dr. LeClair Bissell, director of the Roosevelt Center for Alcoholism in New York.

The Montgomery County Task Force on Spouse Abuse reports:

"All persons interviewed in the legal and law enforcement process indicated that a 'haven' would be most welcome, as it would allow a 'cooling off' period for the principles to get medical attention, to make decisions, to obtain counseling, and to reassess without personal pressures or physical fears."

Betsy Warrior says of the Women's Advocates House in St. Paul, Minnesota, which is usually filled to a capacity, "Residents of the house find it a virtual lifesaver."

In Schenectady, New York, the YWCA sometimes offers a haven for battered wives.

"Battered wives must simply be offered a way out," says Kathy Vilardi, a local task force member. "No woman should have to be trapped into living like a whipped dog."

Maria Roy notes:

"The right of sanctuary came down to us through the churches.

"Our goal is the establishment of a temporary shelter where women can stay for immediate protection while they decide the next step. Once we extricate them from the atmosphere of fear and violence, then they can begin to think clearly and objectively.

"No such shelter exists. Such an undertaking will be costly, almost prohibitively, and so the task of acquiring funding on a large scale is a challenging one."

Passage Crisis Center of Silver Spring, Maryland, provides counseling assistance to battered wives and others in crisis situations. The center is designed to provide immediate intervention and assistance in obtaining long-term counseling.

Clients either call or walk into the center. Passage Center also has a mobile unit that is simply a car with a two-way radio installed. Two staff members drive to help people in trouble in all parts of the county. It does not handle medical emergencies, only emotional ones.

Psychiatric back-up is available twenty-four hours a day and can be provided to people with problems within fifteen minutes.

A minimal shelter facility is available for people needing emergency housing for a night.

On every shift there is one counselor, one nurse, and at least two volunteers.

More such shelters are needed elsewhere. "The point is to break the situation that keeps a woman so dependent on her husband that she has to continue living with him when he is abusive and violent," says Albany's Ms. Vilardi. "Initially, we might just provide the woman and her children with a safe place to sleep for a few weeks while she reassesses things. Eventually, we want to provide much more than that. We envision a refuge that would have room for up to eight women and their children at one time. Each woman would be permitted to stay for two to three weeks, during which time she would receive job counseling and assistance in finding an apartment and obtaining welfare, if necessary."

The Montgomery County Task Force, after studying the questionnaires filled out by battered wives and consulting with persons who deal with battered women, produced a ten-point guideline for an ideal shelter.

In their view, the facility should be:

1. Small, and limited to abused adults and their dependents;
2. Well-publicized, with an emergency telephone number;
3. Staffed 24 hours a day;
4. Secure, with frequent checks by police, and adequate locks and lighting;
5. Flexible in sleeping accommodations for adults, children and infants;
6. Provided with kitchen facilities, basic equipment and foodstuffs;
7. Provided with supplies and equipment for children and infants (toys, disposable diapers, bottles, highchairs.)
8. Equipped with adequate bath facilities and supplies;
9. Equipped with a telephone for use by its clients;
10. Provided with an emergency fund for phone calls, clothing, transportation, and other incidentals.

This same group feels the shelter should provide the following services: A coordinating counselor; medical treatment both for emergencies and continuing problems; liaison with drug and alcohol programs and centers; liaison with the police and district attorney's office; transportation to services such as welfare office, courthouse, police station, and schools for children; and day care for children of women who must leave the haven.

Children are important clients of a battered-wife shelter. Most mothers take their children with them when they are able. This complicates the service problem since the kids can range from infants to teen-agers. A wider range of facilities and services is necessary.

In the long run, providing shelter for the children may be the most important step in solving the battered-wife problem.

Susan Jackson observes: "Though family violence has its most immediate impact on the women, as victims, there is evidence that the children of victims, even when they are not themselves physically assaulted, suffer deep and lasting emotional effects from being forced to witness their fathers' cruelty and their mothers' submission to attacks.

"Erin Pizzey points out the cyclical aspect of family violence: sons of wife-beaters grow up to beat their own wives, daughters grow up with an expectation, often fulfilled, that they will be beaten.

"In order to end the cycle of violence, shelters are needed not only to provide a safe refuge for the battered women but also to provide immediate and continuing psychological aid to the children."

One stumbling block to establishing publicly supported shelters for battered women is that they could be declared illegal because of sexual discrimination. It's ironic that this woman's issue, spearheaded by feminists and exemplified in ERA, could be turned around and used as one more assault by society on the battered women.

The problem is not the admittance of the rare, bona fide battered husband who might seek shelter, it is the exclusion of the violent husband. In order to be effective, it's generally agreed that the shelter must provide protection for the battered woman. She must be able to go there to get away from her husband. If the courts rule that the husbands cannot be legally excluded, then the whole concept of haven goes down the drain. What if the violent husband appears at the shelter claiming *he* is a victim and demands shelter? Must he be admitted? Is it legal for the state to physically block a man's access to his wife and children? Who is to decide who gets in and who gets locked out?

Ms. Jackson observes: "Though the use of public funds to establish shelters for women only could be objected to on the grounds that the exclusion of male victims is a denial of equal protection to men, still female victims of family violence are by far the majority, and shelters for women would provide at least a first step toward ameliorating the problem."

Nevertheless, the thorny legal questions remain and will have to be tested and resolved.

Another area in which concerned citizens can work is in police response to wife beating. Police now view the solution to wife beating as half social work and half police work. Ironically, critics of the system feel that they are putting too much emphasis on the social-work aspect and not enough on the criminal.

The first city in the U.S. to train its entire 790-member police force in crisis intervention techniques was Louisville, Kentucky. The program is considered "Mental Health First Aid" in which police act as mediators in family disputes. They have been settling about 12,000 disputes a year, at the same time significantly reducing the injury and death rate of police officers responding to these calls.

Other cities have followed suit, and it is now accepted police procedure to avoid making arrests and talk the disputants into seeking counseling or advise them to take their problems to the civil courts.

Battered wives who want criminal procedures enforced have a great deal of trouble. Many want a tightening up of criminal procedures.

"Arrests should be made on the same grounds as assaults between unmarried people," says Dr. Straus.

Ms. Jackson argues: "Various legal actions should be instituted against both the police and district attorney, nationwide in any city or county where the laws against wife beating are not fully enforced.

"Specific practices by the police which should be changed include:

"1. Refusal to make arrests for violations of restraining orders.

"2. Refusal to follow through on citizens' arrests.

"Specific practices by the district attorney which should be changed are:

"1. Refusal to exercise discretion by detouring cases of wife beating into the family bureau or,

"2. Abuse of discretion in discriminating against women as one class of complaining witnesses."

To aid victims, the Women's Advocates in St. Paul prepared cards for police to give to battered women when they call. The card contains important information concerning rights, phone numbers, addresses, and procedures.

Similar cards can be prepared for other cities. The St. Paul card reads:

SIDE 1

If you have pain, injuries, or bruises contact your own doctor or hospital. If you don't have one, contact or go to:

EMERGENCY ROOM, ST. PAUL-RAMSEY MEDICAL CTR.
640 Jackson, St. Paul 222-4260

If you make a report to the police, they may transport you to get medical help

If you need help, advice, or emergency shelter, call or walk-in to:

WOMEN'S ADVOCATES, 584 Grand Avenue   227-8284

or call: EMERGENCY SOCIAL SERVICE   225-1515

SIDE 2

If you want to bring legal charges against the person who assaulted you:

1. Tell the police officer you want to press charges.
2. See a doctor as soon as possible. If you are pressing charges,
   photos of injuries should be taken while they are visible.
3. During daytime business hours (8:30–4:30) contact the city attorney's office about filing a complaint:

ST. PAUL CITY ATTORNEY (CRIMINAL DIVISION)
Room 638, City Hall   298-4271
(Kellogg & Wabasha Streets)

Women's groups in other cities are working to change police
procedures concerning battered wives. Probably the most extensive
list of recommendations has been prepared by the Women's Litigation Unit of the San Francisco Neighborhood Legal Assistance
Foundation. These are the changes they want accomplished:

A. Police should formulate written policies and procedures
regarding domestic disputes. These written policies and procedures
should be open to the public.

B. Considering the threat of physical injury, police dispatchers
should assign domestic calls an ''A'' or ''B'' priority.

C. Patrol officers should arrive promptly on the scene of a domestic dispute.

D. Police policy of arrest avoidance in domestic disputes should
be reconsidered. When there is evidence that the situation involves
continuing acts of violence between the parties and the police are
witness to the present crime or the crime is a felony, a police arrest
should be made.

E. Police should inform all victims of domestic violence of the
right to make a citizen's arrest.

F. Police policy requiring a person making a citizen's arrest to
take physical custody of the accused and to deliver the accused to
police should be discontinued.

G. The following steps should be adopted as sufficient for effecting a citizen's arrest:

1. Request to make a citizen's arrest.
2. Identify the accused or give an adequate description.
3. Identify the location of the accused.
4. Describe the crime witnessed.

H. Patrol officers should not discourage victims who attempt to make a citizen's arrest. To do so is a felony or a misdemeanor.

I. Police should make arrests for violations of civil restraining orders.

J. Police should inform victims of their right to reimbursement under the victims of crime act.

K. Where violence does not appear to be a continuing situation, police should continue and increase the practice of on-the-spot problem solving and referral of victims and their families to social service agencies.

L. Police referral manuals should be updated to include the most recent resources available to victims and their families.

M. All police officers who are not currently trained in crisis intervention should be so trained. All new officers should be trained for handling domestic disputes immediately upon joining the force.

N. All levels of police personnel—including supervisory personnel—should be trained in domestic crisis intervention.

O. Police patrol officers intervening in domestic disputes should be monitored on a spot-check basis to ensure that techniques given in training are being used.

P. Female patrol officers should be utilized whenever possible in responding to domestic disputes.

Q. Counselors sensitive to feminist issues and the special needs of women as victims should be utilized by police as referral sources. Feminist counseling agencies should be added as resources to the police manual.

R. Translators for foreign languages should be available to assist police in responding to domestic disputes.

S. Data on domestic calls should be computerized to reveal:

1. Number of domestic calls received by police.
2. The time lapse in police response to each call.
3. Number of arrests resulting from domestic calls.
4. Number of repeat calls.

5. Number of serious injuries and/or homicides resulting from repeat-call situations.

T. Police should assist local community groups seeking funds for shelters that would provide immediate safety and counseling to victims of domestic violence.

Any local task force can adapt this list of reforms to meet their local conditions.

There is much work for a task force or a concerned individual to do in the field of spouse abuse. But the real solution to this problem is more complicated than obtaining police reforms or providing shelters. The root of the problem is our acceptance of violence as a legitimate means of solving problems. It's been said that every time we spank a child, we teach the lesson that violence is acceptable. It is almost universally accepted in America that, under certain conditions, it's proper to spank a child.

"The cliché, 'violence begets violence' is supported in the studies of physical punishment as a disciplinary procedure and its effectiveness in controlling aggressive behavior in children," says Dr. Steinmetz. "Researchers have found that physical punishment tended to increase rather than decrease aggressive behavior in children. This aggressive tendency is apparently retained into adulthood, as child abusers were frequently abused children."

Violence is reflected in our language, and studies have shown that verbal violence is often the forerunner of physical violence. "There must be a recognition that it's wrong to insult, yell, and scream at another person," says Dr. Straus. "This is different from arguing and sticking up for one's rights." Dr. Straus says he's encouraged by communication techniques developed by drug addicts at Odyssey House. "They have developed an elaborate procedure for arguing without hurting others," he says. . . . "When one member does something another thinks is wrong, he has to call it and talk it out in the presence of other people. In marriage you have to have rules. You face the issues and have confrontations—but not by hurting one another verbally or physically."

Three of the leading researchers in the field of family violence, Drs. Straus, Gelles, and Steinmetz, worked jointly on a report entitled *Violence in the Family: An Assessment of Knowledge and Research Needs*. Their assessment of the years ahead is not bright. They foresee developments contributing to, not lessening, family violence. They write:

> A great deal of the physical violence between husband and wife is related to conflicts over power in the family and specifically to attempts by men to maintain their superior power position. One might therefore expect that as families become more equalitarian, violence between husband and wife will decrease. However, this will be the case only to the extent that men voluntarily give up their privileges. To the extent that sexual equality comes about by women demanding equal rights, the movement toward equality could well see a temporary increase in violence rather than a decrease. Aside from struggles over changing rules of the marriage game, there is nothing inherent in an equal relationship which precludes conflict and violence over substantive issues. In fact, in the past, to the extent that women accepted a subordinate position, much overt conflict may have been avoided by not contesting the husband's view of an issue.
>
> As the boundaries between the sexes diminish, there might also be other reasons for an increase in family violence. Under the present sex role definitions, women are expected to be less aggressive and violent than men. The aspect of sex role stereotyping is already changing to a limited degree. For example, the crime rates for women have begun to converge on those for men, especially for violent crime. There was a TV show with an aggressive James Bond type of woman "hero" (*The Avengers*) and a movie *Super Chick*. A study of children's books from 1850 to 1970 found an increase in the proportion of aggressive acts initiated by women, especially in the most recent years.
>
> Turning to radical changes in the structure of the family, there is a widespread belief that such "alternative family forms" will be less violent. In part, this belief is based on the view that, in rejecting the middle class family, there will be a movement away from middle class strivings and aggressiveness. In part it is based on the idea that a larger social group will provide more outlets and alternatives and less frustrations. But on both theoretical grounds as well as the meager empirical evidence which is now available, the opposite might well be the case. The alternative multilateral family forms may provide more opportunities for sexual and other jealousy, even

though they are set up with the opposite intent. In the extent that such families constitute large households, they will require more rigid roles than a nuclear family in order to accomplish the ordinary physical maintenance activities. In addition, many such groups seem to be imbedded with an agrarian romantic ideology glorifying a sharp division of labor between men and women.

More hopeful perhaps, are the words of Dr. Sidney Wasserman, an expert on family violence, who writes:

> The people of the United States have yet to learn how to convert their tendency to violence into compassion and tenderness. We are in danger of losing sight of one of this nation's major social goals, one on which it was founded, that is, to tap the humanity and creative potential of all citizens and to provide the environment and resources necessary for the individual citizen to realize his creative potential. We possess the potential both for violence and for humaneness, and are capable of acting in brotherhood and with understanding.

Changing deeply held attitudes will not be easy, nor will it happen quickly. But because the job is difficult and long, it does not mean that it shouldn't be done.

There is still hope for the betterment of mankind. Helping to make the world a less violent place is worthy of our best efforts.

Bibliography

American Jurisprudence. Vol. 41. 2nd ed. "Husband and Wife to Indictments and Informations: Rochester, N.Y.: The Lawyers Cooperative Publishing Co.; San Francisco: Bancroft-Whitney Co., 1968.

Bach, George R. and Goldberg, Herb. *Creative Aggression*. New York: Doubleday and Co., Inc., 1972.

Bakan, David. *Slaughter of the Innocents*. San Francisco, Cal.: Jossey-Bass Inc., 1971.

Bard, Morton. *Training Police as Specialist in Family Crisis Intervention*. Washington, D.C.: U.S. Department of Justice, 1970.

Bard, Morton and Zacker, Joseph. "The Prevention of Family Violence." *Journal of Marriage and the Family* XXXIII (February 1971): 677–82.

Bennie, E. H. and Sclare, A. B. "The Battered Child Syndrome." *American Journal of Psychiatry* CXXV, No. 7 (January 1969): 975–79.

Biggs, John Michael. *The Concept of Matrimonial Cruelty*. London: University of London, The Athlone Press, 1962.

Biller, Henry, and Meredith, Dennis. *Father Power*. New York: David McKay Co., Inc., 1974.

Blackstone, William. *Commentaries on the Laws of England*. 3rd. edition. Albany, N.Y.: Banks and Co., 1899.

Blum, Lawrence N. "Crisis Intervention Demonstration Project: Mental Health and Police Collaboration and Consultation." Ann Arbor, Mich.: University of Michigan, Institute for Social Research, 1974.

Boisvert, Maurice J. "The Battered Child Syndrome." *Social Casework* LIII, No. 8 (October, 1972): 475–80.

Boudouris, James. "Homicide and the Family." *Journal of Marriage and the Family* XXXIII (November, 1971): 667–82.

Bryant, C. D. and Wells, J. G. (eds). *Deviancy and the Family*. Philadelphia: F. A. Davis, 1973.

Bryant, Flora B. "An Exploratory Study of Child Abuse and Neglect in

Calhoun, Jackson, and Kalamazoo Counties." Unpublished project in Field Studies in Research and Practice. Kalamazoo, Mich.: Western Michigan University, 1974.

Burton, Genevieve and Kaplan, Howard M. "Group Counseling in Conflicted Marriages Where Alcoholism Is Present: Clients' Evaluation of Effectiveness." *Journal of Marriage and the Family* III, No. 1 (February, 1968): 74–79.

Chesler, Phyllis and Goodman, Emily. *Women, Money and Power*. New York: William Morrow & Co., Inc., 1976.

DeFrancis, Vincent (ed.). *Protecting the Battered Child*. Denver, Colo.: The American Humane Association, 1962.

Delsordo, James D. "Protective Casework for Abused Children." *Children* X, No. 6 (November–December 1963): 213–18.

Durbin, Karen. "Wife-Beating." *The Ladies' Home Journal* 91 (June, 1974): 62–72.

Dworkin, Andrea. *Woman Hating*. New York: E. P. Dutton & Co., Inc., 1974.

Eisenberg, Sue E. and Micklow, Patricia L. "The Assaulted Wife: 'Catch 22' Revisited (A Preliminary Overview of Wife-Beating in Michigan)." Unpublished study. Ann Arbor, Mich.: University of Michigan, 1974. (Revised version, *Women's Rights Law Reporter*, Vol. 3–4, Spring-Summer 1977, Rutgers University School of Law, Newark, N.J.).

Elmer, Elizabeth, et al. *Children in Jeopardy: A Study of Abused Minors and Their Families*. Pittsburgh: University of Pittsburgh, 1967.

Faulk, M. "Men Who Assault Their Wives." *Medicine Law* XIV, No. 7 (July, 1974): 180–83.

Field, Martha H. and Field, Henry F. "Marital Violence and the Criminal Process." *Social Service Review* XLVII (June, 1973): 221–40.

Flynn, John (director). *Spouse Assault: Its Dimension and Characteristics in Kalamazoo County, Michigan*. Unpublished Field Studies in Research and Practice. School of Social Work, Western Michigan University, Kalamazoo, Mich., 1975.

Fojtik, Kathleen, M. *How to Develop a Wife Assault Task Force and Project*. Ann Arbor, Mich.: Ann Arbor-Washtenaw County National Organization for Women (NOW), 1976.

Fontana, V. J. *Somewhere a Child Is Crying: The Battered Child*. New York: Macmillan, 1973.

Four Translation New Testament. New York: The Iversen Associates, 1966.

Freud, Sigmund: *Complete Introductory Lectures on Psychoanalysis*. Translated and edited by J. Strachey. New York: Norton, 1966.

Fullerton, Gail Putney. "Marital Conflict: Hostility in Intimacy." *Survival in Marriage*. New York: Holt, Rinehart and Winston, 1972.

Galdston, Richard. "Observations on Children Who Have Been Physically Abused and Their Parents." *American Journal of Psychiatry* CXXII, No. 1 (October, 1965): 440–34.

Gelles, Richard J. "Abused Wives: Why Do They Stay?" Revised version of paper presented at the Eastern Sociological Society, Boston, 1976.

————. "Child Abuse as Psychopathology: A Sociological Critique and Reformulation." *American Journal of Orthopsychiatry* XLIII, No. 4 (July, 1973): 611–21.

————. *Power, Sex and Violence: The Case of Marital Rape?* Paper presented to Western Science Associates, Phoenix, Ariz., 1976.

————. *The Violent Home*. Beverly Hills, Cal.: Sage Publications, Inc., 1974.

————. *The Violent Home, A Study of Physical Aggression between Husband and Wives*. Beverly Hills, Cal.: Sage Publications, Inc., 1974.

Gergen, Kenneth J. "Methodology in the Study of Policy Formation." In *The Study of Policy Formation*, edited by R. A. Bauer and K. J. Gergen, pp. 205–37. New York: The Free Press, 1971.

Gil, David G. "A Sociocultural Perspective on Physical Child Abuse." *Child Welfare* L, No. 7 (July, 1971): 389–95.

————. *Violence Against Children: Physical Child Abuse in the United States*. Cambridge: Harvard University Press, 1970.

Glasser, Paul H. and Lois N. *Families in Crisis*. New York: Harper and Row, 1970.

Gold, M. "Suicide, Homicide and the Socialization of Aggression." *American Journal of Sociology* LXIII (May, 1958): 651–61.

Goode, William J. "Force and Violence in the Family." In *Violence in the Family* edited by S. K. Steinmetz and M. A. Straus, pp. 25–44. New York: Dodd, Mead & Company, 1974.

Green, Kenneth. "The Echo of Marital Conflict." *Family Process* II (September, 1963): 315–28.

Harris, Louis and Associates. Poll conducted for the National Commission on the Causes and Prevention of Violence. 1968.

Helfer, Ray M., M.D. "The Etiology of Child Abuse." *Pediatrics* LI, No. 4, Part II (April, 1973): 777–79.

Helmholtz, R. H. *Marriage Litigation in Medieval England*. Cambridge: Cambridge University Press, 1974.

Hill, Reuben. *Families under Stress*. New York: Harper and Brothers, 1949.

Horney, Karen, M.D. "The Problem of Feminine Masochism." In *Feminine Psychology*. New York: W. W. Norton & Co., 1967.

Kadushin, Alfred. *Child Welfare Services*. London: The Macmillan Co., 1970.

Kanowitz, Leo. *Women and the Law; The Unfinished Revolution*. Albuquerque: University of New Mexico Press, 1969.

Kempe, Henry C. and Helfer, Ray E. (eds.). *Helping the Battered Child and His Family*. Philadelphia: J. B. Lippincott Company, 1972.

———, Silverman, Frederic N., Steele, Brandt V., Droegemueller, William and Silver, Henry K. "The Battered-Child Syndrome." *The Journal of the American Medical Association* CLXXXI, No. 1 (July, 1962): 17–24.

Kennedy, Courtney Stanhope, LLM. *Effects of Marriage on Property and on the Wife's Legal Capacity*. London: Reeves and Turner, 1879.

Kieren, Dianne and Tallman, Irving. "Spouse Adaptability: An Assessment of Marital Competence." *Journal of Marriage and the Family* XXXIV (May, 1972): 247–53.

LaFave, Wayne R. and Scott, Austin W. *Handbook on Criminal Law*. St. Paul: West Publishing Co., 1972.

Lauer, Brian, Broeck, Elsa Ten. and Grossman, Moses. "Battered Child Syndrome: Review of 130 Patients with Controls." *Pediatrics* LIV, No. 1 (July, 1974): 67–70.

Levinger, George. "Physical Abuse among Applicants for Divorce." *Violence in the Family*, edited by S. K. Steinmetz and M. A. Straus. pp. 85–88. New York: Dodd, Mead & Company, 1974.

Loving, Nancy and Olson, Lynn. *Rape and Wife Beating*. Conference information packet prepared by Criminal Justice Staff of National League of Cities and United States Conference of Mayors, Washington, D.C., 1976.

Millett, Kate. *Sexual Politics*. New York: Doubleday & Co., Inc., 1970.

Murphy, Robert B. et al. "Training Patrolmen to Become Crisis Intervention Specialists." *The Police Chief* (December, 1975): 44–45.

Neufeld, E., Ph.D., LIH. *Ancient Hebrew Marriage Laws*. London, New York, Toronto: Longmans, Green and Co., 1944.

Norton, C. *English Laws for Women in the Nineteenth Century,* Printed in private circulation. London, 1854.

Nurse, Shirley M. "Familial Patterns of Parents Who Abuse Their Children." *Smith College Studies in Social Work* XXXV, No. 1 (October, 1964): 11–25.

O'Brien, John E. "Violence in Divorce-Prone Families." In *Violence in the Family,* edited by S. K. Steinmetz and M. A. Straus, pp. 65–75. New York: Dodd, Mead & Company, 1974.

Palmer, Stuart. *The Violent Society.* New Haven: College and University Press, 1972.

Parnas, Raymond. "The Police Response to the Domestic Disturbance." *Wisconsin Law Review,* 914 A.2. (1967).

Paulson, Morris J., Afifi, Abdelmonen A., Thomason, Mary L. and Chaleff, Anna. "The MMPI: A Descriptive Measure of Psycho-pathology in Abusive Parents." *Journal of Clinical Psychology* XXX, No. 3 (July, 1974): 387–90.

Perdue, William C. and Lester, David. "Those Who Murder Kin: A Rorschach Study." *Perceptual and Motor Skills.* XXXVI, No. 2 (April, 1973): 606–16.

Pittman, David J. and Mundy, William. "Patterns in Criminal Aggravated Assault." *Journal of Criminal Law Criminology and Police Science* LV (December, 1964): 467–70.

Pogrebin, Letty Cottin. "Do Women Make Men Violent?" *Ms.* 3, No. 5 (November, 1974): 49–52.

Porkorny, Alex D. "A Comparison of Homicide, Aggravated Assault, Suicide." *Journal of Criminal Law, Criminology and Police Science* LV (December, 1965): 488–98.

President's Commission on Law Enforcement and Administration of Justice, "The Challenge of Crime in a Free Society." Washington, D.C., 1967.

The Public Affairs Offices, National League of Cities and U.S. Conference of Mayors. *Sample News Coverage: Conference on Women Crime.* Washington, D.C., 1976.

Resnik, Mindy. "Counselor Training Manual #1. Ann Arbor, Mich.: Ann Arbor-Washtenaw County National Organization for Women (NOW), 1976.

Reynolds, Rosemary and Siegle, Else. "A Study of Casework with Sado-Masochistic Marriage Partners." *Social Casework* XL, No. 10 (December, 1959): 545–51.

Roberts, J. *The Hardships of the English Laws in Relation to Wives.* London: W. Bowyer, 1735.

Sattin, Dana B. and Miller, John K. "The Ecology of Child Abuse with a Military Community." *American Journal of Orthopsychiatry* XLI, No. 4 (July, 1971): 675–78.

Schafer, Stephen. *The Victim and His Criminal.* New York: Random House, 1968.

Scheurell, Robert P. and Rinder, Irwin D. "Social Networks and Deviance: A Study of Lower Class Incest, Wife-Beating and Non-Support Offenders." *Wisconsin Sociologist* X, Nos. 2 and 3 (Spring–Summer 1973), 56–73.

Schimel, John L. M.D., *The Parent's Handbook on Adolescence.* New York: The World Publishing Co., 1969.

Schultz, Leroy G. "The Wife Assaulter." *Journal of Social Therapy* VI, No. 2 (Second Quarter 1960): 103–12.

Shelley, Sue. "Why Most Wife-Beaters Escape Punishment." *Detroit Magazine* (August 27, 1972): 6–8.

Smith, Selwyn M., Hanson, Ruth and Noble, Sheila. "Parents of Battered Babies. A Controlled Study." *British Medical Journal* IV (November, 1973): 388–91.

Snell, John E., Rosenwald, Richard J. and Robey, Ames. "The Wife-Beater's Wife." *Archives of General Psychiatry* XL (August, 1964). Also in *Deviancy and the Family,* edited by C. D. Bryant and G. J. Wells, pp. 87–94. Philadelphia: F. A. Davis, 1973.

Solomon, Theo. "History and Demography of Child Abuse." *Pediatrics* LI, No. 4, Part II (April, 1973): 773–76.

Spinnetta, John J. and Rigler, David. "The Child-Abusing Parent: A Psychological Review." *Psychological Bulletin* LXXVII, No. 4 (April, 1972): 296–304.

Spitzner, Joseph A. and McGee, Donald H. "Family Crisis Intervention Training, Diversion and the Prevention of Crimes of Violence." *The Police Chief* (October, 1975): 252–53.

Stark, Rodney and McEvoy, James. "Middle Class Violence." *Psychology Today* IV (November, 1970): 52–54, 110–112.

Stedman, Beirne. "The Right of Husbands to Chastise Wife." *Virginia Law Register.* vol. 3 n.s (1917): 241.

Steele, B. F. and Pollock, C. B. "A Psychiatric Study of Patients Who Abuse Infants and Small Children." In *The Battered Child,* by R. E. Helfer and H. C. Kempe, p. 108. Chicago: University of Chicago Press, 1968.

Steinmann, Anne and Fox, David J. *The Male Dilemma.* New York: Jason Aronson, 1974.

Steinmetz, Suzanne K. "Fifty-Seven Families: Assertive, Aggressive, and Abusive Interaction." Unpublished manuscript, n.d. University of Delaware.

———. *Intra-Familial Patterns of Conflict Resolution, Husband/Wife: Parent/Child: Sibling/Sibling.* Ph.D. Thesis. Case Western Reserve University, 1975.

———. "The Use of Force for Resolving Family Conflict: The Training Ground for Abuse." Unpublished manuscript. University of Delaware, 1976.

———, and Straus, Murray A. (eds.). *Violence in the Family.* New York: Dodd, Mead & Company, 1974.

Straus, Murray A. "Levelling, Civility and Violence in the Family." *Journal of Marriage and the Family* XXXVI, No. 1 (February, 1974): 13–29.

Straus, Murray, Gelles Richard J. and Steinmetz, Suzanne. *Violence in the Family: An Assessment of Knowledge and Research Needs.* Paper given before the American Association for the Advancement of Science. Boston. 1976.

Tanay, Emanuel. "Psychiatric Study of Homicide." *American Journal of Psychiatry* CXXIV (March, 1969): 1252–60.

Tinklenberg, Hared R. and Bourne, Peter G., M.D. (eds.). "Alcohol and Violence." In *Alcoholism: Progress in Research and Treatment,* pp. 195–210. New York: Academic Press, 1973.

Tracy, James J. and Clark, Elizabeth H. "Treatment for Child Abusers." *Social Work* XIX, No. 3 (May, 1974): 338–42.

Treatise of Feme Coverts, A., 1732.

Truwinger, Elizabeth. "Marital Violence: The Legal Solutions." *The Hastings Law Journal* 23 (November, 1971): 259.

Turk, James L. and Bell, Norman W. "Measuring Power in Families." *Journal of Marriage and the Family* XXXIV (May, 1972): 215–22.

Warrior, Betsy. *Working on Wife Abuse.* Cambridge, Mass. (46 Pleasant St.), 1976.

Wasserman, Sidney. "The Abused Parent of the Abused Child." *Children* XIV (September–October, 1967): 175–79.

Watlenberg, William W. *The Adolescent Years.* New York: Harcourt Brace Jovanovich, Inc., 1973.

Wayne County Sheriff Police Training Academy: "Domestic Complaints Outline, prepared by Lt. Kurek." International Association of Police Chiefs, Training Key No. 16, Handling Disturbance Calls, 1965.

Winch, Robert F. and Goodman, Louis Wolf. *Selected Studies In Marriage and The Family.* New York: Holt, Rinehart and Winston, Inc., 1953.

Wolfgang, Marvin E. "Husband-Wife Homicides." *Journal of Social Therapy* II, No. 1 (Fourth Quarter, 1956): 263–71.

———. *Patterns in Criminal Homicide.* Philadelphia: University of Pennsylvania, 1958.

———. (ed.). *Studies in Homicide.* New York: Harper and Row, 1967.

————, and Ferracuti, Franco. *The Subculture of Violence*. New York: Barnes and Noble, 1967.

————, Savity, Leonard and Johnson, Norman (eds.). *The Sociology of Crime and Delinquency*. New York: John Wiley and Sons, Inc., 1962.

Words and Phrases, 1658 to date. Vol. 45. War-Willful Negligence. St. Paul: West Publishing Co.

Young, Leontine. *Wednesday's Children: A Study of Neglect and Abuse*. New York: McGraw-Hill, 1967.

Zalba, Serapio R. "The Abused Child: A Survey of the Problem." *Social Work* II, No. 4 (October, 1966): 3–16.

————. "The Abused Child: II. A Typology for Classification and Treatment." *Social Work* XII, No. 1 (January, 1967): 70–80.

Index